FLAMING BLUE

KAREN,

I AM TOLD THAT YOU ARE AN AWESOME PERSON,

Thank you
for your support,

Love
always
&
forever

Third Printing
All characters in this book are fictitious. Any resemblance or real persons living or dead is coincidental.

Writers Block Publishing LLC has edit this book based on the author's standpoint.

www.writersblockpublishingllc.com

Flaming Blue

CHAPTER ONE

"Oh my goodness! What do you want?" River snapped as she answered the phone.

Within the past half hour the telephone had rung incisively as a loud siren. Some of the calls were more important than annoying, because River was trying to get ready for work. The first call was from her publisher wanting to meet with her at noon; that was an important call. The second call was the wrong number; the caller insisted that the number was right,

"I am the only one who lives here," River told the person on the other end.

After realizing how foolish it was to argue with the caller;

"Well, sorry to inconvenience you for being the wrong person," she said sardonically.

The third call was from a telemarketer trying to convince River to switch phone services, another meaningless call. The fourth call was from Jennifer Murdox, a friend and mentor calling to confirm their weekly get-together with hot wings, white zinfandel and literature. To River, that was the most important call of all.

Now the fifth call, the call that seem to have the loudest ring and the call that that broke the camel's back. By the way the phone rang; River could tell that this was the call that was the most meaningless call of all. She could tell who was on the other end. For that reason, when she answered the phone she was going to make it loud and clear that she was not in the mood to talk.

"Is that how you answer the phone?" asked the voice.

Hearing that voice on the other end caused her blood to boil. Her suspicions were right. This call isn't just a meaningless call, but an annoying call. It is her uncle Reuben Massie. Reuben is River's youngest uncle, her mother's step brother. He is five years older than River so they are more like brother and sister arguing and fussing with each other all the time. Reuben would boss River around as if he is her father and River

4

would fuss at him as if she is his mother. What is comical about watching them argue is that both of them are little in stature but have tempers the size of giants. Although they argued, the love between them is genuine. Reuben and River would walk through flames for one another if they needed. However; at this moment, River does not want to be bothered with Uncle Reuben.

"What Reuben?" she snaps.

"What?" Reuben asked. "What do you mean; what?"

"Reuben-," River growled.

Sensing the tone in River's voice, he knows that she is not in the mood for idle banter. Quickly he gets to the point.

"We need to meet the architect today." Reuben said.

"Why?" River asked with a sigh.

"Because one, he has not one but two different types of models and two, you have to sign the check."

"Right," River sighs as she put on her shoes. "What time and where?"

"How about noon at Christie's,"

"No, I have to meet my publisher at noon."

"How long will that be?" Reuben asked.

"Don't know." River told him.

"What time is good for you?" Reuben asked.

"I don't know, Reuben." River said.

"River, I need to know," Reuben said.

He is growing frustrated.

"Oh Reuben," River said whining. "That means I have to look in my planner and it's already in my bag by the door. I will call you later."

"No, because you're won't and I really need to set up this meeting. He is waiting for me to call him back."

River sighs as she goes into her business case and for her agenda planner.

"Okay, one o'clock. But listen to me Uncle Reuben, I don't have all day. I have a three o'clock class."

"Okay, one o'clock at Christie's." Reuben said.

"Okay, do we feel better?" River asked with sarcasm.

"Bye River,"

River leaves the phone off the hook so no one else can disturb her and she can finish getting dressed.

There is not an hour when River Daniels is not doing something. River is a college professor of two subjects. She has her Masters' degree in history and her PhD. in English literature and to add the topping to this dessert, River is a bestselling author of two books, one on the way to the books stores and the other just weeks away from release. River's family is proud of her accomplishments. She is the first one in her family to actually go to college and finish. Reuben is especially proud of his little niece. In his eyes, his niece, the little girl who used to follow him around like a puppy dog has now matured into a lovely successful woman. However, Reuben fails to realize how much his niece admires him.

Once upon a life time, Reuben came close to walking on the wrong side of the tracks. Associating with the wrong crowd and being in the wrong place at the wrong time, his associations landed him in jail for two years. After seeing the disappointed look in his mother's eyes and seeing how he let his niece down, Reuben vowed that once he got out of jail, he would turn his life around. He went back to school and received his Master's degree in business, and that disappointed look in his mother's eyes was now a look of pride. Because River was proud of Reuben's turn around, she offered to help him with anything he needed. When he got the idea to run his own night club, River kept her word. However, as much as it pleases River to help her uncle, his antsy and over anxious demeanor is annoying. Right now her plate is full, and meeting this architect is just another addition. Nevertheless, River knows that if the roles were reversed Reuben would bend over backwards for his niece.

Another fact about River is she is oblivious to her beauty. She may be too thin in her grandmother's eyes, but she is beautiful. River's skin is the color of caramel, her dark brown eyes are not decorated with eye shadows, mascara or eyeliners, but they hide behind glasses. River doesn't wear blush to show off her apple like cheeks nor does she wear lip stick to enhance that natural pout. She wears her long hair in a ponytail or bun. However, she is not a Plan Jane, she does have some sense of style. River's style is very conservative. She usually wears pant suits; wide leg black slacks, fitted blazers and four in high heel shoes or boots

RIVER ARRIVES AT COLLEGE just in time to see her good friend Dave Maroni. Dave is a fellow English teacher who River uses as her personal editor. River and Dave have known each other for almost eighteen years since River was nineteen years and Dave was twenty-five. Together Dave and River worked at a Mexican restaurant. Dave was the waiter, with an English degree waiting for a teaching position to become available. River was a student going to a local community college working as the happy hostess by night. At times, Dave would find River at the hostess station writing or sometimes reading. One day he asked if he could read whatever she was working on. Impressed with River's work, Dave could tell that she had talent as a writer. When it came to critique and advice, he gave his advice and opinion. River was in awe with his intellect. He was the guru of literature. Like an obedient pupil, she listened and made all the necessary corrections.

"Don't forget about me when you're a famous author," He would joke.

"Forget about you! You're going to be my personal editor. I promise." River vowed, smiling brightly.

She became his friend; his Little Friend River. Dave has always had a soft spot for River. He never acted on it because at that time she was too young and somewhat immature, but she looked up to Dave as if he was her big brother. She would follow him everywhere. Whenever the two of them would do swing shifts at work, during their break, they would go to the local book store and buy tons of books. About a year later, Dave finally got that call for a teaching position but it was in Las Vegas, Nevada. It broke River's heart that he was leaving. They promised to keep in touch, although they were just words.

Seven years later, another teaching position opened up at a university in Pittsburgh. By then, he received his PhD. in English literature. He moved back home. Dave wondered what happened to his "little friend" River. Did she do anything with her writing?

Then he saw her at the university.

What a coincidence, he thought.

His "little friend" River was now a college student at the university working on her Master's Degree. At first, Dave almost didn't recognize her. She looked so different. For starters, River had let her hair grow; she no longer had the short pixie cut hair style that she used to sport. Her apparel was different too; she dressed more conservative as if she was going to some kind of business meeting. Her vocabulary was eloquent and proper; she didn't speak using the current slang. This was not the same girl that he had once known. The change was dramatic considering what she had looked like but her new look was also intriguing. No longer the immature girl, she was mature now. River acted older than her actual age.

It was wonderful to see each other again. While drinking coffee, Dave and River caught up on old times. Dave did find out some things that happened that caused her now disciplined demeanor. River lost her grandfather when she was twenty, her mother died two years later and within' four months, her maternal grandmother died. Dave saw that these events were some of the reasons for this new River. He could tell that there was more but she didn't talk too much on the past.

As a matter of fact they never actually sat down to have a heart to heart talk. Their days consisted of getting coffee together and discussing current events. They would give each other teaching advice, laugh at the silly students in their class and admire the smart ones. But there has never been a serious conversation that would give the real reason to the new River.

One thing did remain from the old River to the new; she kept her promise when it came down to her first book. Before she took her manuscripts to her editor, River gave them to Dave to read. And just as he did when they were both younger, he critiqued, gave his opinion and advice. Still to this very day, he is the first to read her work.

RIVER KNOCKS ON THE door to his office and then walks in to see Dave sitting at his desk going over some papers. At forty-three years old he is handsome. He has the typical Italian features; olive colored skin, dark brown hair, but his eyes are the color of sapphire. They are her sapphire eyes. Sometimes just looking into those eyes would ease any tension that River could be going through.

"Good morning, Professor Daniels." Dave said smiling.

"Good morning, Professor Maroni." River said as she poured herself a cup of coffee.

"I've read your book." Dave said putting the manuscript on the desk.

"And," River asked with intrigue.

"Not your best work," he replied.

"Not my best work?" River asked, feeling somewhat insulted.

"Is this book supposed to be a love story?" Dave asks.

"No, but the characters do love each other very much,"

"There is no feeling or emotion." Dave stated. "The love is mentioned but not felt. Maybe you should think about the times you've been in love and relate it to the characters."

River sips her coffee and then shakes her head at the concept of being in love.

"Me in love, I have no time for love." She said with a chuckle.

Dave looks at River, but she doesn't notice. The River that is sipping the coffee in his office is not the River that he met at the Mexican Restaurant. This River is almost detached, unlike the River who was warm and friendly. The River then was happy-go-lucky, very free spirited and energetic. This River breathes, eats, and sleeps work.

"The River I used to know was always in love." Dave told her smiling. "Every time I turned around there was a new boyfriend."

"Excuse me?" River scoffs.

"Come on, River."

River sits down in the chair across from Dave's desk.

"I was a silly teenager who thought life was fairy tale." She said to him.

"And now,"

"Now, I am a writer and a teacher."

"You're a work-o-holic." Dave told her.

"I'm not a work-o-holic. I am just a busy person." River corrects him.

"Want to go to lunch this afternoon, my treat." Dave asked changing the subject.

"I can't I have to meet with Kennedy Bush." River told him.

"That crazy publisher?" Dave asks with a chuckle.

"Yeah, he's good to me. He makes me feel like I am worth more than I really am." River said then winked her eye teasing Dave. She sips her coffee. "Anyway, I gotta go, see you later."

"Bye." Dave replies.

River leaves Dave's office and heads down toward her office. She knows that there will be a ton of messages waiting for her, and most of them would be from Reuben. Her faithful assistant, Bonnie Onesi, a friendly woman who always had a smile on her face, approaches her.

"Good morning, River." Bonnie said.

"Hello, Bonnie." River told her smiling.

As predicted, Bonnie hands River a ton of messages.

"Any of these serious?" River asks.

Bonnie shakes her head no.

"Reuben?" River asked rhetorically, but Bonnie nods her head yes.

"Also, a student wants to interview you for the school paper, and another student wants to interview you for a class assignment."

"When do the interviews have to be done?"

"Well," Bonnie said looking at the class calendar. "Both students are asking to meet with you by next Friday. However, you have busy days next week with your literary class and the Advance Composition class."

"Those are just papers that are due." River replies sorting through the messages.

"Okay, I can schedule both for next Friday."

"Okay." River said.

Bonnie pencils the interviews on the desk calendar.

"So that makes that Friday-," River begins.

"Booked," Bonnie interrupts with a chuckle.

"Okay," River said. "Don't schedule anything else next week. What did Reuben want?"

"He said not to forget to meet with the architect at one." Bonnie answers. "Also he faxed an expense report for the alcohol and food."

Bonnie hands River the faxed information.

"I don't mean to neb, but River, that's a lot of money." Bonnie comments.

"I know," River said as she read the paper work. "Reuben is over the top. But if the roles were reversed, he would do the same for me."

"Well, that's nice." Bonnie said. "You two are very close."

"What class is today?"

"Today is your Wednesday class, Literature. Remember, you're studying *This Side of Paradise*." Bonnie informed.

"Oh right." River told her as Bonnie hands her brief case with her files for her literature class. "Thank you, Bonnie."

"Of course River,"

River takes her brief case and heads off her first class of the day. River loves teaching. She loves to share what she has learned and studied to whoever is willing to listen. It is enjoyable to watch eager students absorb and challenge the information that is being taught. River loves when her students bring new research whether it is for English or history. If River could give up anything, it would be for writing. She loves to write, she loves to create a world that many dream of and tell a story that touches people. Some stories relate to the reality of her readers. River loves the kind of impact her words would have. However, it is the teaching that has a special place in her heart, because she can develop and mold her students' minds. In River's mind, the sun rises and sets on education. There isn't anything more important than knowledge because what can one do it they don't know anything? They can't do anything.

RIVER SMILES AS SHE enters her classroom greeting everyone who is there. A few of her students weren't present.

"Good morning, Dr. Daniels," The students said responsively.

"Good morning," River said. "How is everyone?"

"Hung over," someone shouts.

Various sighs and laughs go throughout the room. As she waits for the other students to come, River begins to organize her files. One by one, the rest of the English Literature class comes in and takes their seats.

"Okay, talk to me," River said. "The adventures of Amore Blane, what is going on?"

"He just broke up with his girl. She dropped him because he's broke,"

Someone began to sing *Gold Digger*, by Kanye West and Jamie Foxx.

Laughter rings throughout the class room.

"How interesting," River said. "However let us try to comprehend this character so far. Here is a typical man, who like some of you gentlemen, is trying to live a good life, has a good woman on his arms, and he is trying to find himself, like some of you.

"I know who I am, Dr. Daniels." said a student.

"Oh?" River said smiling.

The student's remark ignites a spark in River's soul. Words like that are challenging to River. Most students don't know who they are and it amuses her when they think they do. She is ready for them to see the harshness of reality. This kid who spoke up, she is going to let him know that he has no clue to who he is.   It is amusing to watch and truly observe the students who claimed to be independent by the dictionary meaning, and do not know what the role means. Those who claims to be self- sufficient either still lives at home with their parents who are paying their child's way through college or the students that lived in a dorm only to get a taste of what the independent life is about. It is quite obvious to River who the true pupils of independence are. It is the students who do not come to school in the top of the line designer clothes. It is the students who drank faucet water from a left over Pepsi bottle. Who may have cell phones but not the high tech iphones. They are the students who may be in their late twenties to early forties. They know the real value of money and have a sense of discipline, and know what they are in school for. They are tired of working a full time shift making eight to nine dollars an hour only to have their pennies pinched. It is these students who know what they are majoring in. Unlike the silly students who are fresh out of high school thinking they are going to conquer the quest called life.

River is very particular to the students who are maintaining just so they can say, *I've made it.* Because at one time, she was one of those students, as a matter of fact she was both the silly student and the mature student.

So therefore, River looks at this young man who boldly stated. "I know who I am." Jack Mitchell, a nineteen year old who is on academic probation yet manages to speak as if he is actually intelligent. He is in River's Literature class and in her Composition class.

"Okay." Jack begins. "I know that I want to study law. However I want to work pro bono."

"That's good." River said with a grin. "However you must realize the necessary steps to take when it comes to obtaining your law degree. Being pro bono says that you're not out for the big bucks, not out for those big corporations. Tell me, does Amory Blain know what he wants? Yes, however his dreams and aspirations are far from reality and he cannot understand why he cannot achieve them. He is working hard to keep his girlfriend happy. But she isn't happy because her concern is money and being comfortable."

"Well, love don't pay the rent," someone blurted out.

"But it wasn't like they were struggling; she just wanted to live rich," another commented.

Students raise their hands to ask questions and to give their personal insight to the story to get a better understanding, and some nod their heads knowing exactly what River is teaching, and this is what teaching is all about.

"Okay, you know what I need." River said.

Sighs and groans go throughout the class room knowing that now it is time for some real work.

"Yep, I need a paper, one page responding to Amory's situation. You have forty-five minutes."

It is fun to read response papers from students. Some are blasé in the manner of just getting the paper done, and others are insightful and intriguing; these papers are a good read. This is the highlight of River's life.

RIVER WALKS IN TO THE cozy building of Bush Publications. Kennedy Bush is the owner of this local publishing company. Headed up in New York City, New York, Kennedy Bush built a franchise in Pittsburgh, Pennsylvania. Compared to the other publishing companies, Bush Publications is considered to be a small business; however, River is loyal to the company.

Kennedy is stubborn yet kind hearted man who is in his mid sixties, but looks like he is in his early fifties. He has white hair that is beginning to recede. Kennedy has soft blue eyes and wears glasses. He is a proud republican, but he does have a soft spot for a democrat who has redeeming qualities. Like River, Kennedy was a teacher. He taught history in the Pittsburgh Public Schools; now, he is retired from education and now he is the editor in chief of a newsletter called the *Bush Factor.*

River met Kennedy ten years ago at a coffee house both of them being regulars. Kennedy would come by every morning for a cup of coffee and to read the *Post Gazette*. River would come by with her lap top and sit at a little table in the corner writing.   Their conversation began one day when she was in need of a coffee refill.

O

"How are you today young lady?" Kennedy said with a smile.

"I'm okay, and yourself." River said.

"I am well thank you." He replied.

"Another refill, River," Nancy the waitress, asked.

"Yep, and another chocolate chip cookie," River said.

"I just put some more cookies in the oven, so about fifteen minutes okay?"

"Okay," River said as she sat down.

"So, how is school coming?" Nancy asked River.

"It's coming," River told her as she put money down on the table to cover her refill and cookie.

"What are you studying?" Kennedy asked.

"Everything," Nancy joked.

"No, not everything," River said with a chuckle. "I'm working on my Masters in history and my PhD in English Literature."

Kennedy smiled and nodded his head.

"River is also writing a book," Nancy told Kennedy.

"Is that so?" Kennedy asked.

"Yes, maybe my book sales can help me with tuition." River said with a chuckle.

Kennedy grinned.

"River, that is an unusual name for a girl," Kennedy said. "Is there something behind it?"

"Nope," River told him. "I was born in the 70's; disco."

Kennedy smiled.

"I am Kennedy Bush." he told, her extending his hand.

"River Daniels,"

"So tell me how far you are in your book?"

"Actually, I am done." She answered. "I'm just doing a little editing." She told him.

"Really," Kennedy responded.

He then reached into his pocket and pulled out a business card and handed it to River. She read the card out loud;

"Bush Publications,"

"I am interested in working with you."

"When can I set up an interview with you?"

"We're talking now," Kennedy said with a grin.

This was the beginning of their union. Within the next year, River's book became a best seller. Several book clubs used River's book as their book of the month, and Bush Publications was getting just as much recognition. After some time, Kennedy started a magazine called the *Bush Factor*.

○

RIVER ENTERS HIS OFFICE. Inside she finds Kennedy on the phone. He holds up his hand telling her to wait a minute. Also in Kennedy's office is Tommy Helgert. He is a comical individual. A thin man that stands tall, he has dark curly hair and he wears round wire rimmed glasses. He would say that he is "Catching the vision," and if anyone doubted his vision he is quick to argue and fight because the nay sayers are too ignorant to see the beauty that he has created. There are two poster boards on easels in the office.

"Hey, River, how is it going?" Tommy said smiling.

"Can't complain, how you doing?" she said sitting down.

"Good,"

Kennedy gets off the phone and smiles at River.

"Hello River," he said. "A busy morning,"

"I see," River said.

"Tommy has these samples for a cover for your book." Kennedy tells her.

River looks at the samples and shakes her head no.

"What do you mean?" Tommy asked offended. "I worked hard on these."

"They're not working for me." River says coolly.

The room is quiet. River does not fear Tommy's wrath and Kennedy never gets in the middle of their creative disputes. Tommy takes in a deep breath trying not to show that he is getting upset.

"Okay, what do you suggest?" Tommy asks.

"This book is about an adventure with two archeologists." she said. "What is with the beach house setting? I need some artifacts, bones; some one's skull."

"But your characters are on a beach." Tommy said.

"No, my characters are in a desert." River stated. "These covers give the impression of some romantic book."

Tommy looks at Kennedy. Kennedy shrugs his shoulders which told Tommy that he is still remaining neutral.

"Okay, I will fix it." Tommy said pouting.

"Thank you," River replies.

Tommy collects the two posters and leaves the office. River and Kennedy shake their heads. River walks across the office to the coffee maker and pours herself a cup of coffee.

"Jody made that coffee." Kennedy said.

River sighs and pours the coffee back into the pot.

"Why do you let her make coffee," River snaps.

"Oh stop your whining. It's not that bad." Kennedy said. "Here, come here."

As River walks over to Kennedy, he goes into the drawer of his desk and pulls out a bottle of whiskey.

"Why are you trying to liquor me up, what do you want?"

"Why do you think I want something?" Kennedy asked with a grin. "Come sit down."

River smiles at her old friend and sits down in the seat across from his desk.

"Your presence is requested at Hayes Bookstore." Kennedy told her. "When this book finally comes out, do you have time for a book signing?"

River grabs her agenda book from her brief case. She looks through the calendar.

"Okay, once Tommy fixes the cover you should be ready within the next month." Kennedy told her. "So on the first Friday of the month we should be good."

River looks at the calendar and sees that she has two classes back to back. She has a Social Studies class from eight thirty until eleven fifteen, then a history class from eleven thirty until two fifteen.

"I'm good for two-thirty." She said.

"Okay, I will let him know that you will be there at five o' clock. That gives you plenty of time to go home, get some rest and eat something."

"Good." River said. "Did you read my book, Mr. Bush?"

"Of course, my dear," Kennedy told her with a grin. "How is the other book coming?"

"It is finished," River answered in a dreary way. "The manuscript is complete, but my friend Dave Maroni read it and said that it was dull that there was no emotion. So the question is do I need go to back over it?"

"Do you value his opinion?"

"Value, are you kidding? I live by it." River said.

"Do you value mine?" Kennedy asked.

"I exist because of it." River said, then winked at Kennedy.

"You are such a little kiss up," he said.

River shrugs her shoulders nonchalantly.

"Let me read the manuscript."

River reaches into her brief case and hands Kennedy a copy of her manuscript.

"Okay, I will have it read by Monday, and I will call and tell you want I think, and if your friend and I are right, what will you do?"

"Find new friends." River said.

"River," Kennedy admonishes.

"Okay, okay, I will fix it," she murmured.

Kennedy shakes his head at River. She has the driest sense of humor that is both cute and disturbing.

"Okay, now I need a favor." Kennedy said.

"Anything," she said to him.

"I would like for you to write a column for me in the *Bush Factor.*"

"About what?"

"Anything you want." Kennedy said. "Literature, I need a new literature editor. Give me a list of books for the month; different genres, comment on the books. Call the section River Side."

"Very catchy," River smiles.

"Okay kiddo," Kennedy said handing her a piece of paper. "Here is what the next issue is going to be about, and when I call you on Monday, we will go over your column."

"Okay," she said. "Is there anything else?"

"No my dear, that will be all."

"Okay,"

River stands up grabs, her things and leaves.

"Go tell Tommy you still love him," Kennedy said as River walks out of the door.

NEXT STOP IS CHRISTIE'S. Christie's is a local lounge bar in Pittsburgh, owned by Jim Christie, a happy go lucky man in his early forties. He stands at an even six feet and has light blond hair. Jim is an intelligent man; who loves to watch college basketball and play golf. At Christie's, Reuben sits at the lounge with the architect that he wants River to meet, Dana Wilson.

Dana started his own architect firm five years ago. Although business was not where he would like it to be, he was doing well for himself and just the thought of building a night club is exciting to him. Especially now, considering that Reuben's rich niece said that price has no limit.

At thirty-nine years old, Dana is a handsome Afro-American male that stands at five feet ten inches. He has a thin mustache and he weight at an even two hundred pounds and he wears wire rimmed glasses.

Together Dana, Reuben, and Jim sit at the bar, watching the sports channel, looking at the basketball highlights.

"Can you believe that?" Reuben said fussing about the highlights. "Jim, what is wrong with your team?"

"My team," Jim asked in defense. "Come on Ruby,"

The two men laugh.

"You guys going to order or what?" Jim asked.

"I'm waiting on my niece."

"To think, after all the free booze I gave you, you're going to open a club and take my customers away." Jim joked.

"Awe, don't be sore, baby. You can come by have a few drinks and talk to the ladies."

In a joking manor, Jim waves his hand at Reuben as if he was disgusted with him, then goes back into the kitchen.

After Reuben was released from prison, Jim hired him as a bartender. Faithfully, Reuben worked until he was the head bar tender. He still works for Christie's on the weekend. Since Reuben has been working on his club, Jim has been assisting Reuben in getting all the necessary paper work he needs to open his club, from obtaining his liquor license to organizing a menu. Reuben's club is going to be a little different from Jim's lounge. For starters, it is going to open at nine at night, unlike Jim's bar that opens at eleven in the morning. Jim's bar is more of a sports bar, while Reuben's Room is simple a jazz lounge, where folks can enjoy live music, eat, drink, and be merry.

Jim is a fan of River's; he has read all her books. Considering the warm relationship that Reuben and Jim have, River is fond of Jim. They would affectionately get into debates over politics and they would talk for hours.

"So tell me, what made you decide to build a club?" Dana asked.

"Hmm, I love music and I love a get together, so I thought what better way to incorporate them into one. Plus with my niece, price has no limit, as long as I don't get on her nerves."

Reuben looks through Dana's portfolio of the designs he made and the buildings that he had done.

"I am telling you, you are a talented man." Reuben complimented.

"Thank you," Dana said smiling. "Look on page ten; those are my designs for some club ideas."

Reuben smiles as he looks at the designs.

"You know I would love to redo some of the buildings here in Pittsburgh. The buildings here are too old and outdated."

"She is going to love these." Reuben comments.

Reuben looks at his watch. It reads one thirty. River is late, which is typical. He picks up his cell phone and calls her.

"What Reuben?" River said as she answered the phone.

"Where you at girl?" he asked.

"I am stuck in traffic." River said. "I am ten minutes away."

"Okay,"

"Tell Jimmy to put a burger on for me, well done, with mushrooms." River ordered, then hung up the phone.

RIVER FINALLY ARRIVES AT Christie's fifteen minutes past two. She is flush by the noon day traffic.

"There she is," Reuben said smiling. "Come on, River."

"River?" asked Dana suddenly becoming nervous.

"Yeah, River Daniels, maybe you heard of her. She is a writer."

River finally approaches them and is immediately caught off guard by Dana. He is someone from her past. Dana sees that she recognizes him. Dana wants to say:

"Hi, River, how you been," but the cool look in her eyes made him uncomfortable and nervous.

"River, this is Dana Wilson." Reuben introduced.

"Nice to meet you," River replied seeming unruffled.

Does she remember me? He asks himself.

By the way she avoids eye contact, Dana know that she does remember him. Reuben is too excited to notice the sudden tension that is now in front of him.

"Hey River," Jim said poking his head out of the kitchen. "You're burger is ready."

"Hey Jimmy," River said. "Can you make that to go?"

"Sure thing," Jim said then quickly disappears.

"To go," asked Reuben. "I thought you were going to sit down and talk."

"Um, I really can't. I have a class, and with traffic-," River said.

"River," Reuben said. "I want you to look at his designs."

"Um, five minutes and that is it, okay." River says sternly.

Quickly she flips through the pages of Dana's portfolio just to amuse Reuben but really didn't look at Dana's work.

"Looks good," River said to Dana. "Um, we'll call in a few days."

Jim returns with River's food in a to-go bag.

"Um, how much," River said as she nervously began to fidget while looking for her wallet.

"It's on the house, baby." Jim says.

"Reuben, I will call you later. Jimmy thanks for the burger." River says.

River quickly snatches her food and then quickly leaves. Reuben stands shocked trying to make sense of River's sudden strange behavior. Dana takes a deep breath.

"Wait," Reuben said to Dana.

"Reuben," Dana begins.

"No, really, please wait." Reuben said.

Reuben runs after River. By the time he catches up to her, she is at her car.

"Hey," Reuben called out.

She tries to ignore him.

"River," Reuben grabs her arm.

"What?" she snaps.

"What?" Reuben asked feeling at a loss to her bizarre actions. "What was that?"

"What was what?"

"You don't even look at his designs." Reuben cried.

"I did so and I'm not impressed, find another architect."

"Excuse me?" Reuben questioned "What's your problem?"

"Nothing," River snapped.

She tries to open the car door, but Reuben shuts it.

"River, don't tell me nothing." Reuben said. "I told you that I needed you to meet with him. That means that you sit down, talk, get to know him, and look over his designs because he is the one who is going to build the club."

"No he's not." River snaps.

"What?" Reuben asked. "How you going to tell me who is and who isn't going to build my club?"

"Because *Uncle* Reuben, it's my money. Now you either find another architect or find another investor."

River gets into the car and quickly drives off.

Reuben stands stunned with River's sharp words. She only calls him Uncle Reuben when she is frustrated with him. At this point she is extremely mad at him. She never threw up in his face that she is funding this club. She would always refer to it as Reuben's Club. Reuben cannot understand why she suddenly snapped.

RUEBEN LOOKS AT DANA waiting for him.

"Dana, I'm sorry," Reuben said feeling completely confused.

"It's okay, no need to apologize." Dana said with a small grin. "I, ah, think I can explain."

"What?" Reuben asks.

He is now more confused.

"Sit down," Dana told him.

Nervously, Reuben sits down wondering what is next to happen. Also nervous, Dana sits down. He is about to explain something that he thought was ancient history.

"Um, River, I know her." Dana said.

"Everyone knows River, she is a famous writer." Reuben said.

"No, I mean before all that." Dana said. "I used to date her."

"No, no," Reuben said with a chuckle. "River doesn't date."

"River and I dated fifteen years ago. It was only for a few months, but we broke up. I broke up with her. And by her actions I think she is still mad at me."

"Why did you break up?"

"I don't know," Dana shrugged. "I was young, silly, so I ended things."

"So you just dumped her."

"Yeah," Dana said feeling guilty.

"Why?"

"Honestly the truth is that I was falling in love and River had big dreams and goals and I felt that I couldn't compete, so I just broke up with her."

Reuben nods his head. This explains River's sudden crazy behavior. However if this was fifteen years ago why is she still upset? Reuben begins to wonder if there is more to this story.

"Is that it?" Reuben asked doubtfully. "Because Dana, my niece was upset, there had to be more than a simple break up. Did you cheat on her, or-,"

"No, I didn't cheat on her at all." Dana said in defense. "In fact the whole time we were together we spent just about every day together and every night together. Maybe it was timing. I mean her mom had just died and-,"

"Her mom was my sister." Reuben said softly. "She was the first one who accepted me as her brother, not as a step brother."

"I'm sorry, Reuben." Dana said.

Just thinking about River's mother Imani makes Reuben want to cry. Reuben is his mother's only child, but when his mother got remarried to River's grandfather it wasn't the warm and friendly reception for the then five year old. It was very difficult for Reuben to understand this change and adapt into a new family, which included four older siblings that were well into their twenties; Imani and her three brothers. Plus River's maternal grandmother and grandfather had a very turbulent relationship. The brothers didn't understand how their father could pick up and marry a much younger woman and take on a new child. When Imani and her brothers went to meet their step mother and her son, the brothers were intimidating to Little Rueben, all of them standing over six feet tall towering over him. Imani, although second to the oldest, served as the leader. She looked at her brothers and then she kneeled down before Rueben and said:

"I have another little brother, huh?"

Reuben smiled. Imani wrapped her arms around Rueben and welcomed her new little brother into the fold. From that moment, Reuben was in love his big sister.

When River started dating, Reuben played the overprotective uncle. He chased all the boys away. His niece had potential and she was not going to have time for some hormone crazed boy interfering.

How did Reuben miss Dana? He would have remembered intimidating and chasing him away.

"So you basically just broke up with her." Reuben asks.

Dana nods.

"How did she take it?"

"She said she was cool?"

"Can't be," Reuben said shaking his head. "Because what just happened was not cool, and that was fifteen years ago."

"I called her up and told her that we need to talk," Dana began. "She said, 'so talk,' I told her that I would want to talk to her face to face. River was insistent on me saying what I needed to say. So I told her that I want to be friends."

"So were you,"

"What friends?" Dana asked.

Reuben nods.

"I tried to call her, but she avoided my phone calls. So I gave up and moved on, and I never saw her again. I heard about her success, but I kept my distance."

"From her reactions she must have loved you." Reuben said.

"We loved each other," Dana said. "We just haven't said it to each other."

"She loved you, why did you hurt her?"

"Reuben I was twenty-four years old and I returned home from the navy. I moved back in with my parents and I started working with my dad unloading trucks. The day her mother died I had hurt my shoulder, forcing me to file for workman's compensation, however I was not getting any money, some kind of delay with the paper work. Not once did River ask for a dime, she was just happy being with me. We would sit and watch television; whatever. I wanted to do more for her for but I couldn't even do for myself. The best thing that I could actually do for her was buy her penny candy; penny candy! Two months after her mom died, she was getting that insurance money-that money that her mom left her. She was buying herself new clothes and shoes and I couldn't do that for her. Christmas was coming and I couldn't even buy her a present."

"River's not shallow, she would have understood." Reuben replied.

"I didn't want her to understand. Have you ever loved someone and honestly could not do anything for them?"

Reuben nods his head.

"When my sister died, I was in Atlanta. I couldn't afford a bus ticket to come home to Pittsburgh and my pride wouldn't let me ask. My niece needed me and I wasn't there for her."

"I thought it would be best if I ended things before she got tired of me. River had big dreams." Dana said. "I knew I was breaking her heart, but it was fifteen years ago."

"You really messed her up." Reuben said as he shakes his head as if this situation is a tragedy.

"Reuben, we only dated for a few months."

"A few months, a few days, doesn't matter. When you're in love, real love, a few months can seem like a life time. You were her life time."

Dana sighs while he rubs the back of his neck.

"What did she say when you guys were outside?" he asked Rueben.

"Find a new architect or find a new investor," Reuben said. "You must have really messed her up for her to be so mean."

"I'm sorry, Reuben." Dana said. "I can completely understand if you don't want my business. I don't want to come in between you two."

"No, I want your business," Reuben said. "River is very business minded. I'm sure once I've talk to her, she will put business first and put her personal feelings aside."

Reuben and Dana stand up.

"Call me in a couple of days." Dana said.

Reuben nods and he and Dana shake hands.

AS RIVER DRIVES TO SCHOOL, She tries to regain her composure. Dana Wilson, the one true love of River's life. After fifteen years who would have thought that she would bump into him again. The last she heard of him was that he moved to Virginia. Did he recognize her? Of course he did. She saw in his eyes just like he knew that she recognize him. He is still good looking after all these years. His smile is still charming. However this doesn't matter now because Dana Wilson was history. A piece of history that managed to escape the storage from her mind, yet now it will be put back into storage and sealed forever. River shakes her head, erasing any memory that slipped from her mind. What should be on her mind is school.

CHAPTER TWO

Whenever River has such a thing as free time, she spends it with her colleagues and mentors like Dave. Tonight is her night with Jennifer Murdox. Jennifer is the reason why River wanted to be a writer. She is also a Pulitzer Prize winning novelist. Jennifer is sixty-one years old but she looks and acts like a woman in her mid-forties. Jennifer is beautiful. As a writer she takes literature by the rope and swings it around like a lasso.

At that time, River was eleven years old and she was past the fundamental books of her age; she needed something more stimulating. She saw a few of Jennifer's books on her parents' book shelf. Knowing that her parents wouldn't miss the books, River took them and read them, and from that moment, River was engaged into the world created by Jennifer Murdox. From that day on, she wanted to be a writer like Jennifer Murdox. When River was thirty, she decided to do her doctoral dissertation on one of Jennifer's books. River was going to meet her idol.

They decided to meet at Jennifer's home in the suburbs of Pittsburgh. River was beyond nervous. As she walked towards the front door, her heart beat loudly. She knocked softly on the door.

"It's open," said the voice from inside.

River took in a deep breath and slowly walked inside. Jennifer greeted her with a smile. It took so much willpower for River not to cry, but her eyes did well up with tears. She was now in the presence of literary royalty. River wanted to touch Jennifer's skin, to see if she was actually real. Jennifer was beautiful, her skin the color of chocolate, her smile wide and bright, and although she was petite and shorter than River, River felt small and tiny in her presence.

"He-hello," River stammered nervously. "I'm River Daniels."

"It is very nice to meet you," Jennifer said, shaking River's hand.

"Oh, the pleasure is mine, Mrs. Murdox," River said, half tempted to bow and pay homage to her hero.

"Please call me Jenny."

"Yes, ma'am, I will do that."

Jennifer chuckled.

"I was going to make a pot of coffee; would you like some?"

"Yes," River said.

"I am a fool for that international stuff. Would that be alright?" Jennifer asked.

"Sure,"

"Any flavor in particular? I have them all."

"It's doesn't matter. I enjoy them, too." River replied smiling.

"All right," Jennifer said. "Make yourself at home."

As Jennifer left to go into the kitchen to make coffee, River looked around the living room at all the things that Jennifer had. There was an African mask on the wall; maybe she went to the Mother Land and read a poem to an African Prince and his gift to her was a mask that one of the tribal kings wore. There was the famous painting of dogs playing poker.

Total opposites, thought River.

The end table that sat in the back of the living room held a black and white vase; there weren't any flowers in it. On the mantel that was above the fire place, there were few photos. One was a family portrait, with a mother, father and a child. The woman was Jennifer when she was younger, sporting an afro hair style. River grinned at the picture of a toothless baby with a bright smile. There was a picture of an elderly couple that looked both regal, yet warm.

Jennifer's parents, River thought.

River slowly merged into the dining room. The table setting was nice, not too fancy or too dull. The colors were baby blues and creams and scented candles filled the air. River wanted to stay here in Jennifer's world and drink international coffee. Jennifer came out with a tray of coffee and the condiments.

"Have a seat," Jennifer said warmly.

River sat down.

"Where are you from, River?" Jennifer asked.

"Right here in Pittsburgh," River answered.

"What do you do?"

"I'm a student and I am also a writer." River said.

"Oh, do you have anything published?"

"Just a short story," River answered.

"You must forgive me. I am a bit nervous about this interview." Jennifer confessed. "I never have been interviewed for someone's dissertation; interviewed by reporters for magazines but never for one's education."

"You're nervous, I'm nervous," River confessed. "I am a big fan. You would think I'm meeting Michael Jackson or something. I am this close to falling out and fainting."

Jennifer laughed.

"Is it that serious? Michael Jackson?"

"Yes," River said laughing. "You are so talented. The way you write; your words. I became a writer because of you!"

"River, thank you; thank you very much." Jennifer said smiling. "I write how I feel and what I see. I am a simple woman, I like simple things. All those artifacts in the living room, those are from my son, Robert. He is an archeologist living in Africa. He gets masks and staffs; all that kind of stuff and gives it to me. I guess he thinks that because I'm a writer, I am deep and profound, but no."

"I like simple things too," River said.

A beautiful friendship was born. River learned that Jennifer was a widow, her husband, Michael, died of cancer. Both women enjoyed each other's company. They would spend one night a week together, going over literature, eating wing dings or shrimp, and drinking red or white wine, or some kind of international coffee. It was as if they were having their own book club. Jennifer normally leaves her unlocked whenever she knows River is on her way. River's friendship meant a lot to Jennifer because with her husband dead, and her son living across the ocean, Jennifer was alone. River loved Jennifer's friendship as well. River would get writing advice from Jennifer just like she would from Dave. She absorbed Jennifer's advice like water to a sponge. In the years of their friendship, Jennifer became a big sister to River. They laughed and talked about almost everything, but Jennifer noticed that throughout the five years, River never mentioned a man in her life, other than Dave or Reuben. Jennifer noticed that River didn't have a sparkle in her eyes, as if a man had come into her life. Those doors of conversation stayed shut.

O

"ROUGH DAY," JENNIFER ASKS, "Rough day," Jennifer asked, handing River a glass of wine.

Usually River enters saying something clever or funny, but tonight she is quiet and solemn.

"No, just long," River said as she slid out of her shoes.

River sits down on the soft sofa and sips her wine.

"How was your day?" Jennifer asks, sitting down next to River.

River nods.

"It was somewhat okay. First Reuben got on my nerves, but what else is new? Dave doesn't like my book and I have this student on academic probation who thinks he can save the world. Ms. Jenny, how was your day?"

"Quiet." Jennifer answers. "I got some writing done. I talked with my son. He says that he is planning on coming home soon."

"How long has it been since you saw him?" River asked.

"Six years." Jennifer said. "Six long years, I would like for you two to meet."

"I'd like to meet him," River said.

Jennifer gave her a coy smile,

"Maybe you two can hit it off and-," Jennifer hints.

"Oh, no, no, no," River said getting up.

"Oh, River, it would be nice to have you as my daughter-in-law," Jennifer teases.

"Daughter-in-law," River exclaimed. "Jenny-,"

"Come on, marry my son."

River chuckles and walks towards the window. The sun is beginning to set, making the heavens a maroon color.

"Look at that sunset," River said.

"Yes, it is beautiful." Jennifer responded. "It makes me wish that Michael was living, he loved looking at the sunsets."

Jennifer's husband had been dead for ten years and not a day goes by where she is not thinking of him.

"Would you ever get married again?" River asked, not taking her eyes off the heavens.

"No, I am too old to get married again," Jennifer said. "I was a child bride; as soon as I graduated high school, Michael and I raced to the altar. He was on his way to Vietnam, and he didn't want to take the chances of my not waiting for him. So we got married and a month later he was gone.

"Wow, how old were you when did you have your son?"

"I was in my mid-twenties. My momma made sure that I had no babies with no husband so our first month of marriage we were very careful, but as soon as he got home, here comes Bobby."

River chuckles,

"Now, I am ready for some *Jazz*," Jennifer said.

She went into the kitchen to get a tray full of hot wings.

"This is one of my favorite books. Here I come Toni."

FOR TWO HOURS, JENNIFER and River engaged themselves into a world that was not their own by reading *Jazz*, by Toni Morrison. It was like they were snooping into the lives of people whom they didn't know. Jennifer and River became eye witness to everything they saw before them. They were two nosy hens sitting at the window ledge, talking and gossiping about what they did and did not know.

Jennifer notices that River is drinking more than usual.

"*Jazz* is the book that makes you question love." Jennifer said to River. "You know the; I hate you, but I love you."

"Don't sound like love to me." River said coolly.

"Oh, but it is love. You love the person that you're with, but at the same time, the same amount of love that you're feeling you also hate them. And if there was any one better, you take them up in a heartbeat, but at the same time you miss the charge that you had with the other."

"Who has time or wants time for that instability in their lives?" River asked. "Monday, I hate you. On Thursday I love you. Saturday I only like you. Get out of here!"

Jennifer chuckles.

"River, when was the last time you were in love?"

"Never," River said with coolness in her voice.

"Never,"

"Never," River answered back, then bit the inside of her cheek to keep from crying.

"You never had a man that took your breath away?" Jennifer questioned.

"No," River said as she ate a hot wing that had now gone cold. "I dated guys here and there, but nothing serious."

"So you can't relate to Violet and Joe?"

"No, never had that type of drama in my life. No, wait a minute, Reuben. I love him, no matter how much I hate him!"

Jennifer laughs.

"Were you and Mr. Murdock anything like Joe and Violet?"

"No," Jennifer answered. "We never argued, never had a time when we went to bed angry. We talked about everything from the smallest to the greatest."

"The only thing that I can understand when it comes to Violet and Joe is the music." River said. "Jazz music, it represents the unpredictable. You can listen to a smoothing jazz song and no matter what you think about the song it can take you to another place. It may slow down, it may speed up. The music, the emotion of the music represents Violet and Joe.

The instability of their emotions causes the turbulence in their relationship."

"Good insight, River."

"I thank you," River said, sounding like comedian Groucho Marx.

Jennifer laughs.

"I need alcohol," River said.

She gets up and pours herself a glass of wine, then returns to the couch.

"River, what type of music represents you?" Jennifer asked.

"Never really thought about it," River answered. "Would this book be considered a love story?"

"It can be," Jennifer said. "It definitely can make you question love and see where you stand with that person."

"Sounds like love is lethal," River said. "I don't get it. Love is something you don't mess with when you know nothing about it."

Jennifer realizes that the concept of love is somewhat frightening to River.

"Dave said that my book lacked emotion. The concept of *Jazz* is good. This is the blue print I need to help me elaborate on whatever I lack."

Jennifer nods her head agreeing to her idea.

"River, you're too pretty to be alone." Jennifer said to River. "Are you sure that you don't want to marry my son?" Jennifer smiled.

"I'm positive," River said. "Besides, I'm not alone, I have Violet and Joe."

Jennifer and River laugh.

"No more alcohol." Jennifer said.

"Well, I better get going," River said standing up.

She slightly stumbles.

"I have an early class."

"River, you are in no condition to drive." Jennifer told her. "Stay here tonight."

"I'm okay," River said as she slid on her shoes, regaining her composure.

"River," Jennifer replied in a warning tone.

"See you next week, Miss. Jenny, I'll bring the shrimp."

CHAPTER THREE

River avoids the pretty girl. She tries not to go near her and she does not look in her direction. The pretty girl is standing afar looking, watching, and observing. There is something familiar about this pretty girl, but curiosity won't kill this cat. River continues to avoid her.

LOUD POUNDING WAKES RIVER from a comatose type sleep. She lies in bed trying to focus on what is going on. What is causing the noise? Slowly she sits up and looks at her surroundings. She sees that she is at home and in her bed, but she is wearing her coat, her clothes, and she has one shoe on her foot. Slowly, very slowly, she begins to remember the wild night at Jennifer's; the wine, hot wings, and *Jazz*. What time did she get home last night, or this morning for her not to undress herself and get into bed, not dressed properly?

The pounding continues. It is someone knocking on the door. It is too loud. Whoever it is at the door should be arrested for disturbing the peace. River has a terrible head ache; her tongue feels fuzzy as if she had hair growing on the inside. She has all the classic symptoms of a hangover. What is she hung over about? Were the first five chapters of *Jazz* that intense? Slowly River climbs out of bed to answer the door. If she owned any fire arms she would shoot the person who is banging so loudly. She opens the door to see who is on the other side and immediately, focuses her attention on the center of his forehead where she would shoot him.

"Why," she growled.

"What truck ran you over?" Reuben asked, walking in.

She is horrifying to look upon. Her clothes are wrinkled; her long hair is matted over her head and on her face. Also on her face are the indentations of lines from her sheets.

"Come on in Uncle, it is so nice to see you." River said sarcastically to the door.

River closes the door and walks to the kitchen to get an aspirin.

"To what do I owe the pleasure?" she asked.

"You have some explaining to do," Reuben states.

"I think you do, banging on my door this early in the morning," River said as she takes the medication.

"Yesterday, what was yesterday about?"

River thinks for a moment then remembers their meeting yesterday. River quickly turns around and begins making coffee.

"I don't know what you're talking about,"

"River,"

River ignores Reuben. He approaches her and grabs her arms. River jumps and snatches herself back.

"Don't touch me!" she yelled. "Now, if you have something worth saying, speak. If not, get out of my house! You're wasting my time! I have to go to work!"

River walks away and goes to her bed room; Reuben follows.

"Why are you acting like this?" he asked.

"Like what?" she hisses.

"All petty and selfish," Reuben said. "Talking about it's your money. What that's all about?"

"It's about the truth, Uncle. It's my money, and if you don't like it, then find another family member to invest in you. Ooops, I forgot you got me! I am the only person in this family that did something with their life and has money. So I am calling the shots!"

River begins to go through her closet trying to find something to wear.

"Where is my blue and black suit?" she asks herself.

"You're not being fair."

"Grow up, life is not fair. Find a new architect or find a new investor. How hard is that?"

"Because you're being petty over some ex-boyfriend,"

His comment is an arrow that hits her in her chest. She takes in a deep breath to recover from the attack. She doesn't show any signs that she has been struck or that she is hurt.

Instead, River looks at her uncle with cold hard eyes that sends chills through his spine.

"What did you say?" she growled.

Reuben doesn't respond. He's not afraid of her wrath; he just knows his limits with River. He can see that she has reached a boiling point.

"You know what, Uncle Reuben, get out!" she told him.

"River," Reuben said softly.

"Don't River me, I said leave! I'm pulling all of my money, build your own club."

"River stop, Dana told me everything." Reuben said.

Another arrow strikes River in the heart. But this time she groans from the piercing pain.

"Hear me out please," Reuben pleads. "I don't mean any disrespect. I had no clue to who he was. He and I talked after you left. I just want to hear your side. Tell me that he did more than just break up with you. Tell me that he cheated on you; tell me that he abused you, because if that is the case, I will kill him; you know that I will kill him. But please, baby, don't tell me that you are not still mad at him for dumping you fifteen years ago. Men are like buses baby, you miss one; you can always catch the next one."

"Reuben, get out," River said in a cool tone. "If you don't respect my wishes, then you cannot respect me."

"Respect?" Reuben asked loudly. "You want to talk about respect. You throw up in my face on how rich you are and you want to talk about respect? River, seriously talk to me."

"He dumped me, okay, are you happy? You like seeing me weak?" River expressed loudly.

Her body is aching physically from the hangover and it feels like her heart is breaking.

"I needed him in a very difficult time in my life and he dumped me."

"I know, Imani-,"

"Yes, Imani, my mother, your beloved sister, where were you, Uncle Reuben? I don't remember seeing you there paying your respects. Oh, oh, there goes that word again."

"River, I was not in a right place," Reuben defended. Tears form in his eyes.

"I apologized to you and you said you forgave me. Don't make me pay that price again. You said that you forgave me."

"I had no choice, you're family," she told him. "and like most families, they *respect* each other's wishes. Now the odds are in my favor, my dear uncle. No one else in the family is going to give you that much money, so think about it. Now if you don't mind, I have things to do."

Reuben nods his head then walks away. River grasps for air as she tries to regain her composure. It breaks her heart that she has to give her uncle such an ultimatum, but she has to put her foot down.

"OKAY, TALK TO ME ABOUT THE FRENCH AND INDIAN WAR," River said to her early US & History class.

The class is sleepy but focused. This type of history class is based on the history of the United States and early Pennsylvania history. Of all of River's classes, this class is the toughest because it is early in the morning. It is once a week, three hours long. In order to keep her class focused and motivated she puts them into groups and makes them work as a team; and if anyone is a weak link, then it will cost each student in that particular group twenty-five percentage points. River's motto is: Education does not sleep.

Together no one will risk their grade and allow someone to fail in their group. So everyone stays alert and attentive with the help of some form of caffeine or energy drink.

River listens attentively as the six groups of six give their point of view about the French and Indian War, from the events that led up to the war, the significant events of the war and what happened after the war. All are insightful to River, all are intriguing, and today every student does not lose twenty-five points.

"Very nice," River said to her class. "I'm feeling generous today, no homework this weekend."

The class cheers loudly as if they have won some form of prize. In a sense they have, a stress-free weekend from Professor Daniels.

River sits down at her desk to look at her planner and sees that she has fifteen minutes before her next class, Modern US & PA history, the part two of the first class. During her fifteen minutes she decides to work on the articles for Mr. Bush.

Although most students think of River as a good teacher, she is feared by students. When a student finds out that another student has Dr. Daniels, then it is time to lend a hand. Former students warn the new students:

"Pay attention, take tons of notes, and don't miss class."

Students would share information to help out one another whether they knew one another or not. She is tough, she is hard. Homework is reading two or more chapters, writing seven to ten pages, yet nevertheless, at the end of each semester, all of River's students leave her class knowing and learning, if not anything; they learned something.

O

Sundays are the days that River goes to her grandmother's, Shirley Massie, Reuben's mother, to relax. Shirley is a petite African-American woman with a bright and welcoming smile and she is always laughing. Shirley is the step mother to River's mother, Imani. Although they were not related by blood, the bond between them was unbreakable and when Imani died, a part of Shirley died. Things have never been the same since Imani died. In fact, the deaths of Imani, her father, and Imani's mother caused the family to break and Imani's brothers went their separate ways. Shirley was determined to keep her family together; all she had left was River and Rueben. So now every Sunday, River and Reuben are to report to Shirley's home for good home cooking.

River doesn't relax whenever she is with her grandmother. The cell phone never leaves her ear, the lap top stays turned on so she can check emails from students who make excuses on why their homework is not going to be turned in on time, or that they couldn't understand the assignment.

Sometimes River would make class schedules for the next semester, she might check homework papers, or work on her writing. Shirley shakes her head at her over worked granddaughter.

"You need to relax," Shirley would say to her.

"Believe it or not, I am relaxed." River replies.

This particular visit to Grandma's, River wants to avoid. She does not want to deal with Reuben. She hasn't spoken to Reuben since that morning when he was at her house. She wonders if there is going to be any tension. However it doesn't matter she is going to stand by her decision. She is not going to work with Dana Wilson.

Normally Shirley leaves the front door open when she knows that River and Rueben are coming. She chuckles when she hears her son and granddaughter argue as they enter the house together. The sound of their petty bickering is almost musical to her.

"Hush, you two," She would gently but sternly scold them and then greet them with a hug and a kiss.

IT IS QUIET WHEN Shirley hears the front door open. No petty arguing or no threats among the Rueben and River. In fact River comes alone with her cell phone attached to her ear and her brief case in her hands. River smiles at her grandmother and kisses her on the cheek.

"Where is Reuben?" Shirley asks.

River shrugs her shoulders and continues her conversation.

"Okay, just fax that information to my assistant," River says to the person on the other end.

"River, hang up that phone, baby, it's Sunday," Shirley said.

River chuckles, "I gotta go, my grandma says it's Sunday,"

River hangs up the phone.

"Okay, Grandma, I am all yours."

River leans over and gives Shirley a big hug and kiss.

"That's my angel," Shirley says with a chuckle. "I made everything for you."

"Ah Grandma, I could smell everything as I was pulling up."

Together River and her grandmother walk to the kitchen. River sits down at the table while Shirley walks to the stove to check on the food.

"Mmm," River said smiling. "I could smell the fried chicken, salmon and the homemade macaroni and cheese, and green beans. Oh, I know you put your foot in it. You fry the salmon in the batter I like?

"Yes, baby,"

"Oh, grandma, forget the foot, you bathed in it, didn't you grandma,"

Shirley laughs.

"Yeah, Grandma took care of her angel."

"Grandma, you spoil me!" River exclaimed.

"Anything for you, Angel," Shirley said.

River smiles.

"Now, I want to talk to you," Shirley announced in a cool tone.

"About what,"

"You know I love you."

"Yes."

"Reuben called-,"

"Grandma-," River quickly interrupts.

Shirley looks at River and gives her a look that says for River to be quiet.

"Why were you so mean and nasty, especially to your uncle? Now I know your momma didn't raise you like that, neither did I, girl."

"Grandma-,"

"River Lynn," Shirley says.

River sighs. She knows she is in trouble when her grandmother uses her full name.

"Your uncle loves you, loves you!" she stresses. "He would do anything for you; and you have been so nasty because of some man!"

"I just don't want his business." River said. "There are other architects out there."

"Your uncle knows good business,"

"I do too, Grandma," River said sounding like a child competing for her Grandmother's affection.

"Yes, you do, Angel, but don't let some man come between you and your family." Shirley said.

"I am not letting some man come between family."

"No, you are just acting like someone with a stick up their -," Rueben said suddenly surprising both River and his mother.

Quickly River stands up from her seat and storms towards Reuben.

"Let me tell you something!" she exclaims.

"No, no, no!" Shirley exclaims racing over to them.

She stands between River and Reuben.

"River sit, Reuben sit."

Both River and Reuben sit down glaring scornfully at each other; waiting for the bell to ring so they could begin round two.

"Now, I don't want any arguing," Shirley says sternly. "Is that understood?"

"Yes, ma'am," both River and Reuben said practically pouting.

"There is going to be no talk about the club unless you two can be civil."

"Fine by me," River said with a smirk. "I've already said what I needed to say,"

Reuben shakes his head,

"I'm going to watch the game."

Reuben gets up and leaves the kitchen. Shirley sighs as she sits down next to River. River looks up at her. By the way she looks at her grandmother, River looks like Imani. Shirley wonders how her mother would handle this situation; River and Reuben. Shirley waits a moment to speak.

"You mad at me, Grandma?"

"No, Angel," Shirley said with a grin.

Shirley put her arms around River.

"You're so pretty, too pretty to be so bitter."

"I'm not bitter," River said her pretty face turning hard.

"What kind of life you live?" Shirley asked.

"Busy,"

"Busy, you always busy,"

"Yes, Grandma, I am busy, I do fifty million things,"

"Then quit one and do forty nine million. River, you're gonna wear yourself out."

"I like being busy. I like looking forward to having something to do. It keeps me motivated."

"Motivated? Girl, you so simple. You like going home every night to an empty house, no one to talk to."

"Yes, because through the course of the day, I have talked to just about everyone, so when I get home, I have peace and quiet. You see me as lonely, but I see it as being alone. There is no one to worry me to death about insignificant matters, and no one nagging me about some petty nonsense. If I don't want to clean my house, I don't clean it. I don't have to be home by a certain time. There is no one there nagging me, annoying me-,"

"Hurting you,"

"What," River asked caught off guard by Shirley's statement.

"That young man who wants to build Reuben's club, I remember him. You guys started dating each other around the time your mother died. And when she died, that young man came by to see you every day. He was by your side. It was him that brought you peace during that time of chaos. He comforted you in so many ways, especially when you were dating that other knuckle head. What was his name- well never mind. Your mother could not stand him. But this young man, he was good to you-,"

"Grandma-,"

"Angel, I told you that night not to close the door; that he will come back."

River can't believe that she has just let her guard down and allowed herself to go through those ancient memories. She sits up in her chair and gives her grandmother a cold look.

"Grandma, I don't have time for this. I could care less about Dana Wilson. If anything, he did me a favor. After we broke up, I went back to school and refocused on what was really important. An education so that I could get a good job and be established for the rest of my life. And if I had to make a choice between the temporary company of a man or the comfort of establishment and independence, I chose establishment and independence. Plus men come and go."

"But true love lasts forever,"

"What?"

"You loved that young man," Shirley said.

"Yes, loved, with an 'ed', past tense."

"Well, Angel, if past tense, then why not take his business? Let him build your uncle's club and you go on about your business."

"I cannot believe you are taking Reuben's side."

"I'm not taking no one's side." Shirley said. "but baby, let me tell you something about a man. Don't let a man run you or have that much control over you. If you don't accept his business he can always say 'After all these years, you're still not over me,' and that is when he has that control, be it true or not. But if you take his business, you are showing him that he had nothing over you, and it's your money that is putting food on his table."

River looks out the window. She closes her eyes and lets out a sigh. River never thought about Dana once she got focused on school. She got on the train of priorities and rode off never planning to stop to sightsee, but only paying attention to what was important to her.

During her time as a student, the male students would see her in class. They were intrigued by the conservative beauty, they saw her intelligence. After class she quickly gathered up her books and disappeared into the sea of wandering students that walked through campus, going from one class to another. Men couldn't understand how oblivious she was to their subtle hint of flirtation. One would smile at her and ask her;

"What's your name? Where are you from, Can I take you out for coffee?"

Depending on her class schedule, she would rush out of the class saying;

"Let me get back to you, I'm running late,"

If she agreed to coffee, it never dawned on her that she was on a date. To her, she was meeting a class mate, to continue on the debate from the philosophy class, or to comprehend the term paper that they were assigned. Eventually the men would give up on their pursuit, realizing that nothing more was going to come and they would move on to another intriguing beauty. None of this mattered to River, she wasn't turned on to that side of the world, all she knew was the world of books and education.

"Go talk to your uncle, Angel." Shirley said. "If the situation was reversed, he would have built the biggest night club."

River knows Grandma is right. Beside, life is too short for the complications of drama. Just a week ago, River was content with running around teaching her classes and meeting with students, because she is healing the world from the disease of ignorance. Just a week ago she was writing a book and getting the constructive criticism by Dave and Mr. Bush. She argued with Tommy about the cover and Reuben's constant pestering her about the club; from the music to the food. In the middle of pandemonium, she was still able to find comfort and peace with good wine, delicious hot wings and literature with her good friend and mentor. To her, this was the good life; a normal life.

River is in charge, she is in control and she fears nothing. If she is going to do this, she is going to make sure that Dana and she do not share any special moments. She is not going to share a laugh or a chuckle. This is going to be business and not pleasure. River is going to make her dealings quick. Simply build the club and have a good life. The more she rehearses this concept in her mind, the better she can deal with Dana and Reuben, even Tommy on her best day. When it really comes down to everything, she's the boss, she is in control.

REUBEN FINDS RIVER SITTING in the back yard looking over the small garden that Shirley created. The garden is comical to River. One side is a few vegetables like tomatoes, cucumbers, onions, and green peppers and the other side are flowers that are trying to grow. In the heart of the back yard is Shirley's cheap, but pretty patio furniture. The green and cream colored patio furniture is joined by metal folding chairs. River knows that her grandma didn't spend free afternoons sun bathing. But whenever it was nice and warm outside, River would sit in the lounge chair and snooze for a few moments, or until Reuben wakes her and bugs her about something silly.

Reuben pulls up a chair and sits next to her. They share a small grin. That is their way of apologizing to one another.

"I remember this pretty girl that would laugh at the silliest things and she was always smiling." Reuben said. "She was full of life and she was a bundle of energy. Every time she would enter a room, it would light up."

River doesn't respond. Reuben hands a picture to River. It is a picture of River when she was twenty; River chuckles.

"Where did you get this?" she asked.

"Momma found it," Reuben answers as River hands back the photo. "What happened to her?"

"What do you mean what happened to her? You're looking at her." she answers with a chuckle.

"You were the happiest person in the world. You're thirty-seven years old and you act like an old woman. I mean Momma got more spunk than you-,"

"Did you come out here to insult me?" River asks.

"Momma told me about that one boyfriend you had. He was a loser. Then she explained to me how close you and Dana were-,"

"Reuben, look," River interrupted. "I'm sorry I acted the way I did, so if working with Dana is what you want then hire him."

Rueben smiles and River and hugs her.

"You play cold, but I knew you are a sweetie," Reuben said, kissing her cheek.

River tries to pull away.

THE MUSICAL BICKERING AND ARGUING is sweet to Shirley's ears. Together they enjoyed a delicious dinner. Later while Shirley watched television, River and Reuben did the dishes. Reuben didn't stay after kitchen duty was done. He is so excited about working with Dana that he left to call him. River enters into the living room to join Shirley on the couch to watch television.

"I'm glad that you and your uncle worked everything out," Shirley said.

River grins.

Shirley leaned over and kissed River on the cheek, then affectionately tapped her on the leg.

"Sweet Angel,"

"I gotta go, Grandma, it's getting late. I have an early morning." River said standing up.

"Okay, baby, let me fix you a plate." Shirley said, standing up.

Quickly Shirley walks into the kitchen.

"Grandma, I don't need a plate," River said, but she knows her grandmother isn't listening to her.

River reached into her brief case and pulled out her wallet and gathered five one hundred dollar bills. River reaches for her grandmother's Bible and slips the bills into five separate sections within the book.

SHIRLEY HANDS RIVER THE packed plate full of food that's tightly wrapped with foil. Shirley sees River by the front door, carrying her brief case and lap-top in her hands. She hands River the plate and kisses her on the cheek.

"Thanks, Grandma,"

"You welcomed, Angel."

They gave each other a hug.

"I love you," Shirley said.

"I love you more," River says.

CHAPTER FOUR

"OKAY, I'LL CALL YOU tomorrow," Dana says to Reuben.

Dana hangs up the phone and then chuckles to himself. He leans back on the sofa and then turns the mute button off so he can finish watching the basketball game.

River finally got over herself, he thought to himself.

However it doesn't matter. This is business, whether he works for her or not. He has things to do. He thought about her whenever he would read about her latest book in the newspaper. He is surprised that he is thinking of her now. Did she ever get married? Is she did, does she have any children? Dana remembered that River did want at least one son. In spite of her reaction, it was nice to see her. She looks different. River has let her hair grow. She was wearing a business suit and she wore glasses. The River he knew hated to wear her glasses. However, in spite of everything, she is still pretty.

None of this matters now. Dana's number one priority is his baby; his architect firm. Wilson Architect was born five years ago. Dana never thought that he would run his own business. Originally from Pittsburgh, Dana grew up in the suburbs. When he was twenty, he decided to join the Navy where he was stationed in Virginia. After serving faithfully for four years, Dana came back home to go to school and earn his degree in engineering. However Dana never planned on meeting the young woman that captured his heart, but that one Saturday night he did.

It all began as a small get together at a friend's house, Tonya Miller, a friend of River's. Tonya was interested in dating River's cousin, so Tonya arranged for a double date, which included, Dana, River, and the cousin. At first, River was reluctant. She had just pulled a double shift at work and she was tired. After some arm pulling and pleading, River agreed to go to Tonya's house; with her cousin.

Dana didn't expect River to be beautiful. Considering that Tonya was not an attractive woman; why would her friend be? But River was beautiful. Just seeing River caught Dana off guard. Her hair was cut in one of those cute pixie styles exposing her brown eyes. She was wearing a pair of baggy jeans and a baggy T-shirt with the character Bugs Bunny on it. Apparently, River was not dressed for a double date. Her carefree demur was a turn on Dana. She knew that she had gotten Dana's attention, but she was both coy and flirtatious. She was playing hard to get and Dana was willing to play. They got to know each other. Both of them were in dead end relationships. River was not necessarily interested in dating anyone else, but Dana however wanted to move on to someone better.

Later on that evening, River's cousin left, leaving Tonya to be the third wheel, and the small get together went from Tonya's place to Dana's apartment. While Tonya watched television, Dana and River managed to sneak away.

"I want to tell you something," Dana said in a sly way.

"What?"

"I've been told that I'm a good kisser,"

River chuckles,

"I'm glad to hear that, congratulations."

Her joke was cute.

"Can I kiss you?" Dana asked.

"You're not supposed to ask." River said with an impish grin. "You're supposed to take the girl in your arms and kiss her; giving her that rush."

"Is that right," Dana asked walking closely towards her.

"Well, can I take you and give you that rush?"

"I don't know, can you?" River asked with a grin.

Her challenge was intriguing to Dana. He looked her in the eyes, cupped her face into his palms and began to kiss her. Immediately River was taken away. It was a rush that left her without a stomach. He was a good kisser. He was gentle. Dana enjoyed the taste of River's lips, he wanted more, but he knew that just the kiss would soothe his appetite.

After the kiss, they looked at each other.

"Did I give you that rush?" he asked

She nodded her head and nuzzled up to him to kiss him again, and he tasted her lips once more.

For the next month, River spent every Saturday night with Dana. There wasn't sexual intimacy but a bond that will always remain. They would kiss and cuddle and hold each other. It was peaceful falling asleep in each other's arms. River and Dana talked about everything from silly childhood memories to their dreams and goals for the future. She told Dana about her current boyfriend and how unhappy she was and that she was debating if she should stay. Dana told her about a young lady whom he had lived with while he was in Virginia and although he cared for that young lady the long distance relationship was not going to work.

Things seemed to be moving for them; however Dana decided to take a trip to Virginia. He didn't want to tell River the reason for this trip. River came to her own conclusions. She felt he was going to continue the relationship with the young lady in Virginia and end things with River. Although she wanted to know; she didn't ask. Instead, she went along with the way things are going. Dana could tell that River was hurt. He didn't want to lead her on by thinking there is more to their relationship. So before he left, he stopped by her apartment for a visit. River was not going to beg him to stay, or beg him to be her man. If he was going to leave, she was going to let him leave, but not without an opportunity to make him want to stay.

At River's apartment, Erykah Badu's *Baduizm* CD played softly in the background. As Dana sat in her living room, he became intoxicated by the fragrance of French vanilla candles that filled the room. River knew that Dana loved the smell of French vanilla. River didn't look good, she looked delicious. Everything about her was appealing. River wore a tight shirt with strips that showed off her belly button and she wore a pair of black Calvin Klein jeans that hugged her enough to show off the curves of her hips. River remembered Dana's foot fetish. He loved it when a woman had a well groomed pedicure. She painted her toe nails red. Besides looking like a delicious appetizer, she smelled heavenly. River wore Calvin Klein's

Obsession for women perfume. Her whole attire was what she needed. If Dana still wanted to leave he would have the lingering smell and River's beauty to haunt him forever.

Dana had a hard time talking to River that afternoon. Her hypnotic beauty taunted and teased him. But Dana was determined to stay focused. Together they sat down alone on her sofa in her living room. Although she was nervous, River sat on the couch with the hopes that if he came to say good-bye, his plans would change after seeing her, feeling her, and loving her.

"Um, where do you see us?" Dana asked.

"I see you as my friend,"

"I enjoy spending time with you," Dana said he was smiling at her. "It is just that some things in my life are kind of complicated."

"Okay," she said in blasé tone.

She smiled at him. Her smile was both bashful yet flirtatious.

"Are we still going to be friends?" she asked.

"Yes," Dana said quickly.

"Okay," River said with a smile

Dana smiled back at River. She looked so *good* sitting across from him. It took so much self-control not to take her. Dana hoped that there was a reason to accidently bump into her or maybe there was a reason to touch those thighs. He could remove those jeans and just..., Dana shook his head trying to stay focus,

Stay cool, Dana, stay cool. He had to say to himself.

The vanilla scented candles continued to intoxicate him. The red toes were calling him and her hips in those tight jeans taunted him. Her body was amazing. River stood at five feet five inches but she had long legs and a small torso. She was thin; too thin to most people, but she was just enough for Dana to want over and over again. Every time she would move, her shirt would rise exposing her caramel colored stomach. The red lipstick that she wore made her full lips look enticing; they beckoned for Dana to come taste them. He wondered if River knew what she was doing. Her coy and cunning smile said that she did. Yeah, River knew exactly what she was doing.

A LOUD NOISE STARTLED HIM. It is the sound of the alarm clock. He sits up in bed trying to recollect what just happened. Was it five minutes ago that Dana was on the phone with Reuben? Why is the alarm clock going off? Dana realizes that he had fallen asleep dreaming about River, the memories of her scent, the sound of her voice; her touch. Dana turns the alarm clock off, it reads six a.m. The sky is no longer black, but the color of Windsor blue. It is time for Dana to start a new day. While his coffee brews, he showers and shaves. He gets dressed listening to the traffic and weather report. Dana dresses in the normal attire, a pair of jeans with a dress shirt. He fills his mug with coffee, grabs his portfolio and walks out the door to face the world.

It is Monday, a brand new week. He just received a new client, a very rich client, and from this day forward he was going to put all he had into impressing Reuben and his spiteful niece with his designs.

Wilson Architect Firm is Dana's pride and joy. It is a two floor building that was designed by Dana. On the first floor is the reception area. Carol Penman is Dana secretary. She is a cheerful older woman who takes pride and joy in her naturally curly, silver gray mane. Carol never has time for gossip. Life is too short for mindless chit chat. Her life was devoted to Dana. She makes sure that he has nothing to worry about. Carol always has a fresh pot of coffee waiting for him in his office, in spite of the tall mug of coffee he brings in from home. Any file that Dana needs is already in his hands, thanks to Carol. Next on the payroll are two brothers, Eddie and Justin Banks. These men are in charge of the landscaping. The grass is defiantly greener on their side. In charge of the engineering, other than Dana are Nick Vito and Clayton Simmons. They are overseers of construction, the electricians, and the plumbers.

Together, Dana and his dream team would create a vision that was once just a glimmer in Dana's eye. Dana loves his work. He has been known for staying up late to design the perfect building.

Wilson Architect Firm is five years old. Most businesses do not last beyond two to three years, but Dana is determined to succeed. Wilson Architect Firm is not officially out of the woods, just a few more clients and the business will be the success that Dana wants and needs. With the work for Reuben's Room, the success may come sooner.

Dana enters his office. Carol is right behind him. She informs him of the adventures that are in store for the day and gives him his messages.

"Reuben Massie called wanting to meet here today," she says.

"Okay, call him back and tell him that I have two ideas that he just might be interested in and see if he can come in at noon."

"Is there anything else," Carol asks.

"Tell the boys to come into my office as soon as they get here,"

"Okay," Carol said.

Dana cannot wait to tell his dream team about their new business adventure. He wants Reuben and River, if she'll come, to meet his team. He is excited. Maybe River and he can talk like civilized people.

How you been? He would ask. *Congratulations* on your *success. Yeah..., the firm is doing well.*

Dana has dated several women before and after River. Although he was happy with their company, he couldn't find himself fully committing to the relationship, and eventually it would end, leaving him to find security in his work.

As he sits down at his desk and stares out of the window, he begins to wonder if running into River after all these years was destined fate. After all, Dana at one time loved her; she held a special place in his heart. He knew that she loved him. At the time neither of them said those words to one another.

Maybe running into each other again is just coincidence. It has to be. Dana had no idea that Reuben and River are related. She never mentioned her uncle. Now, Reuben and River are just clients. River is just another ex-girlfriend. Just someone he had picked up and dropped off on his journey through life. In a few months she is not going to matter. When this club is built, both Reuben and River will be out of his life.

CHAPTER FIVE

"SET THE STAGE, RIVER," Jennifer said, as River sips on the couch hazelnut cappuccino.

They dine on red velvet cake while engaging into the mind of Toni Morrison; continuing their own interpretation of her novel *Jazz.*

It is Friday night and the ladies have the whole evening for Toni. River is having a problem comprehending the emotion of the characters. She sees no real point to Violet's rage against her husband Joe. To help River better understand the book, Jennifer puts in a jazz C.D. As the music plays in the background, River lounges on the couch. She watches as Jennifer bobs her head and dances to the melody of the music.

"Imagine a man you loved. You have given him everything and then he leaves you for a younger woman; some twenty year old thing,"

"So collect your losses and move on," River says coolly. "Violet is a typical loser. All she needed to do was to clean herself up and find a new love. She had it going on and that was rare for black women in those days; a free lanced hair dresser!"

"You are a tough critic," Jennifer said, looking at River. "However, it is not always that easy. Back in those days it was unheard of for a woman to live life without a man. She was looked on as a spinster. Now days women are so independent, men can be somewhat intimidated by them. A woman can do whatever she wants with whomever she wants. Women today have gotten away from the real purpose of life."

"The real purpose of life?" River questions.

"Yes, a woman was made for the man," Jennifer begins to explain. "to satisfy him in all areas. When he is lonely, she is his companion. When he is hungry; we cook for him. When he is horny; we love him. Now the man's purpose is provided for us; his woman. Now in Violets and Joe's case, they were both entering a season of change in their lives. She was going through *the change*, and he was having a mid life crisis. With them both going through their seasons, neither of them knew how to talk to one another, so he went his way which was to Dorcas and Violet to talking with her birds. Keep in mind, River, back then they didn't have medications to sustain those hormones,"

River takes another sip of her hazelnut cappuccino.

"Please, them old folks had some remedies," River comments cynically. "They mixed baking soda with ketchup," River jokes. "My grandmother did things like that all the time. I'd fall and scrape my knee. Grandma say, 'Put some cooking oil on it, baby.'"

Jennifer laughs at River's joke.

"Yeah, old folks did have some remedies," Jennifer laughed. "When you're sick, tea, honey, and whiskey,"

"You were an alcoholic by the time you're eight years old." River continues to laugh.

"But that cold was gone," Jennifer pointed.

The two ladies laugh.

"But seriously River, have you ever felt unneeded like Violet?"

"We all have," River answered.

"A man in your life who didn't quite understand you?"

"How many men understand women?" River asks with a chuckle.

River stands up and walks to the coffee table where the red velvet cake sits. She cuts a piece of cake. Jennifer looks at River and wonders if there is a man or if there was a man in her life.

"River, can I ask you a personal question?" Jennifer asks.

"Sure," River answers, putting a forkful of cake into her mouth.

"Are you a virgin?"

River almost chokes on that piece of cake.

"What kind of question is that?" River asks, shocked and offended.

Jennifer puts her hands up surrendering.

"I am just asking because I never, never heard you mention about a man in your life."

River looks away.

"Are you gay?"

"Jenny!" River cried out appalled.

"River,"

Both women are quiet for a moment.

"We've been friends for a long time. You can talk to me about anything."

River doesn't respond. Jennifer continues,

"It's okay, if you're gay-,"

"I'm not gay!" River snaps. "I just don't have time for romantic liaisons."

"So you have had sex?"

"It's been a while," River admitted.

"What's a while?"

"I was in my twenties." River answered, embarrassed.

"River, you're almost forty!" Jennifer exclaims. "I cannot believe a girl as beautiful as you has not had sex!" Jennifer said.

"It's kind of hard, Jenny, I'm busy!"

"Too busy for a rendezvous," Jennifer asked.

"I was never one for casual sex." River replies. "Jenny, I am a busy girl,"

"Too busy to take notice in a handsome man, or for a handsome man to notice you?" Jennifer asked doubtfully.

"Jenny, look, my life is not centered on getting laid."

"I don't expect it to be, but don't you get…, urges?" Jennifer questions doubtfully.

"I don't really think it."

"Don't think about?" Jennifer questions again.

"No, when I get up in the morning, the first thing I do is try to remember what day it is and then see what it is I have to do. My day is school, writing and of course, Uncle Reuben. By the end of the day, I may have fallen asleep at my lap top working on some book or I have fallen asleep checking papers."

"Have you ever *noticed* a handsome man?"

"Of course, I'm not blind, but I'm too busy to care."

"Have men asked you out?"

"I've been asked for coffee, but I usually turn it down because I have somewhere to go."

"This life doesn't bother you? Ever think of getting married and having children?"

"Jenny, I'm happy," River said. "My first love is teaching, I love books, I enjoy writing. This is normal to me."

Jennifer nods her head.

"I don't mean to be so nosy or to give you such a hard time." Jennifer says apologetically. "I just worry about you."

"Don't," River said with a grin. "I'm fine, I promise. I've to go, Dave is coming over tomorrow, early, and I can't be hung over."

IF DAVE NEEDED ANY type of book for any reason such as to read, to do research, or to make up a class lesson, he did not go to the nearest library nor did he go to the local book store. Instead he went to River's. She has a wide variety of books, ranging from school books, to best sellers, to encyclopedias.

For the past three years Dave and River have been trying to build a library inside her home. Shelves have been brought, but needs to be put together. However, every time Dave would be at River's house they would begin to organize her books, but end up diving into them, reading and analyzing, and sometimes coming up with a lesson plan. River and Dave would drink, eat, and spend the whole evening together.

River's home is located in a section of Pittsburgh known as Shady Side. Her home is beautiful only because she hired a decorator. The theme colors were maroon and creams, browns and gold. The color combination made her home look luxurious. It is a five bedroom home, with two and a half bathrooms. Outside, the lawn is immaculate. River makes sure that she has someone tending to the lawn. Her home looks exquisite and quite grand, but the large home is not to impress the world, but to store her many, many books. Two of the bedrooms are used as a bedroom; the master bedroom and a guest bedroom. Room three, River has turned into an office. In this room, she would get writing done or school work. Inside the room she has a small desk that holds her computer, and a small end table that holds the telephone and fax machine, and printer. Only a few associates have the telephone number; Reuben does not. In the back of the room there is a naked window. Below it is another desk that holds River's lap top and there are two small book shelves filled with books. The remaining two bedrooms are the rooms that store her many books. There is a living room, a dining room, a basement that River turned into a rec room, but uses as storage for her many books. Once a week, preferably Fridays, River has a cleaning lady come by.

River sits in her office writing; working on her manuscript -the particular manuscript that Dave said that wasn't any good. She has big plans for Dave. If he says that it wasn't any good, then he is going to help her make it good. Her current book is on its way to the book stores in the matter of one month so this particular book needs to be finished.

Dave knocks on the door and then enters. He knows that River leaves the door unlocked whenever she is expecting him. Dave also knows that there will be a fresh pot of coffee. It is early Saturday morning; five minutes past nine.

"Riv-," Dave calls out.

He knows that she not going to answer him. Dave walks into the kitchen and fixes himself and River a cup of coffee. He walks to her office where he knows he'll find her. He smiles when he sees her.

"Hey you, what's up?" he greets.

"Hey Davy," she says.

She looks up at him. Dave hands her the cup of coffee.

"What are you working on?" Dave asks.

"The book that you said wasn't any good," River answers, then takes a sip of her coffee.

"I didn't say that it wasn't good, I said there wasn't any emotion." Dave told her. "I mean the plot is good, the only thing that is unbelievable with your characters is the love they have for each other. You implied that they do love each other. I didn't get that."

River directs her attention back to the computer monitor.

"River read books where there is a relationship with the characters but the relationship is not the focus of the book, but it is the core. So whenever your characters get into a situation they know that they can result to their love for one another to handle the situation."

River sits back in her chair with her arms folded across her chest. She hears Dave talking, but all she can make out of what he is saying is,

"Blah, blah, blah, blah,"

She looks up at him.

"What brings you to my humble abode?" she asks.

"I'm organizing a literary time line with the writers of the Harlem Renaissance and I want to study a little bit of the authors."

"Jessie Redmon Fauset, Countee Culleen, awesome! Can I sit in on this class?"

"So you can intimidate my students, no."

River stands up giving Dave a scornful look. Dave and she go in one of the rooms of books. Every time Dave comes he is taken away by the amount of books.

"Sometimes I wonder if it is safe to come in. Once I am here, I am stuck. Escaping can be a problem." Dave says laughing. "We really need to organize this library."

"I know but who really has the time," River asks, looking through a box of books.

"We have some time today," Dave suggests.

"No, you have to work on your time line and I have to work on my emotionless book."

"River relax, you know whenever I'm here, I am usually here until the wee hours of the morning. I can finish building the shelves and put the books in order, by theme and style."

"David, that can take all night,"

"It shouldn't take too much time. Your boxes are labeled."

"Yeah, but that doesn't mean that the books are in the correct boxes," River said.

Dave sighs.

"Well it's early; let's make a day of it. Plus you can help me construct my time line and I can help with your book."

THE SUN IS BEGINNING to peak from behind the horizon, kissing the royal blue sky. The book shelves are assembled in three bedrooms, including her office. The remaining books that are duplicates are put into storage bins. While Dave assembled the book shelves, River arranged the books by author and categories. River now has a library. Also River assisted Dave on his time line for his class and he assisted her work on her book. Everything took all day and all night.

Dave takes a final look in the library. He is pleased with his work. He walks into the living room and sits on the couch. River sits in her office reading over her manuscript. She is trying to understand where Dave has missed the genuine love her characters share. River combs thoroughly through each paragraph. She sighs and walks to the living room where she finds Dave sitting down on the couch.

"River, this is your book," He takes his hand and covers his face; exhausted from lack of sleep. "Don't change it because I don't see what you see. I'm just one person." He yawns. "Excuse me,"

River looks at Dave. He smiles at her. She notices that he has a five o'clock shadow and that his eyes are red from a lack of sleep.

"I cannot believe you stayed up all night," She replied, sitting beside him. "You want to sleep in the guess room? I can wake you up in a few hours."

"No, I'm okay," Dave tells her.

He looks at her.

"Why are you not tired?" he asks.

River shrugs her shoulders.

"It will hit me later," she says looking away.

"Want to go get some breakfast?" he asks.

"No,"

"Yes you do, come on," Dave stands up.

He grabs River's hand and pulls her up from the couch.

River grabs the books that Dave needs for the Harlem Renaissance and they get into his car and drive to an all- night restaurant.

Dave is tired. He wants to close his eyes and sleep forever, but Dave also wants to spend time with River as much as time permits. He likes her. He practically loves her. However Dave has never told her. River is too busy for him to sit down and talk with her about what he is feeling. Whenever River and Dave would talk, it would be about books, teaching, writing, or studying. They go out to dinner but dinners with River was more like business dinners instead of two friends going out to eat. In the past few years that they have been working together, there was never a good time.

"This air feels good," River says, lifting her head slightly to let the cool breeze tickle her cheeks.

"Yeah," Dave said. "I like this time of year. Spring is here. The winter is lifting its cloud."

"I like this time of day," River said. "It's still too early for anyone to bother me. I can get some work done. No Reuben, no student sending me emails of excuses,"

"Sounds like you need a vacation," Dave said.

"No, I don't have time for a vacation," River said. "I just need to get better organized. Like today, it's Sunday, and after you and I eat, I can get homework checked and organized. Have lesson plans for my classes. I can get some research done from Mr. Bush. I even have time to take a nap. Later on, I will go over my grandmother's for some good home cooking. By six or seven o'clock, I can come home, work on my book and by nine watch re-runs of *Law and Order, SVU*,"

"Sounds like a planned day," Dave chuckles.

RIVER AND DAVE WALK into the restaurant and as soon as they are seated, they are greeted by a waiter.

"Hi, what can I get for you today?" he asks cheerfully.

"We'll have the buffet," Dave says him, "Can I also have orange juice?"

The waiter looks at River,

"I will have apple juice," she says.

"Okay, help yourself to the buffet and I will bring your drinks,"

The waiter leaves.

"Okay, listen," River begins, "You're going to love studying the Harlem Renaissance, I mean really love it."

Dave grins. River looks long and hard at Dave. His five o'clock shadow makes him look dangerous and sexy. Some of the women in the restaurant stop and take notice of him but he doesn't notice. His sapphire eyes are fixated on River.

"I still can't believe that you stayed up all night to organize those books," River said to him.

"It's okay, I had nothing to do," Dave says shrugging his shoulders.

"Nothing to do is an understatement," River comments with a chuckle. "You stayed up all night for me,"

"I like you," Dave smiles, hoping that she gets the hint.

"Well thank you," She smiles back.

River smile confuses Dave. He doesn't know if she sees his subtle flirtation or if it has gone over her head. Knowing his dear friend he knows that his flirting has gone over her head. Will she catch on to his feelings? At times, Dave thinks of himself as a fool. Why waste time on someone who apparently does not feel the same. Why hope and wonder if River would actually look at him the way he looks at her. To the average man, he would be considered a fool. To a good friend, he would be considered the best friend. The best friend doesn't give up on a friend. So he will not give up on the concept of River. He knows that there is something wrong. Something has happened for her to be so opaque. He is going to find out and if finding out takes forever, then forever he is going to give. Dave is determined to find out the mystery to what happened to his Little Friend River.

River pulls out her manuscript from her tote bag and places it on the table.

"What are you doing?" Dave asks.

"I still want to work on my book."

The waiter returns with their drinks and then leaves.

"River it's six in the morning," Dave said.

"What's your point?"

"My point is that we've been up all night."

"Don't get sleepy on me now, Marouni," River said. "You told me that my book had no feeling, so we're going to make it feel."

Dave shakes his head.

"River, I'm getting something to eat."

Dave walks over to the buffet. River follows him. After they fill their plates with food they sit down.

"So tell me," Dave begins. "How is Reuben's club coming along?"

"Okay, I guess," River shrugs. "But that's Reuben's club."

"Aren't you practically funding the whole thing?"

"Yeah,"

"So, it's your club too,"

"Technically," River said. "But that's only because I am buying it. This is all Reuben's thing; not mine. I just want to say, 'Here you go uncle, buy your club, have fun, call me later,' It's like he can't make a move without me. Meet the architect; see his plans, what does that have to do with me?"

"It has a lot to do with you. It's your money." Dave told her. "If I was buying my uncle a night club, I would like to meet the construction team because I like to see that my money is not going to a bunch of sloppy builders. Have you met the architect?"

I've done more than meet him, River said to herself.

"I met him," River said.

"What other buildings has he done?" Dave asks.

River shrugged her shoulders.

"So how did you meet him?"

"Reuben already selected him. He just wanted me to meet the guy, look at his portfolio."

"Did you?"

"Yeah, I glanced at it." River answers.

"Glanced? River, you don't glance at anything you're putting your money in. You need to know if this guy is legit, if the buildings that he has made done well."

"I know all that, but that is Reuben's job to find all that out."

"It's your job too," Dave said. "It may be his vision but it's your investment."River shrugged. "What's the architect's name?"

"Why?"

"Just curious," Dave said. "Maybe I heard of him."

"What do you know about architecture?" River asks with a chuckle.

"I know a few things, girl. I may surprise you." Dave said with a grin as he ate.

"You don't know anyone," River teased with a laugh.

"You think you're the only famous person I know?" Dave asks. "I used to work in Vegas, remember?"

"Yeah, I remember. You came back to Pittsburgh for bigger and better things."

"Right," Dave said. "Seriously, I take it that the architect is not well known." River shrugged her shoulders again. "You're known for helping the local man. Bush Publications is now the top publishing company in the city because of your name. Maybe when word gets out that River Daniels, the niece of Reuben Massie and owner of the hottest club in Pittsburgh, the architect firm might become famous."

"Let's talk about something else," River suggests. "How about you and me start a literature school."

"A what?"

"A literature school for young writers, we can teach them the fundamentals, you know like creative writing. It can be a credited course and transfer to supporting universities. What do you think?"

"I think you need some sleep,"

CHAPTER SIX

DANA PACES NERVOUSLY IN his office. The dream team waits in the conference room. Clear instructions have been given on the set up for this big meeting. Two models of night clubs sit on the large oak table. For each model, there is a well written expense report. Dana had explained to his dream team that this new client is tough. Carol made sure there is a fresh pot of coffee, fresh bagels with cream cheese and bottles of water are sitting in ice.

Dana cannot believe he is nervous. As he paces back and forth in his office, he tells himself;

She is only a client.

He cannot get over the fact that he is letting River Daniels intimidate him. Why let some bitter, petty ex-girlfriend make him fidgety?

Who does she think she is? He asks himself.

River may have been someone special from his past, but that is the point; the past. He may have loved her but he loved her yesterday; and today is today. She is now no one to him. If she would be anything to him, she would be the one that puts Wilson Architect Firm on the map. With her money and her uncle's expensive taste, she will not only bring the firm out of the red zone, but it will open up doors of opportunity. Dana can expand the company. He can put the firm in places like New York, Atlanta, and California. He would be building homes for movie stars.

Dana begins to imagine all of the successful business men that would bring their clients to Reuben's Room, listening to soulful jazz music, eating the shrimp and baby back ribs, making ground breaking deals and admiring the structure of the building. There will be many top musicians and performers coming to Reuben's after a successful energetic concert, wanting to relax and unwind. Once the word gets out that the club was built by a local architect, these same celebrities will want something built. As Dana paces in his office, he starts to see dollar signs.

Maybe, just maybe in spite of River's bitterness, she really is a different person. He'll never know unless he talks to her.

"How you been?" he would ask.

"I'm fine, how you been?" would be her reply.

The telephone intercom buzzes startling Dana from his thoughts.

"Miss. Daniels is here," Carol informs.

"Okay, I'll be out."

Dana takes a deep breath, looks at himself in the mirror and then he leaves to go greet her. He clears his throat as he walks slowly down the hall way that leads to the reception area.

Just be cool, Dana just be cool, He encourages himself.

Dana sees River standing looking out of the window. Butterflies begin to flutter rapidly in his stomach. He hopes that she cannot hear the loud thumping coming from his chest. She looks intimidating in her black pant suit holding her brief case. She wears silver wire rimmed glasses and her hair is pulled back into a bun. River turns away from the window and looks at Dana. Their eyes meet, but Dana quickly looks away. Her eyes are so cold. Dana looks back at her and smiles.

"River," he said with a smile then extends his hand for her to shake.

"Hello," she responds, then shakes his hand.

"I'm glad you made it," Dana said.

River doesn't respond.

"Ah, follow me to the conference room."

The minute walk to the conference room seems like the longest hour in history.

"How are you?" he asks.

"I am well," is the reply.

"How is Reuben?"

"Good,"

Dana opens the door and River steps inside. Immediately the dream team stands to greet her as if she is the Queen of England.

"Gentlemen, I'd like for you to meet River Daniels. River, meet my dream team. Justin and Eddie Banks, my landscapers and Nick Vito and Clayton Simmons are my engineers."

Handshakes and hellos go forth. Dana takes a breath, then walks to the front of the room to begin his well prepared and well-rehearsed speech.

"Shall we get started?" Dana asked. "River, you can sit here,"

River sits down at her assigned seat as everyone else sits down.

"We composed two books because there are two different types of models. Club A and Club B." Dana said.

River looks at the two models on the table.

"Club A is trendy Club B is a little more traditional." Dana continues.

"Which one does Reuben like?" River asked.

"He likes Club A," Dana says to her.

"Then that is the one I want to hear about," she states.

"Okay," Dana replies taking in a deep breath.

He is disappointed that he cannot give his two well-prepared speeches.

Dana quickly removes the model of Club B, while Justin quickly grabs Club B's expense report. Dana can see this is going to be a long morning. He is at her mercy.

AFTER TWO HOURS AND fifteen minutes and numerous cups of coffee, the meeting is over. Everyone looks at River, wondering if she has been persuaded by the presentation. River looks over the well composed expense report. Then she nods her head in an approving manor.

"This is well organized. I am impressed." She states.

I don't want your impression, I want your money, Dana says to himself.

Sighs of relief fill the room and then everyone cheers happily. Dana can see that his boys are tired and they need to stretch their legs. He stands up.

"Okay, boys, order all the necessary equipment and let's get this club built." Dana says to his team.

Without hesitation, the dream team shake River's hand, tells her that is was nice meeting her and quickly they scurry off.

River reaches in to her brief case to pull out her check book.

"Who do I make the check out to," she asks.

"Wilson Architect Firm," Dana answers

River writes out the check and then hands it to Dana.

"Is that everything?" she asks, gathering up all her things.

Dana wonders who is going to relinquish control. The answer is obvious. From her intimidating looks, River is not going to give up any control.

"Congratulations," he said.

Caught off guard, River looks at him.

"Excuse me?"

"I said, 'congratulations'," He said now nervously. "Um, on your success,"

The look on River's face gives him no sign if she is flattered or offended. Her eyes are cold. It is like looking into a block of ice. Dana takes in a deep breath.

"I'm a fan," He said. "I have both your books."

"Is that right?" she asked.

"Yeah," Dana said. "They're really good. I'm not surprised though, you were always talented."

"Thank you," she said. "Well, I have to go, is there anything else?"

"Ah, no. That is everything," Dana said with a grin.

"Good."

Dana watches River leave. It is evident that she is not the same River, from her appearance to the way she speaks. This River doesn't even smile and Dana clearly remembers her having the prettiest smile. River used to wear makeup, not too much, but just enough to enhance her already pretty features. Now her face is plain. Nothing about her stands out. She wouldn't be noticed in a crowd. Regardless of her ordinary features, she was still beautiful.

RIVER DRIVES TO THE school quickly, trying to put the past two hours behind her. She has a creative writing class to teach in an hour, and that can gives her plenty of opportunity to go over a lesson plan for this class and forget about the handsome man that came back into her life. River is pleased at how she handled herself. She didn't overreact and she remained cool in his presence. She kept her focus on the organized expense report that sat before her on the table.

It was also comical at how he complimented her:

"Congratulations," he said. "I'm a fan,"

River knows what he was trying to do. She hasn't been out of the game that long that she can't read any of the plays.

How sweet, Mr. Wilson, but you'll never have control over my soul.

At one time, Dana had full and complete control over her soul. Just one look from his eyes, just one kiss from his lips, just one touch from his hands, and she surrendered everything to him.

As River waits for the traffic light to turn green, she sees that pretty girl. The same pretty girl that was in her dreams a week ago or is she someone else who looks like her? The pretty girl waves at River. River looks around to see who she is waving at. Is she waving at River? River shakes her head, trying to clear her thoughts. The light turns green, River quickly drives off.

Today is going to be a long day, and just the thought of this causes River to get antsy. She can feel her body temperature rise. Every little thing begins to bother and annoy her. Traffic is moving too slow. When it seems to pick up, the person behind her is driving too close. The weather man said that today is going to be a cool and cloudy day, but today seems too hot and the sun is too bright.

Calm down River, she says to herself.

She takes a deep breath, but she is still on edge.

FINALLY AT THE UNIVERSITY, River pulls into her designated parking space. When she gets out of the car, River sees the girl standing across the parking lot not too far away from River's car.

Is she following me? River asks herself.

The girl looks familiar, but River cannot put her finger on where she knows her from. The girl smiles and starts to walk towards River. Nervously Rivers enters the building, the pretty girl follows. River speeds up her walk and the girl's pace quickens. The faster River walks the faster the pretty girl follows.

River needs to get away to hide in her office where she can be buried alive by numerous messages and paperwork. She hopes that Bonnie had stocked the mini fridge with bottled water because right now she is thirsty; her mouth is pasty.

River jumps when she hears someone calling her name.

"River," they called out. "River,"

She hears nothing but her name being called. She sees various students laughing and talking among themselves waiting to go to their next class. River doesn't notice Dave walking behind her. She only sees the pretty girl and hears the sounds of her heart beating. River manages to get to the elevators. She rapidly pushes the up button.

"Come on," River said to herself.

Then someone taps on her shoulders.

"WHAT?" River snaps, turning around.

She catches herself when she sees it is Bonnie.

"Bonnie," River said as she tries to catch her breath.

"I didn't mean to startle you," Bonnie said with a pleasant smile. "Are you all right?"

Before River can fully gain her composure, Dave approaches and taps River on the shoulder, causing River to be startled again, nearly collapsing in Dave's arms. Immediately Dave and Bonnie walk River to an empty chair and helps her sit down.

"I'm okay," River keeps saying. "I'm okay,"

"You're flushed," Dave says as he cups his hand on her face. "And you're trembling, Bonnie, get River some water from the cafeteria, tell them that it's for River. I'll pay them later."

Bonnie quickly leaves. Dave directs his attention back on River. Her face is moist from sweat. He sees her searching for someone. Dave looks around and sees the students looking upon as passer-byes looking, as if they saw an accident on the road.

"Nothing to see," Dave said sternly. "Find something to do and go,"

The students sigh and reluctantly leave the area, leaving Dave alone to cater to River. Dave again turns his attention back to River.

"What?-," River asks.

Dave places his hand on the side of her neck and starts to massage her and trying to ease whatever tension that caused this near breakdown.

"Are you okay?" he asked, concerned.

"Someone was following me." She replies looking for the pretty girl.

"Who?"

"I don't know," River says taking in a deep breath. "But she was following me."

"She?" Dave asked. "What was she wearing?"

Before she could answer, Bonnie returns with a 20oz bottle of water. Dave thanks Bonnie as River drinks.

"Are you all right?" Bonnie asks.

River nods her head.

"I wanted to tell you that I have to leave early, I have a doctor's appointment in a half hour. I left the paper work for your next class on your desk."

"Okay, Bonnie, thank you." River tells her.

Bonnie leaves. Dave looks at River. She is still trembling.

"Maybe you should cancel your classes." Dave suggests.

"No, you're silly," River said with a grin. "I'll be all right."

She takes in a deep breath.

"River, you just said that someone was following you."

"It's nothing, Dave." River said as she stands up.

Dave stands up.

"I'm sure that it was probably a student." River says. "She must have left when she saw all that commotion."

Dave looks at her long and hard in her eyes. He tries to look past the ice that guards any entrance that leads through to her soul.

"What?" River asks trying to break from Dave's intense stare.

"River, you nearly fainted, no more than five minutes ago."

"I'm okay." Dave still looked into River's eyes. "Dave, come on, you're making me nervous. I just lost my cool."

"Let me walk you to your office." Dave put his arm around River, but she moves away.

"David-," River tried to object.

"David nothing," he objects.

River can see that he will not give up. Reluctantly, she takes his hand and together they walk to River's office.

JUST LIKE BONNIE SAID, the necessary paper work for River's creative writing class has been prepared and placed on River's desk.

"Bonnie is too good for me," River said as she put her brief case down on the love seat. "Remind me to do something nice for her."

"Where were you this morning? I wanted to talk about Jessie Redmon Fauset."

"I had a meeting to go to." River said.

She walks to her desk, sits down and begins going over the paperwork Bonnie has left for her.

"What meeting?"

"Um, with Reuben's architect," River answers. "Anyway, did you read anything from Fauset?"

"Yeah, I like her."

"Did you read *There is Confusion*?" River asked.

"No, is it any good?" Dave asked.

"Real good. Fauset's mom died when she was little and her dad married a Jewish woman that wanted to heal the world of racial oppression."

"And that is vital information in an English class because-,"

"Don't know- just a little FYI."

"How did the meeting go?"

"It went well," River said, looking through her drawers on her desk. "It was the type of club that Reuben wants, the cost of materials. There was even a model."

River grabs the copy of Dana's proposal out of her brief case and hands it over to Dave. It was quiet for a moment while Dave leaf through the expense report and River checks her email.

"This is well put together. What is this guy's name?"

"Dana Wilson," River answers.

"Is the company new?"

"I guess,"

"Did you like the presentation?"

"Yes!" River snaps. Her snapping catches Dave off guard. "Sorry," she said letting out a sigh. "It's been a long morning."

Dave walks to River and sits on the edge of the desk.

"Are you sure that you don't want to cancel your class?" Dave asked. "We can play hooky get some Chinese food, watch the *Good Fellows*.

River smiles.

"Sounds tempting, but I really need to clear my head."

"A bunch of students is not going to clear your head." Dave chuckles. "Seriously, River come on, cancel one day. We can go for a walk and forget about Reuben's club."

"No," River said. "Dave I have to stay busy or else I'll be thinking about-," she stops talking and looks at Dave.

She doesn't want to talk or think about Dana Wilson. Dave notices her hesitation.

"I need to stay focused."

She looks away again, in hopes that Dave would give up. It's quiet for twenty seconds. The twenty second silence seems awkward and uncomfortable. Slowly she looks up at him and is hit by his blue eyes staring intently at her.

"What's the matter, River?" his tense eyes are now comforting and trusting.

"Nothing," she said softly.

"You can talk to me about anything, you know that." Dave said.

River nods her head.

"I'll tell you what," River began. "This is my only class today. I'll come over with the Chinese food and we can make it a DeNiro night. *Casino, Godfather,* everything,"

"River-,"

"Dave, come on, I promise. I'm good. I will see you tonight."

"All right."

Dave leans forward and kisses River on the forehead.

CHAPTER SEVEN

RIVER SITS IN HER literature class, watching her students write their rough drafts for their term papers. It is comical to watch these students because they put so much energy in having the perfect rough draft. Whenever they give their work to Dr. Daniels to look over, they wait anxiously for the red pen to stain their well composed paper. If a rough draft had only a few red marks on the paper, then in the student's eyes that is considered to be a good paper. River loves the fact that she can be somewhat intimidating to her students. It's not that she is a mean teacher, River allows her students to voice their opinions and she allows them to have deep and interesting discussions in her class, but she will not tolerate laziness in her class. As tough as River is as a teacher, most of her students cannot say a bad word about Dr. Daniels. They know that she makes them think. The mid-terms and finals are difficult, but only if a student doesn't study. River does not tolerate lazy students with potential.

Dave has tried hard to convince River not to give homework during spring break, but she doesn't budge.

"They'll come back clueless and unfocused." She tells him. "There will be no motivation. Homework maintains their study habits so when they come back, they're just as alert and sharp; and besides, they get enough breaks in between semesters."

Dave shakes his head. Dr. Daniels is the toughest teacher and Dr Marouni is the easiest, yet Dr. Daniels is the best literature teacher at the University.

O

TWO MONTHS HAVE PASSED since River's meeting with Dana at his architecture firm and although River hasn't seen him, she still sees the pretty girl lurking at a distance. Every time River would see her, she notices something more familiar about this girl. Maybe they have spoken in the past. However if she is not bold enough to say anything to River, then River is not going to go out of her way to speak with her. River hasn't told anyone about her.

For two months, Dana and his dream team work from sunrise to sunset. However, the art deco type club is nowhere near being complete and as a matter of fact, Dana and his dream team are behind schedule. As Dana's men work hard to build this dream club, Reuben supervises every detail; almost annoying the staff and crew. Reuben pleads with River to come see the building in progress, but she manages to use every excuse on why she cannot come. She doesn't want to take the chance of seeing Dana. Yet this is her beloved uncle, she needs to put her petty and childish issues behind her and be supportive. After her morning class, she drives to the site of the club for a supportive and brief moment.

RIVER ARRIVES AT THE work site. She is surprised to see how much work has been done. It seems like yesterday that she signed her life away to the man behind this project. She finds Reuben on the grounds overlooking crew men. He waves at her and quickly approaches. They greet each other with a hug. He gives her a brief tour and then takes her to the mobile home that he uses as an office.

"Wanna drink, got a fully stocked bar." Reuben asks as River sits down.

"It's too early to drink," River comments.

"Oh relax, let your hair down and get the bug out your butt!" Reuben teases smiling.

He opens up his mini bar and gives River a wine cooler.

"I got your bug," River says as she rolls her eyes.

Reuben laughs.

"So, what do you think?" Reuben asks. "Coming along good, huh?"

"It's coming along nice," River says, sipping her cooler.

"I've been hiring waiters and waitress," Reuben informs. "As a matter of fact, I have an interview in a half hour."

River grins.

"Oh, man, I can't wait until it opens." Reuben exclaims. "It's going to be jumpin' baby you hear me? Riv, how about once a month, you do a poetry reading,"

"No thank you," River said sarcastically, then chuckles.

"I like to hear some poetry," a voice says coming from the back of the mobile home.

River looks to see who is in the back. Dana comes from the back. River shoots Rueben a look. Reuben takes in a deep breath. Reuben forgot to mention that Dana and he are sharing the mobile home.

"How you doin'," Dana asked.

"I'm well," was River's response.

"We share the mobile home." Reuben explains to his niece.

River looks away;

"Well, I don't want to keep you boys from work." She replies.

River attempts to get up, but Reuben stops her.

"Riv, don't go baby,"

Reuben's cell phone rings. He looks at the caller ID;

"I gotta take this call, Riv wait here, please. I need to talk to you about some things."

Reuben quickly leaves. River sighs. Dana thinks this is too cute. How she avoids him as if he is the devil. Speaking with proper English, "I am well," Who is she fooling? This is not River, especially with that uptight preppy look; those business suits and those glasses. The River he knew hated to wear her glasses. The River he knew wore jeans that showed off the curves of her hips. His River wore those little t-shirts that showed off her belly. Now, this River is tucked away behind her business suits and glasses as if she was going to some business seminar. Her suits give little to the imagination. They hide her legs; the long legs that gave the illusion that she is tall; the same long legs that he used to climb. Wearing her long hair in a pony-tail, her long hair hiding the structure of the neck, the neck he remembers nibbling on. This River doesn't smile. His

River has the prettiest smile. Her smile was her ticket to his heart.

Dana grins as she continues to nurse her drink and wait for Reuben.

"How is the writing coming along?" Dana asks nervously.

"It's coming along just fine, thank you." She answers.

"Anything coming out soon,"

"Had a book released last month." She answers. "but you're a fan so you would know that," River said sarcastically.

Dana senses the sarcasm in River's tone. Considering that the last time he saw her he told her that he is a fan. Fans know when a release of anything new has been released, from their favorite recording artist, actor or actress and well as authors. Dana grins.

"Well, congratulations."

It is quiet. The silence seems eternal.

"How is teaching?"

"Good,"

Dana nods his head. She is hard to talk to; his River was a chatter box.

"River, um, I'm sorry."

River looks at him catching him with her icy eyes. Chills go through his body.

"Excuse me?" she asks.

"I'm sorry," he says again. "For any resentment you have towards me."

Touching, she said to herself.

River doesn't have time to be spoon fed by tasteless words. River gives Dana a grin.

"Tell Reuben that I had to go. Whatever it is he needed to discuss will have to wait."

River quickly leaves. Watching her leave, Dana realized that there will be no solution to melting the ice that has guarded her soul.

Once she is outside, the cool spring air begins to relax her. The bright sun is almost blinding, but not blinding enough to see the pretty girl standing across the street. River ignores her by shielding her eyes from the sun light and walking across the parking lot. She greets the landscapers with a friendly nod. As she gets into the car she sees that today is going to be a lovely day to sit outside and write. River had fixed that "emotionless" book and it has been shipped to Bush Publishing. The idea of sitting around for hours writing seems very ideal to River. She can create characters and erase her mind of Dana and his sorry apology.

I'm sorry for any resentment you have toward me. His words echo in her mind.

"HA!" River laughs out loud.

River takes a deep breath. Unintentionally her mind wonders to the past when she would hear the sweet words and the smooth lines. They would be from Dana and the other men from her past. Men would always come into her life. Ironically they would come when she would be focused on her priorities. Foolishly, River believed that she could juggle a steady boyfriend, attend school and establish a writing career.

These men would be captivated by her beauty and her witty personality. They pursued her and managed to win her heart by their musical words and soft kisses. They date for months. They tell her that they love her, and they cannot imagine a life without her. They introduce her to their families and their families would fall in love with River. Everything seemed to be perfect; the perfect boyfriend, the perfect girlfriend. They would spend every moment together, indulging each other with love. Their indulgence would cause River to lose focus on her schooling and on her writing. She was too consumed with her boyfriend. Life was blissful, but then suddenly, there was a halt.

"I think we should be just friends," the boyfriends would say. "I don't know what it is, but I think we should slow things down a bit."

The sudden halt caught River off guard. River knew what their reasons were and no matter how vague and confused these men claim to be, she knew that they knew the real reason. During those days, River was pure. She was innocent to the touch of a man's hands and inexperienced to their caresses. After a few dates, she would tell them:

"I'm a virgin,"

The fact of having fresh meat in their reach seemed stimulating to her boyfriends. They would smile and welcome the challenge of being the beauty's first lover. At first they would be the perfect gentlemen, not forcing or trying to talk River into doing anything she wasn't ready for. After a while her intriguing innocence became a hindrance, and soon the boyfriend would leave, breaking her heart.

She would hope and pray that they would come to their senses and want her back, but they never called. River would slowly get over the lost love focusing on her schooling and writing, until another distraction came along.

One day River decided to take control, she met a man named Jerry Simms. Jerry seemed to be a nice guy. He was good looking, intelligent, had his own house and he had a good job. Jerry was seven years her senior and he had two children. He was experienced. He was a man compared to the boys River had dated. At twenty-one she decided to not tell him that she was a virgin. She was going to wait if they got serious. If not; no love lost. However Jerry found out sooner than River had planned.

River decided to surprise him one day by showing up at his home. River looked sexy that night. She wore a royal blue baby doll style dress. Jerry turned the surprise visit to a romantic evening. They sat in his game room with the light low. Jerry kissed River with strong, yet gentle passion. He touched and caressed her in all the right places. Although her body responded positively towards him, she wanted him to stop. River can tell by the way he kissed her and the way he touched her that he was not going to let up. Her body surrendered fully and complete. Tonight is going to be the night. Maybe he wouldn't notice. As they kissed and caressed each other, River made the decision to go all the way. On the couch in his game room, Jerry ripped through her virginity.

Then suddenly her body jumped with pain and his body now frozen from tension.

"You're a virgin," he said in shock.

"I was," River said sardonically.

She was trying hard not to reveal that she was uncomfortable.

Immediately Jerry pulled himself from River. Quickly he stood up and put his pants on. River sat up also.

"You didn't have to stop," she said.

"Yes, I did," Jerry said coolly. "Get dressed."

Jerry walked away. She laid on the couch feeling like an idiot. Maybe she should have told him. There wasn't much for River to do but to put on her underwear back on. She walked up stairs that led to front door.

"Did I hurt you?" Jerry asked coming from a back room.

"No," River lied.

"Why didn't you say anything?" he asked.

"You didn't ask."

Jerry approached her. He wrapped his arms around her. He leaned in to kiss her.

"Let's go upstairs and do it right,"

River grinned. The idea of this man making gentle love enticed to her. Jerry took River by the hand and he escorted her upstairs and into his bed room. As their second time became a redeemed first time, River finally believed that she had control of a man. However, she was so naïve; she being the prey and Jerry the predator.

During the year of their relationship Jerry used her innocence to fulfill his overrated sexual desires. His desires were too overwhelming for River. But in order to keep her man, River performed any sexual need that Jerry requested. She thought as long as she performs when requested he would stay; he would love her. But Jerry came and went as he pleased, leaving River to be forgotten about and waiting for his call. River would cry endlessly at night, wondering if he would ever love her.

After a year and a half, River grew tired of being used. Once again, she got her priorities in order and she started writing again, and if Jerry called, he called, and if not, she was not going to lose sleep over it.

Then one summer night in August she met the man who captured her heart forever.

Now, like Jerry, she is trying to make him a distant memory. It has taken too long for River to erase the ghost of boyfriends from the past from her mind. It took long for River to stop thinking about the concept of relationships. Now her body is cold as if she has no soul. No one will feed her bland words of love.

SHIRLEY IS SURPISED TO see River at her home during the middle of the week and in the middle of the afternoon on just a social call. Something tells Shirley that River is bothered by something and she needs her grandmother's wisdom. After they greet each other with a hug and kiss, Shirley fixes River something to eat.

"You been drinking this early in the day?" Shirley asks.

"Grandma, how can you tell?" River asks.

"Grandma knows, baby," Shirley said with a grin.

"I was at Reuben's. He fixed me a complimentary drink." River confesses with a sweet innocent smile.

"How is it looking?"

"Actually, it is looking really nice," River said. "It's spring break right now, the students are eager to go to some beach down south and indulge into some kind of drunken sexual immorality and come back to school all refreshed and experienced."

Shirley laughs.

"So how is the writing coming along?"

"It's coming," River said.

"You know, that Grandma is you're biggest fan."

"What are my books about, Grandma?" River asked, doubting her grandmother's devotion.

Shirley laughed.

"You know grandma reads your books, your characters are so mean."

River laughs.

"My characters aren't mean." River said.

Shirley grins. The telephone rings Shirley answers it.

River finishes eating and then goes into the living room. She sits down on the couch and turns the television on. She finds an old *Golden Girls* episode on. River chuckles as she watches Blanche get into some kind of love triangle. Rose tells a long and dull story about her days in St. Olaf, and not far behind, Sophia getting into some mischief and Dorothy is scolding her for it.

Shirley enters the living room and sits next to River. River rested her head upon her grandmother's shoulder. River closes her eyes and breathes in the familiar smell of fabric softener and cheap perfume. River remembers hiding on Grandma's lap, escaping a spanking from her mother whenever she would get into trouble. Shirley would softly stroke the side of River's face and in a soft voice reprimand the child.

Shirley softly strokes and caresses River's back. She is the beloved, the only grandchild. She was her grandfather's angel. His River could do no wrong in his eyes. Tears well up in Shirley's eyes as she caresses River, her beloved River has been through so much, losing dear loved ones before she was twenty-three. Shirley wishes that she can bare the pain that her beloved carries. Maybe then she can see River smile again.

"What's the matter baby?" she asks in a soft tone.

River doesn't respond right away. She keeps her eyes closed; staying in the safety of Grandma's arms. The silence doesn't bother Shirley. River will talk when she's ready.

"He apologized," River said softly.

"What baby?"

"He said that he was sorry for any resentment that I had towards him."

At first, Shirley doesn't know what River is talking about, but then she realizes.

"Dana?" she asked. "When?"

"Today at Reuben's,"

"Well, River that's nice."

River sits up and looks at her grandmother.

"Nice? What's nice about it?"

"He trying to make amends for breaking your heart."

"Amends?" River asked. "What do I need an amend for?"

"He wants to make things better between you two," Shirley said. "He knows that he was wrong for the way he broke your heart-,"

River sits back on the couch.

"He's fifteen years too late, don't you think?"

Shirley grins.

"Better late than never, baby,"

"Grandma, why you defending him?" River asks annoyed with her grandmother's optimism.

"I'm not defending him, River," Shirley says with a smile, "it's past due. He broke up with you over the phone, not giving you an explanation, but it is nice that he did. He was not too proud."

River remains quiet. Shirley continues.

"Maybe he will tell you why he broke your heart and maybe the two of you can be friends."

"I don't think so," River chuckles walking toward the window. "It took me too long to erase the memories of him and every man that hurt me. If my mom was here she would be proud of me. I am an accomplished woman," she turned toward her grandmother, "I am a powerful woman right now."

Shirley shakes her head in a disappointment.

"You're proud!" Shirley said.

"No, I'm powerful, students fear me. I am the bestselling literary author right now. My books are being studied. I am a millionaire who humbly lives in Pittsburgh, I don't need Dana's apology to make me somebody!"

"Your mother would be very proud of all of your accomplishments, but your heart is black. She wouldn't have been proud."

"My heart?" River exclaims, shocked by Shirley's comment.

River looks at her scornfully.

"I have nothing but the biggest heart!" River defends. "I give and contribute to every charitable organization. I bought - not loaned my uncle a million dollar club that is being built by my ex-boyfriend. My heart is not black, I am the nicest woman in the world, Oprah and Mother Theresa have nothing on me!"

"But you're bitter and cold," Shirley states sternly. "I haven't seen you smile in years. All you had to do was smile for your grandfather and you had him in the palm of your hands."

"I'm not bitter nor am I cold." River said turning back to face the window. "I'm just busy,"

"Busy running from reality, running from love, and hiding behind your work."

"My work doesn't disappointment me,"

Shirley stands up and walks to River.

"What did you say when he apologized?"

"I told him to find the nearest bridge and jump." River replies.

"River-," Shirley admonishes.

"I didn't know what to say," River confesses. "It came out of the blue."

"Where was Reuben?"

"Using the phone. Anyway, I need to write, I'll be in the backyard."

CHAPTER NINE

RIVER WAITS PATIENTLY IN the office while he sits in his chair reading the article that she submitted. As Kennedy reads, River gets up from the chair and looks around his office at the photos and plaques on the wall. Some of the pictures are the warm family portraits like photos of the grandchildren with Mrs. Bush. There are photos of Mr. Bush, taken with people of nobility like the mayor of Pittsburgh and other city councilmen. River looks back at Kennedy. She is growing impatient. He sits perfectly still, not moving as he read thoroughly over the article. His face is stern.

"Come on, Mr. Bush, it's not that serious." River cries.

Kennedy peeks over his glasses and gives River a look that tells her to sit down and be quiet. Seeing the look, River grins and quickly returns to her seat and waits.

A HALF HOUR HAS passed. Finally Kennedy finishes the article. He sets the paper down on his desk and looks at River. She gives him an innocent yet impish smile.

"Very nice article, River," Kennedy says.

"Thank you, Mr. Bush," River says sweetly and politely, "Is that it?"

"What is your rush, a hot date?"

"Yeah," River chuckles then winks "A hot date of grading finals and throwing away my money into my uncle's night club."

Kennedy chuckles at River's sadistic sense of humor.

"Well, I need your time. Is that all right?"

"Yes, Mr. Bush," River says as she added more sugar to her sweet act.

"Good, help yourself to some coffee and relax."

"To Jody's coffee; no thank you. If I wanted to commit suicide, I'd just shoot myself in the mouth, why suffer?"

"Hush, it's not that bad," Kennedy replies.

"It's poisonous, Mr. Bush." River states.

"It's not that bad," Kennedy assures.

"If it not that bad then why do you spike it?"

"Because I am sixty-seven years old and I will spike anything I want. Now close your mouth for a few minutes because I am this close to spiking you."

River sits up in her seat. She is smiling that sweet, yet mischievous smile. Kennedy shakes his head, then sips his coffee.

"Your book is making a lot of noise," Kennedy informs her. "It is making noise in New York, L.A. and in Miami, and bookstores are requesting your presence for book signings, photos and all that good stuff."

"Is that right?" River asked smiling.

"Yes, a book tour, for six weeks, what do you say?"

"I say yes!" River exclaimed.

"You will interview with some of those morning shows as well. Do some talk shows promoting the book."

"Sounds like an adventure!" River smiles.

"Good, you leave next weekend. First stop to New York. What are your plans?"

River looks through her day planner. She looks thoroughly at the next six weeks. She has plans but nothing that River can't cancel. She hasn't confirmed her teaching schedule for this upcoming semester. The book tour is exactly what she needs. She can see certain parts of the country that she has always wanted to visit but never had the time because of her schedule. River is going to buy souvenirs and hang them on her walls just like Jennifer. Most importantly she is going to escape the pretty girl that has been stalking her.

Then again, what if she hears of the book tour and decides to follow River. She would be standing in a distance watching River. Maybe this tour may not be such a good idea. It would be much safer for River to be stalked here in her home town, instead of some unfamiliar place. Quickly, River shakes off the paranoia. Who is she to run? Especially from some girl who has been too much of a coward to say anything to her.

Hmph, River said to herself.

This is now a challenge to River, a challenge that she is going to take. However; she is not going to take this challenge alone, after all, she is being stalked.

"Um, can I ask for security?" River asks.

"Security?" Kennedy questions.

"Yes, you know; someone to watch me as I go to my car and to the bookstore or to my hotel?"

Kenny reads directly between the lines. River sees him reading. Kennedy sees that she sees him reading. River pretends that he reads and sees nothing. Instead she grins and takes in a deep breath.

"Someone giving you a hard time," Kennedy asks her calmly.

"Um no, not necessarily," River said trying to be elusive. "It's just that I am a known writer and maybe a fan might want me to sign their book whenever I want to be left alone."

Kennedy nods his head accepting that she doesn't want to talk.

"I can assign a security guard to escort you every place you go, from the book store, to your car, to your hotel." Kennedy says.

River nods and grins. She takes a deep breath and looks away. This is a side of River that Kennedy has never seen. Her evasive manner worries him. Considering her tough nature, Kennedy knows that she is not going to discuss anything with him. She sits before him trying to be brave against whatever has worried her. Kennedy is going to make sure that River is protected.

"Set everything up and call me later with more details. I have to run. I'll talk to you soon."

Quickly River leaves and gets into her car, not looking for her to the left nor to the right. She doesn't want to take the chance of seeing that pretty girl. River decides to drive to Dave's house to tell him the good news and ask him to join her.

DAVE'S HOUSE IS A typical modest home. Three stairs lead to the porch and there is a swing on the right side of the porch.

There is a small table that holds books. On the door is an ornament that says, "Welcome," The home used to belong to Dave's parents. He promised that he would never sell the house so when they died, he moved in.

River sees his car parked in the driveway. She gets out of the car, walks to the front door and knocks. He opens the door and greets her with a smile. He looks good in his red T-shirt that shows his muscles and he wears dark blue jeans.

"What's up?" Dave said, as River entered in.

"Nothing much," River said, smiling.

Together River and Dave walk into the living room. River notice Dave had been eating lunch while watching basketball highlights on ESPN. She sees the half eaten sandwich and a can of soda on the coffee table.

"Want something to eat," he offers.

"Um, sure," River says as she sits down on the couch.

Dave goes in the kitchen to fix River a sandwich. She waits patiently, looking at the television. Within five minutes Dave returns with a sandwich for River. Together they eat in silence and finishing watching the basketball highlights. Once they finished, River tells Dave her good news.

"So I was in to see Mr. Bush today," she begins.

"Yeah,"

"Yep," River said. "And he wants me to go on a book tour, to New York, L.A., and Miami."

"Wow, River, congratulations," Dave says smiling sipping his soda.

"Thank you," she said. "There is more,"

"What?"

"I want you to come with me." River asks.

"Come where?"

"On my book tour silly," River replies.

"I don't think so," Dave chuckles.

"Oh come on, we can sight see, go to authentic museums, go see plays, and just have fun."

"Fun?" Dave asks doubtfully.

River doesn't have fun.

"Fun," River states smiling.

"I don't know, River." Dave stands up, collects the plates and soda cans.

"Dave, come on," River pleads following him into the kitchen.

"River, I will get in the way." Dave said.

"No you won't. You're my best friend, my first editor. I wouldn't be on a book tour if it weren't for you."

"Me?" Dave chuckles. "You're the writer not me."

"I know that," River said. "But before my works goes to Mr. Bush, it goes to you."

"Really?" Dave questions, surprised.

"Yes, you know that. Why do you think I give you my manuscripts first?"

"Because you're my friend,"

"You're more than my friend David. You're my mentor, my editor, my colleague."

Dave smiles; River continues.

"Dave, have you noticed that I don't send anything to Mr. Bush until you like it. You help me create my characters, my plots. Did I not fix the last book because it lacked *emotion*, and did I not take the suggestions you gave?"

"Wow, I didn't know that I had that much input on your work." Dave smiles.

"Why do you think I thank you in every one of my books?"

"Because I'm your friend," Dave said.

"Okay, well stop being my friend and come with me." River snaps.

"What?" David asked with a chuckle.

River realizes what she just said.

"I mean, come with me, please, I need a friend by my side."

Dave playfully punches River on the cheek.

"How long will we be gone?" Dave asked as he sits on the edge of his kitchen table.

"Six weeks," River answered smiling. "I'll pay for everything-,"

"You don't have to pay-," Dave interrupts.

"Be quiet," she cuts him off. "We'll stay at the best hotel, in a big roomy suite."

Dave takes in a deep breath,

"Okay, I'll go,"

River cheers loudly and wraps her arms around him. Dave laughs as River and he embrace. It is nice to see her smile.

"You can be my personal assistant, you know?"

"You're goofier!" Dave chuckles. "Is that why you want me to go?"

"No, Dave, I really do need a friend with me. Plus, as an assistant, you can just make sure I meet all of my appointments and things like that."

"Okay," he said again.

She smiled at him.

AFTER DAVE'S, RIVERS NEXT stop is Jennifer's House. River wants to tell her the good news. When she gets to the door, River sees that Jennifer left her front door cracked open. River entered and calls out for Jennifer but there was no answer.

"Jenny," River calls out.

River walks to the back of the house. She sees the new items like ancient artifacts on the coffee table. River looks out the window that leads to the back yard and sees Jennifer talking with a gentleman. That must be Robert, Jennifer's son. He is visiting from Africa. River is able to recognize him from the photos that Jennifer had shared with her. River smiles as she walks to the back yard.

Jennifer's back yard looks like a small paradise. The rich green lawn always takes River's breath away. The garden is full of asters, baby breaths, and bell flowers. In the center of the lawn is a small gray bird bath. In the spring time, Jennifer loves to watch the robins take a bath in their little tub. On the other side of the garden is a thick beautiful red maple.

Jennifer laughs at something funny that Robert has said. She turns around and sees River slowly approaching.

"River," Jennifer calls out smiling. "Come meet my son!"

Robert stands up and he shakes River's hand.

"Very nice to finally meet you," Robert says smiling.

"Nice to meet you too," River says.

"I heard a lot about you." Robert informs.

"All good I hope," River says with a chuckle.

"Of course," Jennifer laughs.

Robert Murdox is an attractive man. From seeing the photos of his late father Michael, River can see that Robert favors his father. He stands tall at an even six feet. He has broad shoulders. He wears a white t-shirt that shows every muscle on his upper body. His skin was the color of bronze and his smile was wide, bright and friendly. He has long dread locks that are pulled back into a pony tail.

"Well, your mother has told me all about the many adventures of your days in the jungles of Africa." River said smiling. "When did you get in?"

"Last night," Robert said. "And mom has not stopped feeding me or hovering over me."

"That's what mothers are for," River says smiling.

"River, what bring you this way?" Jennifer asks.

"I have some good news, but I will tell you later."

"Nonsense River, have a seat."

Robert's cell phone rang.

"Excuse me, I need to take this call."

Robert leaves the table.

"So," Jennifer said smiling. "Isn't he handsome?"

"Yeah," River said in a blasé manor.

"What do you mean, 'yeah'?" Jennifer asked. "I'm glad you came by today, I was trying to call you last night, were you home?"

"Yeah, I was doing some writing, well at least trying to. I have writer's block."

"Whenever I have a block, I write a letter to someone, anyone, about anything. It can be about what you did today, yesterday, ten years ago. It can be about what you saw, or something silly or serious, just write. I write to my characters asking them about the situations, explain it to me, maybe I can understand about what I'm writing about."

River nods her head taking in every word.

"I was thinking," Jennifer said with a grin. "Maybe you can take Robert out-,"

"No,"

"River, listen to me. He is only in town for the weekend and then he is off to do more work in Arizona, then he's back to Africa. I just need you to show him around."

"Show him what? This is his home town, his home country."

"He hasn't been here in ten years."

"Then you take him out." River replies.

"I have a meeting to go tonight."

"I have plans too," River said. "That is why I came over to tell you."

"What?"

"I'm going on a book tour, starting next weekend. I'm going to Miami, New York and L.A.,"

"River, that's wonderful," Jennifer said smiling. "Book tours are very exciting."

"Yes, I am very excited. So I don't have time to escort your son around his home town. I have to shop, buy new clothes, shoes and everything."

"You can do that another day, tomorrow." Jennifer suggested. "Please, I am asking for one night."

River sighs,

"Okay,"

"Good, it's a date!"

"No, no, no, no!" River objected quickly. "This is not a date. Miss. Jenny, just me doing a favor and boy you will owe me big!"

"Okay," Jennifer said with a bright smile.

"Tell him that I will pick him up tonight at seven, we'll go somewhere."

River gets up and walks away.

"Stop smiling Jenny!" River calls out.

Jennifer tries to stop smiling, but she has a bright smile on her face. River can't believe that she has agreed to take some man out that she doesn't know. Other than the stories that Jennifer would tell, River doesn't know him personally and really didn't want to know him personally.

DANA CANNOT WAIT TO get home, relax with a cold beer, and watch television. Today was a long day of going over contracts and going over designs of buildings. He enters his home and sees the mounds of work that he had left on his dining room table. He sighs. There isn't going to be relaxing with that cold beer or watching television. He has to organize the files on the table. The files on the table are the files for Reuben's club. The last thing Dana wants to do is think about Reuben's club or his niece. She is still beautiful, but he shakes his head trying to erase the haunting image of those cold eyes staring through him. He orders a large pepperoni pizza and returns to his paper work organizing the files for Reuben's Room. Dana wonders if River is seeing anyone. If so, does she look at her man with those cold eyes, or does she look at her man with warm eyes, the same way she had once looked at him? Eyes that said:

"I love you, I am happy that you're with me. I trust you."

Do her eyes tell him to have his way with her, the same way her eyes used to speak to Dana?

Will he see her smile again? The thoughts of River's smile hypnotize him. Dana is feeling warm. He opens a window for fresh air. The cool breeze is comforting. As he focuses on his paper work, he smells a familiar scent. The cool air carries the scent of lilies inside his home. River smelled like lilies. It was some kind of perfume that she wore. Dana had loved that smell, it was calming to him. Dana tilts his head back and inhales the scent. This is strange. Where is the scent coming from? It never crosses his mind that the neighbor's flower garden has lilies in the yard.

SHE LAUGHS AT THE adventures that Robert tells her. As much as she did not want to take him out, she is having a good time.

"How is everything?" Jim Christie asks. "Hot wings okay?"

"Hot wings are fine," Robert says smiling.

"Good," Jim said. "River, who's your friend?"

"This is my friend Jennifer Murdox's son, Dr. Robert Murdox." River introduces. "He's an archeologist living in Africa. Robert, this is Jim Christie, the owner."

"Wow! Where do you live in Africa?" Jim asks, impressed.

"Right now I'm living in Kenya doing some research on an ancient queen."

"Wow," Jim says.

"Robert is only in town for a few days," River informs. "So I'd thought I take him to get the best hot wings this side of the Atlantic."

"They're only the best whenever you get them free." Jim jokes.

River laughs.

"Yeah, free chicken is great chicken." River laughs.

Jim and Robert laugh.

"Enjoy the rest of your night," Jim smiles. "Nice meeting you Robert."

"Nice meeting you as well."

Jim leaves. Robert focuses his attention on River. He watches as she sips her coke and eats a few French fries.

"Are you having a good time?" River asks.

"Yes, I feel horrible that my mother put you up to this." Robert says.

"How did you know?"

Robert raises an eyebrow; River chuckles.

"River, my mother has been trying to set us up for years. Give in to her way, we are married with-,"

"Four children," River laughs shaking her head. "R.J., Tia, Isaiah Michael, and Yvette, whom she would call Bunny."

"Why Bunny?" Robert asks.

"She wanted us to have that baby in the spring."

Robert laughs shaking his head at his mother's logic.

"Are you serious?" Roberts asks laughing.

River nods. Robert continues to laugh as River sips her soda. He raises his glass of soda. River raises her glass of soda.

"To my mother and her wishful thinking,"

"To Jennifer," River smiles.

Robert smiled at River.

"Tell me, River, why is a nice girl like you single?"

River chuckles at the question.

"I'm a work-a-holic, I guess." River confesses. "Don't really have time for a relationship. I teach five English classes and two history classes. I teach them at two different schools. I write for a magazine and I have three books in the book stores."

"Yes, you are busy." Robert comments with a chuckle.

"Yep,"

THE LOUD KNOCK AT the door interrupts his thoughts. Dana sighs and then answers the door. Immediately he is bombarded by his co-workers Nick Vito and Clayton Simmons and their girlfriends. They carry boxes of pizza and cases of beer. They take over his home.

"What's all this?" Dana asks.

"Friday night, NBA highlights!" Clayton exclaims. "Red Zone,"

"You got cable." Dana rebukes.

"Cut off," Nick confesses with a shrug.

"Plus, you need a break, you been working hard on that Daniels-Massie Project" Clayton replies.

Dana grins.

"Dana, I'd like you to meet someone," Clayton said. "Katrina Robinson,"

Clayton winks at Dana as he shakes hands with Katrina.

"Hi Katrina nice to meet you," Dana replies.

"The pleasure is mine," Katrina replies with a smile. "I am told that you are a very good architect."

"I do all right." He replies modestly.

"Ms. Katrina is a lawyer looking to start her own practice," Clayton informs with a grin. "from scratch,"

"From scratch?" Dana asked looking at Clayton.

"Scratch," Clayton says then walked away.

Dana looks at Katrina. She is a beautiful African-American woman. She has dark brown skin and her eyes are the color of amber. She has long dark hair. There is something familiar about her.

CHAPTER TEN

"**GRANDMA, YOU OUT DID** yourself," River exclaims looking in the pot got of green beans.

"River get!" Shirley scolds swatting River away.

Quickly River runs from the pot as her grandmother shoos her away.

"Everything looks and smells good Mrs. Mass-," Dave begins.

"No Mrs., baby, I'm Shirley." Shirley interrupted.

"All right," Dave said smiling.

River chuckles as she watches Dave fall in love with her sweet grandma Shirley. It has been a long time since he had a grandmother in his life to shower him with love and stuff him with home cooking.

This Sunday dinner is special. River told her grandmother of the six week book tour and for dinner, Shirley made no exceptions on preparing River's favorite meals, fried and baked chicken, baked tilapia that was smothered in butter and baked salmon and her famous roast beef. Shirley's roast beef is so famous; the neighbors come by whenever she makes it. There are corn bread and biscuits, green beans, corn on the cob and macaroni and cheese. For dessert, Shirley made apple pie and peach cobbler. With Dave joining them this afternoon Shirley also prepared a few of Dave's favorites, lasagna and garlic bread.

"When was the last time you had some home cooking, baby?" Shirley asks smiling at Dave.

"It's been a long time," Dave answers.

"Oh, please, Grandma. He has tons of girls bringing him home cooking." River teases.

Dave blushes.

"No, come on, River, you'll have your grandmother thinking I'm some kind of ladies man."

"If you learned how to cook he can be your man, lady!" Shirley scolds River.

"My grandmother is trying to set us up." River mumbles to Dave.

I wouldn't mind, Dave says to himself.

"Well, dinner is almost ready," Shirley announces. "Where is Reuben?"

"He's on the way," River answers.

"That club had made him a work-a-holic," Shirley says stirring a pot of green beans. "He don't call any more. I could be dead and you and Reuben wouldn't know it."

"Grandma," River admonishes. "Don't talk like that!"

River's cell phone rings. Answering the phone, River walks out of the kitchen. Shirley sighs and shakes her head disapprovingly and continues to prepare the food.

"That girl is going to run herself into an early grave." Shirley comments.

She looks up at the heavens.

"Imani, it was hard enough burying you. If I have to bury our angel, they bury me too."

Dave observes Shirley talking at the ceiling; calling out to a woman who has been dead for fifteen years. Shirley looks at Dave.

"Forgive me," Shirley says with a small grin; embarrassed by her behavior. "You must think I'm crazy."

"No," Dave smiles. "Just concerned,"

"River is all I got left of Imani," Shirley says with tears in her eyes. "She wasn't my blood, but she was my heart. I promised her momma and her granddaddy that I'll take care of our angel."

Dave's grin assures Shirley that he understands her concern for River. She continues.

"Her granddaddy, he loved him some River. She was his angel." Shirley informs, tears falling from her eyes.

She takes a tissue out of her apron and dabs her eyes.

"I miss them both," she confessed.

Shirley takes in a deep breath.

"Do you still have your parents?" Shirley asks.

"No," Dave replied quickly.

River returns into the kitchen.

"That was out hotel reservation," she says to Dave. "They wanted to confirm our suite."

"Everything okay," Dave asked.

Yep," River said smiling. "Grandma, I am so excited. I'm going to send you a post card every day and bring you back nice clothes back from New York, L.A., and Miami. Would you like that?"

"Baby, you spoil me." Shirley says caressing River's face.

"Momma," Reuben calls out as he enters the house.

He walks into the kitchen,

"Hi Momma, River,"

"Hey Rue, this is my colleague and my friend Dr. David Maroni."

"How you doin," Reuben says to Dave shaking his hand.

"Good,"

"Hey, Dana said that the club will be ready next month."

"That's wonderful, Reuben!" Shirley said.

"Yes, ma'am," Reuben said.

Reuben grabs his mother in his arms and starts dancing.

Everyone laughs watching Shirley trying to two-step with Reuben. Dave looks at River. She is relaxed with her family.

"Reuben, you are so silly," Shirley says trying to catch her breath.

"River, Dana needs to talk to you about some information."

Dana watches the smile leave River's face.

"Whatever information he needs he can fax it to me." She states coolly, then walks out the kitchen.

Dave grins, then follows River into the living room. Together they sit down on the couch. River turns the television on.

"Are you okay?" he asks.

"Yeah, why," River asks.

Her face fixed on the television as she channel surfs.

"You seemed a little distracted." He comments.

"I'm good," River replies. "Just ready to eat,"

"Good, the Cleveland Cavs are playing,"

Dave grabs the remote from River's hand and turns the basketball game on.

"Cavs baby," Reuben cheers entering the living room. "Dave, you're a man after my own heart."

Reuben sits down. River gets up and returns to the kitchen to help her grandmother with dinner. River sets the table. She sees that her grandmother has laid out the good tablecloth.

"The good tablecloth," River replies.

"Oh yes, baby. My granddaughter is a famous author." Shirley winks.

River grins.

"So do you think you and your friend-," Shirley questions evasively.

"Grandma," River admonishes repulsed by the idea.

"Well, baby, he likes you." Shirley says.

"Grandma, we're just friends." River replies.

"Those make the best lovers," Shirley says with a wink.

"Grandma," River said almost offended. "It's not like that with us. He and I are just friends,"

"Okay, okay, okay, baby." Shirley surrenders. "Are you excited about Reuben's club?" Shirley asked.

"Yeah, but don't tell him." River answers with a small grin.

Shirley laughs,

"I'm joking Grandma, I'm real happy for Reuben."

DINNER IS READY. FOR ten minutes everyone passes food around to each other filling up their plates. They sit in silence, eat and sigh with delight.

"Grandma, every time," River attempts to compliment but she closes her eyes and enjoys her food.

"This is really good, Shirley." Dave agrees.

"Momma, you out did yourself. What is the occasion?" Reuben asks.

"River," Shirley coaxes.

"I'm going on a book tour." River said smiling.

"A tour," Reuben asks.

"Yep," River responds.

"Congratulation, River. When are you leaving?" Reuben asks.

"This weekend,"

"How long," Reuben asks.

"Six weeks,"

Reuben's heart broke knowing that River is not going to be around for the opening of the club. River continued to talk about her trip.

"I'll be in New York, L.A., and Miami," she says.

River doesn't notice that Reuben is heartbroken.

"You're won't be here for the opening." Reuben comments.

"I didn't plan on it." River says in a blatant manor.

She continues to eat.

Reuben is shocked by her cool demeanor.

"Excuse me?" he asks.

"Excuse me what?" she questions. "Reuben, you don't need me there."

"You're my niece," Reuben said. "You're the reason why I have the club!"

"Reuben, you did the work, what am I going to do there? Plus, I'm working."

"I was working when I came to your first book signing."

"Reuben, did you even read the book?" River asks irritated with Reuben.

"No, but that is not the point! River I was there for my one and only niece."

River sighs as she looks at Dave.

"Do you see what I go through?"

"Sounds like you're more important here than what you think you are." Dave comments.

"No, it sounds like I am being pulled in every direction." River snaps looking at Reuben

"Okay, okay, okay," Shirley intervened. "Let's finishing eating and maybe we can work something out later,"

No one speaks. River, Dave, Shirley and Reuben push their food around on their plate. River wants to talk about her tour, but flaunting would be wrong. Rueben has worked hard on his club. He has worked long nights organizing menus. He's hosted dinner parties trying out new food dishes. Some of these parties she would attend, most she would not. River knew that Reuben has worked hard on establishing a good working crew, from waitresses and waiters, the head chef and the rest of the kitchen crew. She understands the blood, sweat and tears that Reuben put into making his vision come to life. What about her blood, sweat and tears that she would put into her books? But River knows that if she really needed Reuben he would be there for her without question or hesitation.

"I can look at my schedule, but I won't make any promises." River finally breaks the silence.

Reuben smiles as River grabs her Blackberry and looked at her calendar.

"I will be in California the night of the opening." She announces. "With the time difference, I can come in for an hour, but I have to leave."

"Perfect," Reuben said smiling.

"Rueben, that is too much for River, she will be jet lagged." Shirley says. "River, don't push yourself." Shirley looks at Reuben. "Reuben, you know that she's busy."

"I will be fine," River said as she put the date down in her calendar.

O

Katrina Robertson is a successful defense attorney. Originally from Chicago Illinois, she studied law at Harvard graduating Summa Cum Laude. She served as second chair in litigation for a major law firm in New York City. Her reputation as second chair quickly promoted her to first chair. Katrina's reputation as a defense attorney brought the firm a lot of new clients. This made Katrina one of the best lawyers that law firm has seen in a long time. Within two years of working at the same firm, she was offered a position as partner which included a nice salary and benefits. Katrina declined the offer. Her heart was in starting her new firm. Katrina turned in her two weeks' notice and moved to Pittsburgh. She was asked why Pittsburgh. Why not start a law firm in a major city, like Atlanta, Los Angeles or stay in New York.

Her answer: she enjoys practicing law. She does not need to be a high powered attorney. Considering her reputation, her clients will come. So she brought property and now she is looking for someone to build her firm.

Katrina is the type of woman that got what she wanted. She is not a spoiled little rich girl who asked her daddy for everything. Katrina worked hard for all of her accolades. When she set her eyes on the prize, she did what she needed to do to get that prize. She is shrewd. She does not under mind. She is not cunning or crafty. Katrina is that woman that simply gets what she wants. She wanted to be a lawyer, so she applied herself in school and became a lawyer.

Once her firm is established, her next conquest is marriage. She wants a husband who works as hard as she does and who will not be intimidated by her success.

When she met Dana Wilson that Friday evening it was nice to know that he started his own business. Katrina likes the fact that he is handsome, down to earth, and a hard worker just like she. That evening she talked with him about the ideas for her firm.

They met a few times at Christie's and talked on the phone about constructing the perfect building for her. Just like with River, Dana and his dream team had a meeting in the conference room at Wilson Architect Firm. He showed her two models of buildings that he thought would best suit her. Dana appreciated the fact that she listened to two presentations for her building, unlike River who cut him off and only listened to one. Within two weeks, neither Dana nor Katrina realized how much time they had spent together. They looked forward to returning each other's phone calls.

As much as they enjoyed each other's company, Dana tried his best to maintain a professional relationship-she is still a client; a beautiful client. Katrina is a voluptuous beauty, a woman of the Amazons. Katrina looks like a model that has graced the cover of *Sports Illustrated, Vogue,* or walked the catwalk with Naomi. Katrina has long chocolate legs. She has brains and beauty.

Their next meeting, Dana asks if she could meet at his home. It was Sunday afternoon, and he needed a few contracts signed so he can get started on her building. While waiting for her, Dana opens up the window to let fresh air come through the house. It is a warm May evening. The weather man said that the temperature would be in the eighties with high humidity, which was good for him, because he cannot be distracted by the scent of the lilies. Dana needs to talk with River for more money. Reuben added an extra room to the club. Although Dana does want to see her, he doesn't want to look into those cold eyes.

The knock at the door distracts Dana's thoughts. Dana answers the door. Katrina stands outside smiling. She wears a tight T-shirt and a pair of tight hip hugging jeans. He watched her hips sway from left to right when she walks. Dana takes in a deep breath.

"Hi," he says almost speechless. "Can I get you something to drink?"

"Yes, alcohol," she said smiling.

"Um, okay," Dana chuckles. "I have wine."

She smiles.

Dana walks into the kitchen to pour Katrina and himself a glass of wine. Katrina looks around in the living room. She admires the organized home. Dana approaches Katrina with the two glasses of wine.

Katrina smiles as he hands her a glass. They toast.

"To a successful working relationship," Katrina says smiling.

They gently tap the glasses together and begin to drink the wine.

"You know, I am so excited that that you're making this building for me." She answers as she walks to the couch and sits down.

"Why did you pick law?" Dana asks.

He walks to the couch and sits next to her; far enough to remain professional.

"Someone has to defend the guilty, no matter how guilty they are," she says sardonically. "Architecture?"

"One day, I want to reconstruct Pittsburgh." Dana says.

They are comfortable, both Katrina and Dana are enjoying each other's company. Talking with each other is easy and relaxing. They are unaware of the time. With the wine in their body and their relaxed demeanor, neither noticed that they had drunk two bottles of wine and three hours have passed. The paper work that Katrina needs to sign is still sitting on the table.

BY THE EVENING, THE HUMIDITY outside has broken and the spring night releases cool air. Dana smells the familiar fragrance of the lilies. The scent begins to hypnotize Dana. He looks at Katrina and moves in closer to her. Her smiles welcomes to him and she moves closer to him.

"Defense attorneys aren't supposed to be beautiful," Dana says softly.

She giggles and smiles bashfully at the comment. She looks at him and for a moment they look into each other's eyes, slowly inhale and exhale. The fragrance of the lilies and the alcohol has impaired his judgment. Quickly he leans forward to kiss her on the lips. He kisses her passionately. To his surprises, she is receptive. As he kisses her, Dana knows that this is not a good idea, but his desire out weights his logic. Will their business relationship survive? The way she is kissing him, she is not offended by the advances.

They look at each other for a moment. She looks at him. Her brown eyes seductively tell him that she wants him.

SHE RESTS PEACEFULLY IN his arms. Although he gently caresses her back, Dana cannot recall how Katrina ended up in his bed. He remembers kissing her. He remembers her kissing him back. Dana remembers how good she felt to him, but how did this happen? Katrina is a client. As good as he feels, he has regrets.

"This feels nice," she whispered. "You feel nice,"

The scent of lilies lingers in the room. Did Dana open his bedroom window?

As they lay in bed, Dana's mind wonders to his first time with River. He returned home from his weekend in Virginia. He had missed River. He couldn't wait to see her. He went to Virginia to tell his then girlfriend that it was over. Dana wanted to come home and be with River. However while he was gone, River's mother died. Dana came back to a broken and emotional River. He felt so bad. Dana made sure that she ate and that she got sleep. A few days after the funeral, River visited Dana at his apartment. She was dressed very casual, wearing a pair of baggy sweats and a baggy T-shirt. Dana could tell that she wanted and needed to be held. She lied on his bed with her head resting on his chest.

"Thank you for being there for me," she said softly.

"It's okay," he said.

As he held her he softly kissed her forehead. Dana wanted her, but considering all that she had just been through. He didn't want to push her, but as he kissed her, River didn't resist him. They kissed each other and that night they made love, it was wonderful. When it was over, she rested her head on his chest and listened to his heart beat. He glided his hands along her back.

"Are you okay?" Dana asked.

"Yes," she answered back.

"Are you sure?"

"Yeah,"

Dana kissed her forehead. River sat up and began to climb out of the bed.

"What are you doing?"

"Going home," she said reaching for her clothes
"Home," Dana asked reaching for her, "Why?"
She shrugged her shoulders.
"River, you okay?"
"Yeah," she said. "It's late-,"
"You don't have to leave." Dana said. "Come here,"
River moved closer to Dana. He leaned forward to kiss her.
"This wasn't just sex for me," he said.
She grinned.
"I really like you," Dana cupped her face in his palms and leaned to kiss her cheek. "Stay the night, please,"
He pulled her back in bed, wrapped his arms around her, and they went to sleep.

AS KATRINA LIES IN Dana bed, Dana sighs softly, wishing that the woman softly kissing his neck is someone else.
"Dana," she said softly,
"Yeah,"
"That was nice,"

DANA WOKE UP TO the smell of bacon. Without opening his eyes, he reaches in the bed hoping to wrap his arms around River. He dreamed of her. Dreamed of her smiling at him, the sound of her laughing that is like a lullaby, and her scent is the comforting fragrance that relaxes him. But as he reached across the bed, there is no one lying next to him. Dana sits up and begins trying to recall the night before and comprehend the dream. Slowly he remembers one name; Katrina. Is she in the kitchen cooking? Slowly Dana inhales. The smell of bacon covered the sweet smell of lilies. Quickly he gets out of bed, put his pants on and goes in the bathroom to freshen up. Then Dana walks to the kitchen. Katrina greets him with a smile. She put on those tight black pants and the T-shirt. He smiles back.
"Good morning," he said.
"I made you some breakfast." She said cheerfully.
"Thanks," Dana said.

"After last night, I figured you would be hungry."

Dana sits down at this table. His head is aching from alcohol and his heart is aching from love. Katrina sits a plate of food with bacon, eggs and toast in front of him. Then she hands him a cup of coffee.

"Everything looks good," he said.

"I would have made more but you didn't have much food." Katrina smiles as she sits down.

"I'm a bachelor, I'm not supposed to have food." He joked as he takes a few bites.

"But how are your girlfriends supposed to fix your breakfast in the morning; especially after a wonderful night like last night."

"I'm usually over their house eating their food." Dana jokes as she sipped his coffee.

Katrina laughs.

"Katrina, this is all very nice and I hate to eat and run, but I have a meeting in about an hour."

"Okay," Katrina said softly.

Feeling somewhat disappointed, Katrina stands up to leave. Dana stands up and takes Katrina in his arms.

"You don't have to leave just yet. Let's eat."

She grins and together they sit down and continue to eat breakfast together.

AFTERWARDS, DANA WALKS KATRINA out with the promise that he would call her later on. He wonders if trying to start something with Katrina is wise. Questioning this concept seems pointless considering that they just spent the night together. Dana does like Katrina, but does he want to start a relationship?

CHAPTER ELEVEN

THERE HAS BEEN A mistake at the luxurious Platinum Island Hotel in New York City, the reservations were made in enough time to secure the hotel suites. For some reason there is only one available. The hotel receptionist taps away rapidly at the key board trying to find out why Dave's room had not been secured. The confirmation number from River's credit card shows that the suite had been purchased but is not available. The room that is available is the suite that Bush Publications purchased for River.

"Unfortunately Dr. Daniels, we cannot explain the mistake." The receptionist said. "We will definitely give you a full refund and if there is a vacancy within the two weeks that you're here, it will be yours free on the house."

River looks at Dave,

"Would you mind sharing a room with me?"

"Room with a girl, gross," Dave jokes.

River smiles,

"Sure, it's okay." Dave says smiling.

River turns to the receptionist.

"Okay, we'll take the room,"

"Okay, Jimmy," the receptionist said to the bell boy. "Please take Dr. Daniels and her associate to their suite. Dr. Daniels, again, we're very sorry for the inconvenience."

"It's okay," River says with a smile.

As the bell boy escorts River and Dave to their suite, they couldn't help but be in awe at the lovely hotel. It looked like a grand estate that the very rich and the very important stay in.

"I fell like a royalty," River whispers to Dave.

He chuckles.

"This is nice," Dave replied. "Mr. Bush set this up,"

River nods.

"Nice," Dave replies.

Once inside the suite, River looks around the room as Dave tip the bell boy. The suite is beautiful. A gold and crystal chandelier hangs in the center of the ceiling. The living room is large. The walls are white and the couches, love seats and chairs are the color of a soft, cool gray. The gray gives a nice contrast to the soft blue coffee and end tables. The dining area has a similar style and theme. The dining table is a large black glass octagon table. It seats four with soft black, white and red chairs. The suite has three bedrooms, the master bedroom and two guest rooms. The master bedroom has its own bathroom and there is another bathroom that connects the two guest bedrooms. Off towards the back of the suit adjacent to the living room, is a small office.

Dave sees River standing on the balcony, it appears that she is captivated by the view, but actually she is staring hard at the pretty girl that stands a far in the distance. This girl is definitely a stalker. The word has been out about the book tour. The bookstores in New York, LA., and Miami have advertised of her appearance. Interviews with national morning television shows have been scheduled. This girl has heard about the tour. River is afraid, but she manages to hide her emotions.

"This suite is big enough for the both of us," she says to Dave as he approaches her.

She doesn't taking her eyes off the pretty girl.

"I mean, if a room becomes available, you don't have to leave it you don't want."

"That's two weeks, Riv, you sure?" Dave asks.

River finally looks at Dave.

"Yeah, I need you here."

Dave smiles River smiles back.

"Let's unpack and get organized. I have to get up at the crack of dawn for that morning to be at the book store." River said.

As River and Dave walk back in the room, there is a knock at the door.

"You expecting anyone?" Dave asks as he answers the door.

"Um, a body guard," River answers vaguely.

"A body guard?" Dave asks caught off guard.

He opens the door and standing in front of him a tall thick and stocky African-American man. He towers over Dave's six feet five inches.

"I'm Mike Shawl from the New York Protection Agency. I'm here to see Dr. River Daniels."

"I'm Dr. Daniels," River walks to him.

"I will be out here if you need anything." Mike the Bodyguard informs her.

"Yes, thank you." River says.

Dave shuts the door and Mike the Bodyguard assumes his position outside the hotel suite. Dave looks at River.

"Why do you have a body guard?" Dave questions.

"Because I'm famous," River answers, as if Dave's question was silly.

"River since when did you become someone who can't walk down the street without a mob of fans chasing you."

River doesn't answer him. Instead she grabs her suitcases and walks in the master bedroom. Dave waits a moment in the living room. He begins to ponder on River's body guard. Then suddenly he remembers the incident a few months ago when River thought that she was being followed. Dave goes in the bedroom.

"A few months ago you said that someone was following you. You were really stressed out that day, remember that?"

"Yes," River answers unpacking her suitcase and putting her things into the dresser.

"You said that it was a girl." Dave continues to interrogate.

"Yes Dave,"

"Is there still a problem?" Dave questions.

"She's been around." River answers in a vague manor.

"How long?"

"Since the end of January,"

"January, River, it is May!"

"Dave-," River admonishes him.

She is growing irritated with his questioning.

"River, why am I just hearing this?" Dave asks.

"Because she hasn't really done anything," River answers. "She just stands and stares at me."

"Do you know who she is?"

River answers by shaking her head no.

"Has she said anything to you?" Dave interrogates

"No," River answers.

"Does she know about the tour?"

River doesn't answer. Her lack of answering means to Dave that River has seen her.

"Okay," Dave said. "Do you think this tour is safe?"

"Yes, we have security." River pointed towards the door.

"Security? What security? Mike the Bodyguard?" he asked in a cynical manor.

River rolls her eyes.

"A security guard will be posted at every book store."

Dave doesn't respond. One part of him wished that he never came on this tour because it had the potential to be dangerous. River is a stalked celebrity. Anyone can harm her or kill her. Does she understand the seriousness of this whole situation; River has just put Dave's life in danger. Knowing River, Dave knows that she understands everything and maybe that is why she invited him for support. Mike the Bodyguard standing out the door or book store security guard cannot give her the personal and intimate protection that a supportive friend can give. If he was not on this trip and something would happen to River, it would kill him. River becomes aware of Dave's nervousness. She looks at him. River takes his hands and forces him to face her.

"Dave, I'll be okay." River says. "I'm not going to let some person, one woman keep me from living."

"What does she looks like?" He asks coolly. "Does she look familiar?"

"It's too hard to tell, I would have to see her up close."

River continues to unpack as Dave nervously paces in her room.

"Dave it's not a big deal." River says with a dry chuckle.

"Not a big deal? River, Mike the Body Guard is standing outside!"

"I understand that but with you here, and the guards, she won't do anything."

"What does she look like?"

"Why?"

"Why?" Dave asks shocked at her evasiveness. "Because if she is stalker and she *is* here,"

"I never told you she was here-,"

"You don't have to-." He snaps cutting off quickly.

River sighs. A moment passes between them. River doesn't understand Dave's hostility. He has never raised his voice with her before. Dave couldn't grasp her detachment she has on reality. River doesn't seem fazed by this so called stalker. Why was she so uneasy and unsettled that day in school? She must be scared if there is an unusually large man standing outside the door. So why the cool demeanor? Because River is not going to show any sign of weakness. Dave takes a deep breath.

"What does she look like?" he asks her again.

"She's about five feet six, five seven, she a black woman with short curly hair."

"Have you seen her here in the hotel?"

"Dave, I can't think of this right now, okay, I need to-,"

"River-," he interrupts sternly her again.

"Don't act crazy." She warns.

Dave puts his hands up in a form of surrendering. River can see in his eyes that he is not going to be cool about this situation.

"I will tell you if I see her." She says sternly.

"Thank you." He replies.

Dave walks out of the room and enters the living room. He sits down on the couch. He thinks more on the description. A five feet and six inches African-American woman.

Ah River, Dave cries out to himself. *That could be anyone!*

For a writer she wasn't too descriptive.

KATRINA WALKS THROUGH THE construction site where Dana is working for Reuben's club, wearing a tight pencil skirt and five inch stiletto heels. She ignores the construction crew who has stopped hammering, assembling, and plastering, to watch her walk in that tight skirt and high heels.

Who is this Amazon beauty? They wonder.

Their question is answered when they see her smile at only Dana. She sees him looking over his clip board and discussing information with a few members of his crew. He smiles when he sees Katrina, he holds his hand up indicating for her to wait a moments. She nods, grins and patiently waits.

Katrina and Dana have been spending their evenings together. She cooks dinner for him in the evening, makes love to him at night, and in the morning, has breakfast for him. As good as things appear to be, he still remains hesitant to completely enjoy her company. Every night after dinner, he convinces himself that Katrina is good for him. Here is a woman that is very good to him. She is allowing him the distance he needs to focus on work, and she herself is an established defense attorney. Katrina is sweet, she is nice, and she is sexy.

Dana dismisses his crew and walks to Katrina.

"So this is the famous club," she says looking around. "It is coming along nicely."

"Thanks, but we're behind schedule." Dana says with a sigh. "It opens in a month."

"Oh," Katrina said. "What's the problem?"

"Reuben added an extra room and there has been an addition for the outside and balcony. And on top of that, Reuben is still hiring staff."

Reuben walks over to Dana. Dana hands Reuben another expense report and watches as Reuben eyes enlarged.

"Oh man," Reuben said. "baby girl is going to have a stroke."

"We need more money," Dana states. "We need to get these permits."

"She just signed a check over to me before she left." Reuben sighs.

"I know Reuben but considering your additions we must meet safety regulations and this is what is needed." Dana explained.

"I know, River is not in town though,"

"When is she coming back?" Dana asks.

"July," Rueben said. "River is on a book tour."

"Can you call her?" Dana asks.

"I can call her but-,"

"Excuse me," Katrina interrupts. "Is this River Daniels, the author?"

"I'm sorry, Katrina, this is Reuben Massie, Reuben this is my friend, Katrina Robinson." Dana introduces them.

"You know her work?" Reuben asks.

"Know it, I'm a fan!" Katrina says smiling.

Dana closes his eyes then massages his temples,

Why, he asked himself. *Of all the writers in the world, why be a fan of River Daniels?*

"A fan huh?" Reuben asks, then glances at Dana.

"I've read all three of her books." Katrina says smiling. "How do you know her?"

"She's my niece," Reuben answers.

"Your niece," Katrina exclaims. "Dana, you didn't tell me that you're working with River Daniel's uncle."

Because I'm debating if I am going to keep you around. Dana said to himself.

"Do you think I can meet her, maybe she can sign my book?" Katrina smiles.

"I'll see what I can do," Reuben says. "Dana, I will try to get in touch with River."

Reuben walks away with the expense report. Dana turns to Katrina who is now smiling from ear to ear.

"Have you ever met River Daniels?" she asks.

Met her quite a few times, he says to himself.

"Yeah, she is buying the club for Reuben." Dana said.

"This is the million dollar client, you mentioned?" Katrina exclaims.

"Yeah," Dana says coolly.

"She is that rich?" Katrina asks in a whisper.

"What's up?" he asks changing the subject.

"Sorry," she grins "I came by to see if you want to get lunch."

"I really wish I could, but things are a mess here?" Dana tells her. "How about dinner, I'll give you a call later."

"Okay," Katrina smiles.

Katrina gives Dana a kiss and then she walks out the same way that she walked in; with the eyes of the construction crew watching her.

Dana watches Katrina leave. He shakes his head and regains his focus on his clip board. Reuben approaches Dana.

"Very nice," Reuben says with a smile.

Dana grins bashfully.

"She's a big fan of River's." Reuben teased.

"Yep," Dana ignores Reuben's jeering as he looks over his chart on his clip board.

"I take it she doesn't know about you and River."

"Me and River; what about me and River?" Dana asks, being vague.

"That she was your girl," Reuben replies.

"Does it matter?" Dana questions "Besides, she was more like a childhood friend."

"A childhood friend?" Reuben asks almost offended. "You told me that you're were once in love with her."

"Yes *was,* not still," Dana said. "River was over a decade ago."

"Look, I don't expect you to still be in love with her," Reuben said. "but the look on your face when you found out that your lady was fan was not a happy look. It was a look we brothas get when we get caught."

"I will always care for River," Dana confesses. "I'm just trying to be cool about this whole thing."

"What whole thing?" Reuben interrogates.

"This whole thing." Dana said. "River, you, now Katrina,"

"What?" Reuben's asks, confused.

"Since I started building this club, I have been wondering if all this is a coincidence or fate. I've been thinking about River and me. What are the odds that this is just a coincidence? I mean fifteen years later, I am faced with a woman that I was with, building her uncle's club, and now my girl is a fan of her work."

Reuben nods his head in an understanding manner.

"You feeling something for River," Reuben asks.

Dana shrugs his shoulders.

"I don't know,"

"You know what is sad?" Reuben asks.

"What?"

"This- whatever this thing is, River hates your guts." Reuben says with a chuckle.

Dana doesn't find his joke funny.

"Come on, I am just messing with you. This is just a coincidence, unless you want to get back with River,"

"Please, every time she looks at me, chills go up and down my spine."

"River is scary," Reuben aggress. "But if you feeling River then tell her,"

"I don't know what I am feeling for her," Dana said. "I just don't want her to look at me as if she wants to kill me."

"Well you know what they say; hell has no fury...,"

"They also say, forgive and forget." Dana said.

"If you want, I'll get River to sign your girl's book."

"Thanks."

IT'S THE MORNING FOR the first book signing. Before Dave, River, and Mike the Bodyguard go to the book store, Dave informs Mike the Bodyguard of the alleged stalker. Dave describes her based on River's description.

"That could be any girl," Mike said with a dry chuckle.

"I know, but that is what River told me." Dave said.

"Okay," Mike said as he shrugged his shoulders.

River appears before Mike and Dave looking stoic and reserved.

"Tubbs, Crocket, I'm ready to leave." She says.

THE FIRST BOOK STORE is Ansani's Book Store. The manager is a petite red head named Cindy. River smiles shaking Cindy's hand and introducing Dave and her bodyguard. Ansani Book Store scheduled River's book signing and reading from the hours of ten am until three pm. Cindy escorts River to her assigned seat with a table full of books. River sits down at the table, Mike the Bodyguard stands at the front door. Dave gets River a cappuccino at the book store's coffee shop. River watches Dave. His eyes are shifty and she can see that his body is tense. She knows that he is looking for her mysterious friend.

"Dave relax," River says.

She smiles at him, he smiles back at her. Dave takes in a deep breath. He looks around the book store then hands River and himself a cup of coffee.

"Thanks," River says. "Listen -,"

"I told Mike," David interrupts.

"What did you go and tell Mike for?" River asks horrified.

"For the very reason you hired him," Dave hissed.

"I don't need you here acting paranoid getting Cindy and the customers all alarmed and they not buy my book. Mike is my protection, the security guard in the back that is eating his pop tart is Cindy's body guard, you, you're here as my personal assistant."

River raises her cappuccino and winks at Dave.

"Seriously, Dave, relax, and let's have fun."

Dave surrenders. River sits down at her table with her books. Dave sits next to her in the vacant seat.

DAVE DOES NOT SAY anything to River. Throughout this day, he remains in the background; a silent figure, watching every African-American woman that comes to the book store. He notices the tall ones, the short ones, the thin ones and the not so thin. He looks for them to have short hair. However, the African-American women he sees, none of them fit the description of the woman who is stalking River. Dave watches River's reaction to any African-American woman who comes to River to get their book signed. He watches to see if she is uncomfortable. River noticed Dave watches cop persona. She waits for the last person in line to get their book signed.

"Will you stop?" River admonishes. "You are really putting the ugly in racial profiling."

Dave sighs. He runs his finger through his hair.

"I'm sorry," he says.

INSPITE OF DAVE'S RACIAL profiling, the day has been quite eventful. Several book store owners had come by to get their book signed and to request for a book signing at their book store. A teacher from a community college brought two dozen of River's books so she can pass them out to her class for a literature reading. Consider that she is being used for education, River purchase the books herself and autographs the books.

By the end of the day three P.M seems like nine P.M. River, Dave, and Mike the Bodyguard are tired and hungry. River thanks Cindy for the hospitality and Mike the Body Guard and Dave escort River to her car and the chauffer drives the three back to the hotel. During the ride everyone is silent. River rests her head on Dave's shoulder and eventually falls asleep. Today has been eventful. Dave is beyond exhausted and this is just day one. As River rest her head on his shoulders, she looks vulnerable, far from the strong stoic look. Is she in real danger?

The car finally pulls up to the hotel. Dave feels bad waking River. He watches her stretch. The chauffer opens the back door for Dave, River and Mike the Bodyguard to get out, and together they walk inside the hotel. The receptionist approaches them.

"Dr. Daniels, there have been quite a few phone messages for you." She informs her as she hands River the messages.

River thanks the receptionist. As the three get on the elevator, River looks over the stack of messages. One is from Shirley, another from Mr. Bush and the other ten are from Uncle Reuben. Waiting on their floor is Jeff Wilson, from the Protection Agency to relieve Mike the Bodyguard. Dave and River enter in the suite. Overwhelmed by the day, Dave takes a shower and River returns phone calls.

"Why am I just hearing from you?" Kennedy asks.

"I'm sorry, Mr. Bush, I've been busy." River explains.

"How did everything go?"

"Everything went really well." River says smiling. "All of my books sold out at Ansani's."

"Congratulations, my dear," Kennedy said. "Tomorrow you're going to a book store in Long Island."

"After that I want to go to a museum, do you recommend anything?"

"The Met," he recommends. "And after that, get some rest."

"Sure Mr. Bush," River smirks.

"Okay, dear call me tomorrow with a report." Mr. Bush instructs.

DAVE COMES FROM HIS shower feeling revived. He enters the living room to find River looking over the room service menu.

"What do you want to eat?" she asks.

"A steak, well done, smothered in mushrooms and onions, a baked potato soaked in butter." Dave answered as he sat down on the couch.

"That sounds good." River says.

River orders the room service and then she takes a shower. Dave sits on the couch and turns the television on so he can watch the basketball highlights. After the highlights he channel surfs for a good action adventure movie with tons of explosives and pretty women. River comes from her bedroom looking like a different person. She wears a pair of baggy gray sweat pants and a navy blue T-shirt. Her wet hair hangs down

her back. She looks so different. He looks down at her feet.
She is bare foot, her toes are panted the color of hot pink. Her
big brown eyes are not hidden behind her glasses. Without
realizing his actions, he stands up to greet her.

"You look comfortable," he finally says, feeling like a
nervous school boy meeting the prettiest girl in school.

She grins.

A HALF HOUR PASSES. Room service knocks on the door.
Dave answers the door to allow them in. Dave tips the waiter
and within minutes, River and he are eating dinner. They
discuss the events of the day.

"While you were racial profiling, many people wanted to
book me for readings." River informed. "If my schedule was not
so crazy with school, I may have made appearances."

"Well, maybe you'll consider it. You don't have to teach
every English class," Dave says, sipping his wine.

"I enjoy teaching."

"It was nice to see you not in teacher mode though,"
Dave replies. "You seem carefree and relaxed."

This is the River that Dave remembers.

"You know you gave me an idea with your Harlem
Renaissance time line." River said.

How did River manage to turn this into a work dinner?

"River how did you turn this into work?" Dave asks.

"I'm working," River answers. "I'm on a book tour."

"You're done for the evening." Dave said. "Enjoy your
New York steak and relax."

River shrugs her shoulders and eats her steak.

"River, what is your favorite song?"

"Don't have one," she answers putting a piece of steak in
her mouth.

"Your favorite song is, *Let's Stay Together* by Al Green."

River shrugs her shoulders indicating that she has no
recollection of the song.

"'I, I'm so in love with you, whatever you want to do, is all
right with me. Cause you make me feel so brand new, and I

want to spend my life with you…,'." Dave sings pieces of the song to River.

She looks at Dave as if he is strange. Dave sighs and stops singing.

"River, what do you do whenever you come home from work?" Dave asks.

"Grade papers, work on lessons plans, or work on my book. I go over to Jennifer's house once a week. We get drunk and read books."

"Any locker room talk?" Dave asks suspiciously.

"Locker room talk," River asks.

"You know when you women talk about boyfriends, tell lies about how they didn't satisfy you-,"

"Dave what are you talking about?" River asks horrified. "As much as I love Jennifer, I don't want to know the details of her and her husband."

"That is not what I am talking about," Dave replies frustrated. "River, you're my best friend and I know nothing about you."

"Yes, you do," River said. "You know my work and you know what I like."

"Yes, yes, I know your work. I can look at a sentence phrase and know you wrote it. I know how you like your coffee and I know what you like on your pizza. But River, I want to talk to you, not my co-worker. We don't have anything to talk about unless we're talking about books or work."

"Dave, I think you need some sleep." River says. "You seemed stressed out."

"Yeah, I'm stressed out." Dave stated. "You have some girl stalking you for five months and I knew nothing about it. I don't know you!"

"I didn't want to tell you!"

"So you wait until we're fifty million miles away from home and tell me."

"I wasn't going to tell you. You got paranoid when the bodyguard came to the door. All day today you were looking for her, making me nervous. I told you, I am not going to let someone prevent me from doing what I need to do. I'm going to bed."

Dave watches River walk to her bedroom. He wonders if she heard anything he said. Knowing River, she heard nothing.

CHAPTER TWELEVE

AFTER THE BOOK SIGNING in the bookstore in Long Island, River convinces Dave to let the bodyguard go home for the day, and they went to The Metropolitan Museum of Art, better known as The Met. The assigned docent introduces himself, Damon Williams. There is something familiar about him. He is an African-American male that stands five feet ten inches. He wears wire rimmed glasses and he has a nice smile.

Damon takes them through the museum showing classic paintings and scriptures giving full detailed information and historical facts about the exhibits. River and Dave pay close attention as if they are going to be tested on the information given. Damon has a laid back and carefree demeanor. He makes River and Dave laugh as he goes through each exhibit. There is something intriguing about his charming personality. River is drawn to him. She doesn't feel any kind of physical attraction but there is mental stimulation. Damon was speaking in her language. As cool as his manner is, Damon is very articulate, and he shows passion by the way he speaks of historical facts and the educational background. River likes intelligent people, people like Dave until he started talking crazy last night about not knowing her or whatever it was he was talking about.

A particular exhibit catches River's eye. It is a series of twelve paintings of a horizon in the colors of blue and red; beautiful royal blue waters, under a captivating red sky. The sun is white, but hiding behind maroon colored clouds. The borders of the paintings are black. To the average person looking at these paintings one would think that they were bland and boring, but to River there is something intriguing about them. In each painting, the blue and reds look darker, until the final painting that is black. Damon and Dave notices River's interest in the paintings.

"This is our Flaming Blue series," Damon informs.

"Flaming Blue?" River asks.

"Yes, by Evenly Payne. Her story is that she was having an affair with a rich aristocrat, but unfortunately he ended things, leaving her heart broken. Each painting represent each month. Each shade of blue shows how depressed she was until the black. This exhibit did receive rave reviews, but she killed herself after the display. The black symbolizes her heart."

"Was she that depressed?" River asks horrified.

"Yeah," Damon said. "Evelyn was very beautiful. As a matter of fact she had many admirers. "

"The shades of red in each painting," Damon begins.

"The passion," River answers.

"Yes," Damon responded.

River's eyes are distant as if she has been hypnotized by the display and the artist's background.

"River, you all right?" Dave asks.

"Her story, it's sad, interesting but sad." River answers. "Is there any other work from her here?"

Damon shakes his head.

"Most women are drawn to a love story." Damon said to Dave.

"This is not normal," River comments. "Did that guy ever know that this paintings was because of him?"

"Reports say that he was very blasé about the matter, saying that her death was not the cause of him, but saying that she was a depressed woman. That was one of the reasons why he ended things with her."

"He just didn't care?" River asks shocks.

"Reports said that he felt it was tragedy, but-," Damon answers.

Dave sees that Damon is ready to continue with the tour. Dave places his hands on the small of her back.

"River," Dave says.

"I'm sorry," she said shaking her head coming out of her trance.

Damon grins and together they finished the tour. River and Dave thank him. When they get outside, their car is waiting for them.

"Where to?" the driver asks.

"I need alcohol," Dave comments

"I know a nice bar and grill in the city." the driver suggests.

"Then off we go!" River exclaims.

The driver drives River and Dave into the city. While riding along, the driver has the radio on. Dorothy Moore's version of *Misty Blue* comes on.

"I've heard this song before." River says listening.

"Yeah, that's an old classic. Nobody does it like Dorothy Moore," the driver says.

River listens to the lyrics of the songs and remembers when she first heard the song. The version she heard was from R & B singer Monica. River was with Dana. They had been dating officially for a week. Dana planned a romantic evening together at his apartment, and after dinner they slow danced. Their romance was new and sweet. Dana and River had become inseparable. They didn't want to be in different rooms, let alone away from each other. He loved holding her in his arms and she loved to be held. Jerry never held her, never offered comfort to her, with Dana she was relaxed.

"Just the thought of you, turns my whole world, misty blue." River sang off key.

Dana chuckled as he held River closer.

"Promise not to turn my world misty blue," River said smiling.

"I promise," Dana said kissing her upon her neck.

As they danced, he twirled her around and dipped her.

"Dana, this is a sad song," she said laughing. "You're not supposed to dip to a sad song."

"River," Dave calls her disturbing her thoughts and bringing her back into reality.

She looks at her surroundings, the driver had pulled up to the bar and grill that he recommended. River grins. Dave and she get out of the car and enter the restaurant. The song on the radio has long been over, but it echoes in River's mind.

Oh it's been such a long, long time
Looks like I got you off of my mind
But I can't, just the thought of you
Turns my world, misty blue

Just the thought of Dana Wilson has turned her perfectly normal yet chaotic life upside down. She hasn't thought of him in fifteen years and now she hears a song that she had once danced to with him. River is not on a book tour to think about Dana, but to promote her book. River remembers the phone messages from Rueben. She knew they are about that club. As soon as that club is finished, the sooner she can move on with her life. As Dave and she walk in the restaurant, River takes her cell phone and call Reuben.

"It's about time you called back." Reuben says.

"How did you get the number to the hotel?" she questioned.

"I bribed Momma. I told her that I would repaint the house." He confesses. "How's New York?"

The hostess approaches Dave and River. While River fusses with her uncle, Dave informs the hostess that they need a table for two; non-smoking.

"What do you want?" River asks.

"Dana said that we need more money for additions." Reuben said. "Dana said that he is willing to email you an expense report."

The hostess grabs two menus and leads Dave and River to an empty table.

"How much," River asks through her teeth.

"A couple of grand," Reuben asked. "If you wire the money, we can get started.

"Fine," River sighs.

"So tell me, how is New York?"

"Nice, until I heard from you," River says rudely.

"Oh, niece, you love your Uncle Ruby," he teases.

"You owe me big, really big, and it is more than just money."

"I know, I know, Niece, and I promise I will take care of you."

"Email me the information, bye."

River and Dave sit down at the table. The hostess informs them of the specials, then leaves.

River and Dave begin to look over their menus.

"Uncle Ruby irritating you again?" Dave asks.

"It's like he's a child," River complains.

"I know you will be so glad when this club is finished." Dave says.

River nods his head. The waiter comes to the table.

"Hi, my name is Eric, what can I get you two to drink?"

"Whatever you have on tap," Dave says.

"I need a Long Island." River says with a sigh.

Eric grins, then walks away.

"What did Reuben want?" Dave asks looking over the menu.

"More money," River answers. "He is making some extra additions."

Dave doesn't respond. His lack of commenting bothered River.

"Don't say anything Maroni."

"I didn't say a word." Dave says with a chuckle.

"You don't have to. I can read your mind." She smirks with a wink.

"You put more into his club-,"

"I know, I know," River said. "but if the roles were reversed, he'd do the same."

"River, you do this for anyone, not just your uncle." Dave said. "You're a good woman, with a pure heart."

"Stop sweet talking me, Marouni," River says sarcastically. "I might be foolish enough to fall for it."

Eric returns back with their drinks.

"You guys ready to order or do you need more time?"

"I want the buffalo chicken salad, with ranch dressing, sub the tomatoes for black olives." River said.

"Just give me the cheese burger with fries." Dave said.

The waiter nods his head. He takes the menus and then leaves to put in the order.

"We did what I wanted to do today. Is there anything you want to do?" River asks.

"Yeah, the Knicks game, they're playing the Lakers tomorrow."

"I can ask our driver where we can get tickets. While we're there, I can look for something for Christies."

"See, that is what I was just talking about." Dave says smiling. "You're always looking out for someone. When are you going to look out for yourself?"

"Tomorrow," River answers.

AFTER FIFTEEN MINUTES THE waiter brings their food. River and Dave eat in silence.

"So with Reuben making more additions, I take it that you're comfortable with the architect."

"I'm comfortable with helping my uncle." River responds.

"Where did you say the architect was from?"

"Pittsburgh," she answers.

"How did Reuben find him?"

"He opened the phone book and said, 'enny, meeny, minny, mo!'." River replies sarcastically.

Dave chuckles.

"What other buildings has he done?" he asks.

The song *Misty Blue* echoes in her mind:
> *Just the mention of your name*
> *Turns a flicker into a flame...,*

River thinks about that Flaming Blue collection,
> *Ooh, Baby, I should forget you*
> *Heaven knows I tried.*

Fifteen years, she went fifteen years without thinking of him and now she is here giving him her money, and Dave making casual conversation about him. River wonders if she should tell him about Dana. When she looks up from her plate she sees the pretty girl standing across the room.

"River," Dave said disturbing her thoughts.

"What?" she asked. "Um, I'm sorry, I was someplace else."

"Where were you?" Dave asks. "I was asking-,"

Dave's voice fades out. River looses Dave, she's not paying attention. She looks at the girl standing up against the wall. Why hasn't anyone noticed her? Waiters and waitress walk past her as if she is not there, no one asking her if she needs help with anything such as: finding her seat or speaking with her server or a manager.

"River," Dave asks again.

"What?" she snaps. "I'm here, I'm here,"

Dave notices her looking at something, he looks around.

"What are you looking at?" he questions.

"Nothing," she says. "Tomorrow I am going on the Autumn O' Neil Show. Did you know she is doing one of my books for her book club?"

"Autumn O' bad mouth men," Dave comments. "And-,"

"And what?" River asks interrupting Dave. "She teaches women to be independent, prepare for circumstanced-,"

"As if there aren't enough movies and how-to-books on teaching women not to need their men."

"She is a leader," River points.

"She is bitter old spinster," Dave states with a smile.

River laughs.

"You have the prettiest smile." Dave said smiling at her.

Pretty smile, echoed through her mind.

River heard those words before. She heard them too many times, years and years ago. "You have a pretty smile," the men would say.

She smile bashfully and they kiss her, promising their love and devotion. No matter how pretty they thought her smile was, they still broke her heart.

River unintentionally looks at the pretty girl. Still, no one seems to notice her. Dave looks at River. He sees her eyes wandering; searching the room. Is she looking for someone? Dave puts two and two together. River's little friend is here.

"She's here, isn't she?" he asks in a soft tone.

River doesn't answer verbally; her eyes said yes.

"Where is she?" Dave asks still in a soft tone.

River shifts her eyes. Dave slowly turns his head to see her, but he sees no one. He only sees the waiters and waitress. No one fits the description of what River told him.

"River, where is she?" he asks.

"Don't make a scene," River whispers.

"Just show me where she is," he replies.

River doesn't respond. She sips her Long Island Ice Tea.

"Do you want to go back to the hotel?" Dave asks.

"Would I seem weak if I said yeah?" she asks.

Her eyes are pleading asking for help.

"No baby," he says, shaking his head no.

Dave reaches over and caresses her hand. Then he calls for the waiter to pay for their meal.

"WHERE TO?" ASKS THE driver.

"Back to the hotel," Dave tells him.

Dave and River are quiet for the long ride back to the hotel. They sit looking out the window. Dave can't understand why he couldn't see the girl. He looked exactly where River's eyes led him, but he didn't see her. In fact, come to think of it, he has never seen her, not at the school, not at the restaurant. Is she that good that she manages to not be seen? Dave looks at River. He wants to hold her, but he returns his focus to the window.

"SHALL I STAY?" THE driver asks once they arrive at the hotel.

He holds the door open for Dave and River to get out of the car.

"No," Dave answers. "Thank you,"

Ignoring the front desk, Dave leads River up to their suite. Once inside, the atmosphere changes. River sits down on the couch. Dave walks to the bar to pour her a glass of water.

"You didn't see her did you?" River finally speaks.

Dave doesn't answer her. He hands her the water then sits beside her.

"Sometimes I see her and sometimes I don't,"

"What do you mean?"

"I see her, as clearly as I am looking at you, but then whenever I look away, just for a second, she is gone. Then I wonder if I ever saw her or did I think I saw her." River drinks the water and sighs. "But whatever, I've got things to do, I don't have time to think if I have seen her or not."

"Too busy for a stalker?" Dave asks with a chuckle.

River grins.

"Anyway, you seem to like that Flaming Blue collection," Dave said.

"Yes, that exhibit was disturbing," River replies. "That red in the sky was like blood. Painting sad paintings because some guy dumped you? Move on. You heard what the tour guide said. She had guys loving her, but she wanted someone who didn't want her; pathetic!"

"You're so harsh, Dr. Daniels." Dave comments.

River shrugs.

"Come on, you see it all the time with the silly girls in school. They have their head in the clouds, thinking about their boyfriends instead of focusing on their education."

"Were you always that focused?" Dave questions.

"No, I was just as goofy as those girls. I was flunking out of community college with my head in the stars. But after a while I grew up, focused on what was really important and now I am a millionaire living the dream."

"The dream?" Dave questions.

"Yes," River says.

"You are successful, but do you ever get lonely?" Dave asked.

"No," River said. "Why would I get lonely, when I have you and my stalker?"

CHAPTER THIRTEEN

Reuben puts the finishing touches on his club as Dana oversees the construction on Katrina's Law Firm, making sure that minor details become major priorities. Like Reuben, Katrina uses a mobile home as her temporary office. In her office she promises clients that she will do her best that they don't do jail time.

Dana enters the trailer hot and hungry. Katrina smiles at her man. She is in love. He makes her smile, he makes her happy. If he tells her that he loves her today and asked her to marry him, her answer would be yes. Like high school girls, she doodles his name on her legal pad, and plays with her name: Katrina Robinson-Wilson. Katrina is ready for Dana to meet her parents. Is it too soon?

"How are things coming?" she asks, getting Dana a bottle of water.

"Everything's coming along good." He answered. "I'm just tired."

"I'd be tired too if I didn't sleep at night and worked all day," Katrina comments.

Dana doesn't respond to Katrina's comment. For weeks Dana has been dreaming about River; dreaming it is River that is sharing his bed and not Katrina. Dana dreams of the River that he fell in love with, the River that used to smile at him. Dana and Katrina don't make sweet passionate love, they hump rapidly; just enough for Dana to scratch the itch and Katrina to enjoy his energy.

Dana knew that this is wrong. As good as Katrina is to him, he feels bad because he doesn't like her the way that he can tell that she likes him. By the way that Katrina looks at him, Dana can tell that she loves him, but he is not in love with her. Truth be told he doesn't want to be with her but he needs her to help him forget about River. Katrina is a means to an end.

As Katrina complains about the amount of work her latest client has her doing. Dana wonders what River is doing. How is the book tour? Rueben said that she'll be gone for six weeks. She may not be at the opening. It hurts that she hates his guts.

River doesn't want to be in the same room as me. He says to himself.

He looks at Katrina, nodding his head making it appear that he is listening to her. Will she hate him the same way River hates him?

"Well, I gotta run," he replies.

Dana kisses Katrina on the cheek.

"See you later," she says

Dana quickly walks out of the mobile home and drives to Christies.

JIM GREETS DANA WITH a smile.

"What can I get for you?"

"Something strong; rat poisoning," Dana says sardonically.

"Your day that bad?" Jim chuckles as he fixes Dana a glass of coke.

"My life is complicated."

"River," Jim comments

Dana looks at Jim surprised that he knew what is going on.

"I overheard you and Reuben talking that day you guys first met. Plus Reuben talked with me, he was worried that River was-, well anyway. You two have history."

"There's no history," Dana corrects him. "River and I dated in the past, almost two decades ago."

"If there is no history, then why is life complicated?"

Dana looks at Jim.

"You like Isaac from the *Love Boat?*"

Jim chuckles.

"Okay, River and I are the past. One of the girls you dated and really cared about, but when the relationships ran its course. You still care about her, but it's the past. I loved her whenever I was with her, but we were young. I never thought that I would see her again, but for some strange reason, she is back in my life. I find myself thinking about her and now I am wondering is it fate or coincidence."

"How do you feel about River?" Jim asked.

"It's hard to say, when I think of her from the past, she was a breath of fresh of air."

"Now?"

"She's scary, all stoic and frosty."

"Frosty?" Jim asks laughing.

"You know, she's cold."

"The River I know isn't cold, she more conservative, but not cold."

Dana nods his head sips his coke.

So River is only cold towards me.

"Maybe it's fate intervening to bring you closer." Jim suggests.

"What kind of closer? River is out of town. When she comes back, the club will be finished. I will probably never see her again."

"You'll see her again." Jim said. "Because all this here it's not settled and until it is, you will see her again."

"Do you know hard it is to look at that woman?"

"Women always hate the men that broke their hearts," Jim says.

"But that was almost twenty years ago." Dana said.

"Twenty days, twenty years, it could have been yesterday, the fact is that you broke her heart."

"So what do I do?"

"Unbreak it," Jim said with a chuckle. "If you're as done with the relationship now as you were then; then don't worry about it. If you're not then sit back and let fate do its thing."

Just sit and wait. – Dana meditates on Jim words.

Dana wonders if he should ends things with Katrina, because if River and he are meant to be, she will only be in the way. Then again, fate will remove Katrina and he wouldn't have to do anything.

THE TRIP TO MIAMI promises more excitement than New York. Driving along the coast, Dave and River watch everyone on the beach soak up the sun. River feels revived, ready to conquer the world with her knowledge. Their driver and escort is a Latino man named Paul. Instead of a hotel, Bush Publications rented a beach house. The house is a two floor home with three bed rooms and one and a half baths. The first floor has a kitchen, a living and dining room that lead to the back porch that leads to the beach. The beach house is very intimate and reserved. Just what River needs; her little friend cannot find her here. River looks out on the back porch and sees the little children playing in the sand, women sun bathing in their tiny bathing suits. A bodyguard is posted in front, his name is Carlos.

River does not have to be at the bookstore until noon the next day. Dave and she have the whole day to themselves. Paul suggests a night club down on the main stretch.

"Live music; lots of dancing," Paul encourage.

River shakes her head, detesting the idea, but Dave loves it.

"We need a change of scenery." Dave says to her.

"We have a change of scenery. We went from New York to Miami." River stated.

"That is not what I mean," Dave told her. "We went from bookstore to bookstore, one stuffy museum to another. I want to party and get sloppy drunk."

"You're free to do whatever you want," River says.

River grabs her luggage and goes in her room.

"Come on," Dave whines, following her. "You had a successful two weeks. Let your hair down. Relax and unbutton the top button on your shirt and get loose."

"Dave, I don't have time, I have to work on my next book."

"Work on your book when you get back," he told her.

"Dave,"

"River," Dave said. "Come on, give me two hours, then we can come back and stay up all night, talking and reading literature."

"You're so full of it!" River says laughing. "By the time we get back, you'll be too drunk."

"River, please," Dave complains.

"Fine," River surrenders. "What does one wear to this club?"

"Not that stuffy pant suit," Dave comments.

He goes through her suit case tossing her clothes around.

"David!" River exclaims. "Do you know how much these suits cost?!"

River tries to stop him. He holds his hands out blocking her off.

"I will shred these suits!" He says holding one up.

River looks at him horrified her eyes intense as he holds her Chanel pant suit.

"David that suit cost six hundred dollars!"

"You spent six hundred dollars on a pair of slacks and a blazer?" Dave questions.

"Don't judge me! I had a meeting. Give me my suit!"

"Do you own any sexy clothes?"

"No, who am I being sexy for?"

"It's not about being sexy for anyone. It's just good to have some sexy clothes for an occasion." Dave said. "Let's go shopping."

"Well, I have fitted blazers and straight leg pants," she defends.

Dave shakes his head and grabs her hand and they leave the beach house.

THEY TOUR THE DRESS shops along Lincoln Rd. River feels like a fish out of water looking for skimpy dresses to wear to a night club. River can't remember the last time she wore a dress.

"What do you plan on wearing to Reuben's club?" Dave asks.

They enter a dress shop.

"One of my suits," River answered.

Dave shakes his head. A pleasant sales associate approaches them smiling.

"Hello is there something in particular you're looking for," she asks.

"Yes something to sex her up," Dave says, smacking River on the behind.

Embarrassed by his words and actions, River shoots Dave a look, but he smiles and winks.

"Excused me," the young lady replies.

"My friend here needs to loosen up and she needs a very sexy dress to show off some thighs, cleavages, and a little emphasis on this area," Dave smacks her on the rear end again.

"Will you stop that?" River hisses.

The young lady giggles at River and Dave.

"We have some nice dresses this way," she says leading Dave and River to a section in the boutique.

Before their eyes are several dress rounders full of small, yet very sexy dresses in many colors from bright reds to light blues. From spaghetti straps dresses to the strapless dress, all of them are short and cut to reveal any information that the woman is willing to tell. River is not allowed to turn down any dress. Dave makes her try all the dresses that the sales associate selects. River goes in the dressing room and tries on a dress. She hesitates on coming out of the dressing room.

"River," Dave calls out.

She sighs. Slowly she steps out of the dressing room and stands before Dave. His eyes widen to the size of quarters and his mouth stands agape. The sales associate stares. She wears a flowing, black silk dress that is long enough to grace her thighs and short enough for Dave to drool.

The silence makes River nervous.

"Well?" River asks.

His eyes still glued on River, Dave hands the sales associate his credit card.

"You take American Express, right?"

SMOKES FILLS THE ROOM and the smell of sweat and alcohol is a stench in River's nostrils. The live band plays loudly while the women move their hips from side to side and the men shake their rear ends to the rhythm of the beat. It is an amazing sight to behold to River. She has never seen such madness. If she could, she would have everyone in the club committed to a mental ward. To what others see as pure innocent fun, River sees as an episode of epilepsy. Dave leads River to a vacant but dirty table. Many men watch River as she walks to the table. She is the unintentionally sexy woman that wears a dress that made Dave forget about his credit. He also brought her four inch heels black sandals. In pure River fashion to hold on to some source of identity, she her wears hair in a bun.

"Want to dance?" Dave asks.

"Um, no, thank you," River answers with a chuckle.

"Why not,"

"I just don't want to," River says defending herself.

"What's the matter, you can't dance?" Dave asked jokingly. "I thought you people had rhythm."

"Ha-ha," River said laughing.

"Come on, let's dance," Dave leads her to the dance floor.

"I can't dance to this music," River said.

"Come on it's easy,"

Dave begins to dance like everyone else, moving his hips, swaying them from side to side, shaking his behind. River stands guarded, watching and wondering what has come over his senses. She looks around embarrassed, not knowing to say or what to do. Dave places his hands on her hips and moves them with the beat. Dave takes her in his arms and moves her with his body along with the beat. River can't help but to giggle and laugh. To River, this is all a game and she doesn't understand the rules, but as long as she is with Dave, she is willing to play. Soon, she begins to fill the rhythm music and within the hour, she is moving her hips and swaying from side, to side just like everyone else.

CARRYING THE FOUR INCH shoes in her hand. River and Dave dance back to the beach house. Dave turns on the radio, music plays.

"I'm tired now," River says.

"Come on," Dave said. "One more song,"

Dave takes River by the hand and they begin to dance. Standing on her tippy toes, River watches her feet move along with the rhythm. Dave smiles at her as he watches her move. Then a slow song comes on. River tries to keep up with the beat, but she stumbles and steps on Dave's feet. He pulls her in close to him and he whispers in her ear.

"Relax and just feel the music."

River nods her head.

"Follow my lead," he says.

River follows Dave's lead and begins to dance. He watches her watch her feet.

"River," he says softly.

She looks up.

"Relax," he said with a smile.

River smiles back.

"Why are you smiling?" she asks.

"This," he answers. "You, I got Old Lady Daniels in a dress."

River laughs.

"Old lady?" she laughs. "Is that what they call me?"

Dave spins River around. She laughs.

"You look so beautiful tonight," he tells her.

River is not paying attention. She looks down at her body move along with Dave's. She watches her hips move with the melody.

"River, when was the last time you danced with a man?" Dave asks.

"Um, wow, I was uh?" she thinks for a moment. "I really can't remember."

Getting lost in the music, River closes her eyes and thinks of the last time she danced with a man. She remembers it was with Dana. He was the last guy that she dated. He was the last guy that held her close as they danced. River doesn't realize that she snuggles up to Dave. She doesn't take notice when he pulls her in closer. River remembers the feeling whenever she was in a man's arms. River is feeling good at this moment.

No longer off beat, but swaying gracefully with him, River has allowed the music to rapture her. She giggles as hands move to the small of her back. She looks at him, but she doesn't see the sapphire eyes looking at her. She is looking into the dark brown eyes that once loved her. He leans in to kiss her. As he kisses her softly, a familiar feeling has awakened in her after being asleep for so many years.

Immediately comes from back from the past. Was she just kissing Dave while thinking about Dana? Quickly she pulls back and looks at her surroundings wondering where she lost her grip of reality to the point she ended up making out with Dave. River is shaken; there is a frightened look on her face.

"River," Dave calls her name softly.

"I think we had too much to drink." she chuckles nervously.

"I wasn't drinking," he tells her.

"Then I had too much to drink. I'm going to turn in," she says to him.

River attempts to walk away, but Dave stops her.

"We need to talk," he says.

"I'm willing to forget if you are," River grins.

"I don't want to forget," Dave said.

River doesn't like the look in his eyes. He had an unfamiliar look to her.

"I have something to say to you. Something I wanted to say for a long time."

As tears form in her eyes, River shakes her head. The strange look in Dave's eyes is the look that man gives a woman when he is about to tell her that he loves her. River also sees his eyes hoping that she will feel the same.

"River," Dave says softly.

He has to tell her that he loves her.

"No," she whispers weakly.

"I lov-,"

"Stop," she hissed.

River walks to the window that views the beach.

"River,"

"Dave don't," She closes her eyes trying to fight any emotion from pouring out from her.

"Don't what-," Dave asks.

River doesn't respond. He walks to her. His body aches. He wants to hold her. He almost had her in his arms.

"River, I always had feelings for you, ever since we worked together at the restaurant, but you were too young, but now...," he hesitated. "I wondered what it would be like to love you, for you to love me. I dropped hints, lot of hints, but you never got them. At first I thought you may not have been interested, but at times when you looked at me, or the times it seemed like you needed me. I knew that it was a matter of time when we would talk about this."

River finally looks at Dave. He smiles.

"Why do you think I like spending time with you?" he asks.

"Because we're friends," she softly said.

"Yes, of course, but I am also crazy about you." He says to her.

River doesn't respond. She turns her attention back towards the view.

"River, look at me," Dave takes his hands and gently turns her head to face him. He sees tears in her eyes. "What's the matter?"

"Your words are like soft sweet music, like a beautiful love song." She says. "I can see in your eyes that you're sincere. I wish you told me how you felt then, you could have saved me a lot of years of heartache."

Tears fall down her cheeks. This explains everything to Dave. The seriousness of her character, the concept of not knowing what love is, and why she has never caught on to Dave hints. Because the love that once lived inside of her died leaving her body cold and numb.

"Who hurt you?" he asks.

"Every one," she answers softly.

Her face wet with tears.

"What happened?" Dave asks.

Standing up straight, she wipes away her tears and grins.

"It's not important. It was many, many years ago."

"It is important because you're dead," Dave says her. "I bet you any money that what just happened hasn't happened for you in a few years."

River sighs and attempts to walk away, but Dave grabs her arm.

"Don't walk away from me. We need to settle this," Dave says.

"Fine," she snaps. "It was the first time in years because I'm dead, but you're very much alive!" she points to his groin.

"Very cute," he replies.

"I'm sorry," she felt bad about her remark. "Dave, I don't give myself anymore. My love, my heart belongs to my work and my books."

Although he is hurt, he is not surprised. The River he knows now would never consider him for a lover.

"You know every time I look in your eyes, I see sapphires. I see beauty and I see peace. When the chaos of my life takes over, just knowing I can look into your eyes relaxes me and gears me up to deal with the chaos. You will always have a special place in my heart. If you told me how you felt back then, maybe you would have been a possibility. Who knows, you could have been my first lover. Showing me what true love is really about and having a broken heart would have been unknown to me."

Dave takes her hand and kisses them.

"Too little too late," he replied.

"No, life is just dealing us a bad hand," She told him. "I am getting the wild card and you get the king of hearts. But I appreciate everything you've done for me. It's been a long time since a man held me the way that you did or even kissed me."

She looks at the clock and looks back at Dave.

"I'm turning in." she says.

Dave nods his head.

"Good night,"

DAVE AND RIVER ENTER the book store holding hands and smiling at everyone. The bookstore is crowded. Hector Sanchez, the manager of the bookstore approaches them smiling. Hector escorts River to the table where her books are displayed. As River takes her seat at the table, many fans line up for River to sign their copy of her book and Dave takes his place in the background watching every woman, hoping to see if one of them would be River's little friend. River didn't have the courage to tell him that she saw her this morning and it would only be a matter of time that she might see her again.

River smiles at her fans as she signs their book. As focused as she tries to be, the events of last night flood her mind; the dancing at the night club, the kissing of a best friend while thinking of another, and her best friend telling her that he loves her. There is no physical attraction to Dave, but he had awakened feelings in her that she thought died many years ago. The touch of a man felt good to her. Cold chills run through her blood leaving her body feel cold. She closes her eyes trying to morph her body back into her comfort zone. She is now numb to the warm feelings that she felt last night. To think she almost let her guard down and gave in to a man with charm. The thought that she had almost allowed a man to take her into a sexual abyss enrages her. River immediately jumps up from her seat startling the middle aged woman who wanted her book signed.

River's quick and strange reaction immediately catches Dave's attention. He rushes by her side. River catches herself and looks at her surroundings and sees the strange looks on everyone's face.

"Is everyone all right?" Dave asks River.

Hector approaches.

"I'm sorry, I just wanted my book signed." The woman says looking at Dave

"River," Dave says looking at River.

River inhales, then exhales.

"Okay," she says with a weak smile.

There is no one else in line. River quickly signs the lady's book. Dave insists that she take a break and go outside for some fresh air.

"Dave, it's humid out," River says.

"A break, River," Dave states sternly.

River sighs, surrendering.

"Give us an hour," Dave says to Hector.

Dave leads River to a quiet secluded section on the beach. Hardly anyone is around but just a few passer-bys.

"What happened?" he asked handing her a bottle of water.

"Actually, I saw a spider," She lied.

"Are you going to tell me the truth?" Dave asks looking at her intuitively.

River sighs.

"I, ah, just lost focus, that's all?"

"Why?" Dave asks.

River shrugs, then sips her water.

"Was it thought of last night?"

River didn't respond.

"River, I know I stepped over the line last night, but I hope-,"

"Dave, last night, it's okay." she said taking his hand.

"So we're okay?" Dave asked.

River nods her head with a smile.

"What's the matter? And don't tell me nothing and don't be vague. I know you, I know when something is bothering you."

River chuckles at Dave. He does know her.

"Last night, you opened up doors that I wished stayed closed." River admits. "Now I am thinking of past loves that I buried in the depth of my mind."

"Why did you bury them?" he asks.

"Because in order to move from past pain you bury it."

"In order to move past the pain, you deal with it." Dave tells her. "River, talk to me,"

"It's too complicated," River says.

"Then make me understand," he requested.

River looks at Dave.

"I'm stronger this way," she says.

Dave sits listening to the wave of the ocean clap their hands and the sea gulls sing. As River sits quietly trying to forget about them; all of the boyfriends that broke her heart, she sees her, that pretty girl that has been haunting her for months. There she is standing in full view for Dave not to miss her. There is no more seeing and not seeing her now. She stands still on the beach just staring at River.

"Dave," River whispers.

"Uh, huh," Dave says, getting hypnotized by the sun.

"There she is," she whispers.

"What?"

"Dave, she is here!"

Dave's eyes scan the beach. No one is walking around, no one is swimming.

"Where," he asks.

River looks at him.

"Right there,"

Dave continues to look, then realizes why he has never seen the girl who has been following River. Everything begins to make sense, even from her quick disappearance back at the college. There is no stalker, there isn't a pretty girl following River. River has been hallucinating.

River quickly gets up.

"Why don't you see her?" she questions.

"River-," Dave said.

"Don't River me!" she shouts.

River looks at the girl and yells.

"You have something to say to me?"

"River," Dave calls out.

Quickly, River runs to the bench. Dave jumps up and follows her.

"How hard is it to see one woman?" River exclaims.

River is going to get to the bottom of this. She is going to find out who this girl is and what she wants with River. Once River and Dave get to the beach the girl is gone. Frantically, River searches for her causing her, to go around in circles like a madman.

"Where is she? Where is she?" River screams. "I just saw her!"

The commotion brought attention to that section of the beach. People come out from where ever they were to see what the disturbance is about.

Dave stands still not knowing what move to make. River looks at Dave.

"Why don't you see her?" River questions, her eyes intense with fear and anger. "She was just here!"

"Okay," Dave says softly.

"Don't okay me," River says through her teeth.

River is so angry that she punches Dave on the chest.

"Don't okay me. I just saw her!"

River continues to punch on Dave, angry with him because he doesn't see her. He grabs her arms and tries to pull her close to him. At first she fights him, but then she gives in letting him hold her. As she surrendered herself to him, she cries in his arms.

"I saw her," she cries. "I did, I saw her,"

"Okay," Dave said softly, "okay,"

He loves her too much to tell her that she is seeing things. He holds her in his arms and rocks her back and forth. His dear friend is over worked, tired, and heartbroken. River pulls back from Dave's arms.

"I'm going back to the book store." She tells him regaining her composure.

"I'm taking you back to the beach house." Dave states.

"I have an obligation to my fans," River tells him. "I am not going to let you or some girl stop me."

Dave watches as River storms off. She is determined not to be a wimp and let someone intimidate her. There will come a day when they will meet face to face.

CHAPTER FOURTEEN

RUEBEN SCURRIES AIMLESSLY AROUND his club making sure everything is perfect because tonight is the opening of Reuben's Room. Finally, the art deco style club is complete. There are three major sections of this club.   The VIP Suite is exclusive for private parties. The walls are white with gold colored boarders. The two chandeliers that hang on the ceiling are Swarovski crystal and gold. Twenty tables; ten round tables that seat four and ten square tables that also seat four. The tables and chairs are made of oak wood and the chairs are covered in mahogany colored leather. There is the Boardroom, a section for business and women who can come bring their clients, and make major and important deals. Like the VIP Suite, the colors are gold and white, oak floors and tables but the chairs are covered in black leather. Last, but not least, the Dining Room, the major section of the club. The Dining Room holds twenty-five booths, ten dining tables that seat from two people to four people and five large round tables that seat ten. The colors are metallic gold and silver, along with oak tables and oak floors. The chairs are covered in black leather and the booths are the color of maroon leather. On the tables are cream colored table clothes to match the cream colored walls and navy blue cloth napkins and cloth place mats. Three Swarovski gold and crystal chandeliers hang on the ceiling. This room is for formal dining- when the men want to romance their ladies, or maybe when business men come to win over a client making big and major deals. In the front of the dining room is the stage for the live band, the band leader is a laid back and friendly, bass player known as Down Home Davis.

Waiting at the door are three hostesses waiting on Reuben's cue to open the door and to greet and seat the customers. A.J., Kevin, and Randy, the bartenders, stand prepared to serve drinks, and waiters and waitresses stand with their serving tray in their hands. The cooks are in the kitchen stirring the soup and seasoning the beef. Jim Christie has taken the night off from his lounge to assist Reuben in this opening. Reuben cannot be more grateful.

Reuben closes his eyes and takes in a deep breath. Jim pats Reuben on the shoulders encouraging him to relax. Reuben needs this first night to be a success, and more importantly, he is hoping that River will keep her promise and show up.

"Dana Wilson is at the front door," one of the hostesses announces.

"Let him in," Reuben says.

Dana enters. Tonight, he wears a very fine black silk suit, white shirt and a navy blue tie. He hopes that River comes. Dana smiles as he approaches Reuben. The two men shake hands.

"Dana," Reuben says smiling.

"What's up, baby," Dana smiles. "How you doin' Jim,"

"Hey Dana," Jim smiles and shakes Dana's hand.

"I just came to make sure that everything is okay," Dana replies. "It's my policy to be at the buildings on opening day. Reu, there is a parking lot full of people."

"Really," Reuben asks with a smile.

Dana nods his head.

Reuben looks at Jim. Jim smiles at Reuben.

"Congratulation," Jim pats Reuben on his back.

Reuben turns to Down Home Davis and the band. Reuben gives one nod of the head; they start to play and instantly music fills the air. Reuben calls out to his hostesses:

"Open the door ladies," Reuben is smiling brightly.

The young girls unlock the door, and soon the crowd enters in Pittsburgh's newest night club. As they look around, they are in awe at the awesomeness of the club. They are fascinated with the chic, yet very welcoming atmosphere.

"Welcome to Reuben's Room," Reuben greets. "I am Reuben."

The guests smile as they are escorted by the lovely hostess to a table or booth. They snap their fingers and bob their heads, listening to Down Home lead his band in up tempo jazz tunes.

REUBEN'S ROOM IS CROWDED, every table and booth have customers in them and there are guests waiting to be seated. The waiters and waitress as move quickly, attending to tables by refilling their drinks and making sure that everything is all right. Shirley is at the club, sitting in a booth drinking apple juice and eating a baked chicken breast with season rice and steamed broccoli. She was not going to miss this night. Shirley is so proud of Reuben. Looking back, ten years ago, if someone had told her that her son would be a night club owner, she would not have believed it. Now, she is watching her son, go from table to table, introducing himself and receive congratulations and well wishes. Her baby boy is becoming a successful business man!

"Momma, don't cry," Reuben says, taking his handkerchief from his pocket drying her tears.

"I am so proud of you baby," she says crying. "Your daddy would be so proud."

"I love you, Momma." Reuben said. "I love you,"

She hugs Rueben tight.

Shirley notices him occasionally looking at the front door.

"She's coming baby,"

Reuben smiles as he takes in a deep breath.

River would keep her word. Reuben said to himself. *She won't say that she would do something and not do it. She knows how much this night means to me. So where is she? Why isn't she here yet?*

Reuben's eyes continue to scan the club hoping, that he'll see her in a stuffy business suit and her long hair in a bun, but so far he doesn't see anyone. The only thing that would keep her away is Dana. Reuben looks back at Dana who is seated at the bar with his girlfriend. Would she not show in spite of him? Reuben shakes his head. River will show up; she'll come.

No matter how River feels about Dana, he did a good job on the club. Dana has a gift. He is a creative person. River should come out and see what her investment did. So what if Dana is her ex-boyfriend; Reuben chuckles to himself thinking of the ex-girlfriends that he ran into. His eyes scanned the dining room wondering if any of them are here.

"HEY KATRINA, THANKS FOR, coming out," Reuben greets. "You're looking good tonight."

"Thank you," she smiles.

Reuben has to admit, Katrina is a beautiful woman, especially in that tight light brown dress. She is wearing her hair down and her arms are around Dana.

"Dana is so nervous tonight," Katrina tells Reuben smiling.

She rubs Dana on the back.

"Hoping that the roof won't cave in," Reuben jokes.

"Yeah," Dana chuckles.

"This is a wonderful turn out," Katrina says smiling.

"Yep, real nice," Reuben scans the club.

Come on River, don't let me down.

Dana wonders if River would show up tonight, but he is afraid to ask.

"EXCUSE ME," SAID A familiar voice to Reuben.

He turns around from the bar and sees the face that he longs to see.

"Where can I get some service?" she teases.

"Service, I got your service," Reuben hugs his niece. "Thank you so much for coming." Reuben steps back to admire River. "My, my, my, look at my little niece." River looks away bashfully, "You look beautiful."

River's dress is a long black A-line dress with spaghetti straps. Her neck, her ears and her wrist are graced with diamonds. River is not wearing her glasses and she is wearing makeup and her nails are painted red. Her long hair is not pinned in a bun: tonight, she wears her hair down and she has curls in her hair. River looks absolutely beautiful. Is she wearing lip stick?

"Want a Long Island?" Reuben offers.

"Yep," River answers quickly.

With the noise from the crowd and music, River doesn't notice that she is sitting next to Dana, and with his back facing her, Dana doesn't notice River either.

Reuben points to the bartender.

"A Long Island Ice Tea," he says to the bar tender.

Reuben returns his eyes to River,

"So tell me how the tour is," Reuben said.

"It's been good," River says to him. "New York is amazing and Miami is sizzling. Signed books all day and I saw a few potential aunties," River winked at Reuben.

Reuben chuckles. The bartender sets the Long Island Ice Tea in front of River. She smiles, thanking him and takes a sip.

"Playing matchmaker for your uncle, you check their line of credit?"

"Yes, all clear uncle, you're going to the pent house."

River and Reuben laugh.

"Riv, want some wing dings?" Reuben asks.

"Yes, I am starving," River tells him.

Reuben grins at the same bartender and tells him to get River a dozen of hot wings.

"Come on, let's go see Momma,"

Reuben takes River by the hand and leads her to Shirley. Shirley smiles when she sees her River and Reuben walking to her. She stands up and hugs River.

"Reuben, look at our angel," Shirley says smiling.

"Yes, Momma,"

River notices that Shirley eyes are wet.

"Grandma, why are you crying," River asks as she shakes her head and smiles.

"She's been crying all night," Reuben comments.

"Ruby hush," Shirley said drying her tears. "Tell me about the tour baby,"

"Very nice, signing books, meeting fans," River says.

"Did Dave come with you tonight?" Shirley asks

"No, he's in L.A., getting things set up for me."

"Your uncle has been waiting for you. Waiting by the door like a dog waits for his master,"

"Is that right?" River questions, smiling.

"No, I was just greeting my customer," Rueben says looking around.

River and Shirley laugh at Reuben playing coy.

"Well, I am glad that I have both of my babies here. Now I am going home and going to bed."

Shirley hugs and kisses Reuben and River. They escort Shirley out of the club. Outside Reuben has a car waiting for Shirley to take her home.

"Grandma at the club," River jokes.

Reuben laughs.

"Want me to show you around?"

Reuben takes River by the hand and shows her around the club. River smiles as Reuben shows off his club, he is a child showing off his new toy.

"Reuben, this is beautiful." River tells him.

"All because of you," Reuben says.

"I didn't build it," she tells him.

"No, but your money did," Reuben states.

River shrugs her shoulders and looks away.

"Riv, I'm glad that you were able to work with Dana-,"

"I didn't work with Dana-,"

"No, but it was your money-,"

"Ruby, I'm sorry for acting-,"

Reuben leans in forward to kiss River on her forehead.

"I love you niece,"

River smiles up at her uncle. She is happy that she is able to help Reuben achieve his dreams and Reuben is grateful that she was able to get past whatever issues that she had with Dana. Together, with hand in hand, Reuben leads her back to the bar where her wing dings are waiting for her. As they approach the bar, Jim stands at the bar talking with a few customers. He notices River and smiles at her.

"Look who decides to grace us with her presence," Jim says, taking River by the hands.

"Hey Jimmy,"

"You look, wow…," Jim is at a loss for words.

"The old girl cleans up good," Reuben jokes.

"I came by for Reuben's opening," River replies. "But I'll be leaving back out tonight."

"How is the tour?" Jim asks.

"The tour is going well," River said. "Seeing nice places, buying nice and expensive clothes,"

"Just like a woman to shop rather than work," Jim teases. "Would you like to dance?"

"Um, no thanks," River answers with a polite grin and with the fear of ever dancing with a man again.

"Come on," Jim said smiling.

"Sorry, I have wing dings waiting for me," she said.

"Oh please forgive me," Jim said humbling bowing at River. "How dare I come before a lady and her free hot wings?"

"Free," Reuben playfully cried. "Who said anything about being free?"

Together, Jim, River and Reuben laugh.

"Come on," Reuben says, taking River hands.

"See you later Jim," River said to Jim.

"If I don't get a chance to see you again tonight, have a safe trip, babe." Jim says, then gives River an affectionate kiss on the cheek.

Reuben escorts River back to the bar. Dana sees River; she sees him but pretends that she doesn't notice. The only empty seat is the seat next to Dana. As River sits down, Reuben walks behind the bar to get her food. He looks at the clock. She only has forty-five minutes remaining of her promised hour. She is half tempted to take her wings to go, but tonight is about Reuben. Reuben returns with the dozen of hot wings and new Long Island Ice Tea.

Dana cannot take his eyes off River. She looks lovely tonight in the black gown and sparkling diamonds. The outfit is not over done. River could not have looked more perfect tonight. Dana looks at Katrina and sees that she doesn't compare to River. Katrina notices that something has caught Dana's eye. She looks to see what the something was. She sees the something is a someone; it's River Daniels.

"Excuse me," Katrina said with her brightest smile.

River slowly turns her head toward the voice and then sees the exotic, Amazon beauty. "River Daniels," Katrina said. "I'm Katrina Robinson. I am a huge fan of your work."

"Is that so?" River asked with a well formed polite grin.

"Yes," Katrina answered. "I had no idea that Dana was building your uncle's club!"

River shoots Dana a glance and then let out a chuckle. *This is Dana's date?* River says to herself as she smiles at Katrina.

Dana is reading River's smile. He knows that inside she is laughing at him.

This is comical to River. Seeing Dana with this voluptuous woman who is wearing too much make up and whose dress is too small for her body is disturbingly funny to River.

Oh how the mighty have fallen, River says to herself.

"I'm sorry, what did you say your name was?" River asks.

"Katrina, Katrina Robinson,"

"Attorney at Law," Dana adds, smiling, hoping to remove the Joker-like smile from River's face.

"Katrina, it's nice to meet you and thank you for your support," River replies.

Dana is embarrassed by his date. Although both women are beautiful in their own way, their outfits determine who has the most class. Katrina's dress hugs her body emphasizing her curves, yet it is too tight for her voluptuous frame. River's dress looks as if it was tailored made. She looks like an elegant princess. Dana tries hard not to look at River, but it is too difficult to ignore.

Reuben and River make eye contact. He mouthed the words:

"Be nice,"

"When is your next book coming out?" Katrina asks. "I hear that you are on a book tour. Will you be doing any book signings here in the city?"

"Babe, let River eat," Dana chuckles nervously.

"I'm sorry," Katrina says still smiling a smile that is almost blinding to River.

"It's okay," River says to Katrina. "I am actually still on tour, I just came back tonight for Reuben,"

Reuben is nervous. River's temper is unpredictable. He smiles at Dana, River and Katrina. Katrina notices the nervous smile coming from both Reuben and Dana. She also notices Dana looking at River. His looking is more than an occasional glance that one would give when they are watching two people have a conversation; his eyes are locked on River. Is he looking at her because she was *the* River Daniels, or is there something more?

"Hey," Katrina whispers to Dana.

"Hmm," Dana replies finally looking at Katrina. "I'm sorry, I ah-, looking at the building."

"Making sure that the building doesn't cave in," Reuben comments.

"The building is beautiful," Katrina replies.

"Yes, it is," Dana says softly, shooting a glance at River.

"So, um River, do you write full time?" Katrina asks, seeing Dana looking at her again.

"No, I am also a teacher," River answers.

"Oh wow, what grade?"

"College," Dana chimes in.

Katrina looks at Dana. He grins nervously.

"Ah, she is a college professor." Dana replies.

"What subject?" Katrina asks, looking back at River.

"English," Reuben answers.

"I can speak for myself," River said looking at Reuben and Dana. "Katrina, I have my doctorate in English and my masters in history." River said.

"My niece works at two colleges," Reuben said, winking at River.

Katrina sips the drink that she has been nursing on.

"You teach two subjects and write," Katrina says. "What do you do in your spare time?"

"Find spare time," River jokes.

Reuben and Dana laugh nervously. Katrina looks at them suspiciously.

For some reason, both Reuben and Dana are acting strange around River. What is the issue? Is she more than just a client of his? Katrina is a client of his. Is River or was River his lover? Like Katrina is his lover. Dana doesn't look at her the way he is looking at River. He may look at Katrina with a smile, but the look Dana has towards River is more. It is as if River is the only one in the room. Katrina rationalizes Dana's actions. Maybe he is impressed at her celebrity status.

"Well, I am looking forward to your next book." Katrina said smiling. "It was nice to meet you."

"Nice meeting you too," River says to Katrina.

"Dana let's dance." Katrina says.

Katrina takes Dana's hand and leads him to the dance floor. River lets out a sigh of relief. Then she scornfully looks at Reuben.

"You didn't tell me he was going to be here, Uncle." River hissed.

"Don't you Uncle me," Reuben hissed back. "He didn't bite you!"

River rolls her eyes, sips her drink and finishes her meal.

On the dance floor, Dana and Katrina dance to a slow song. They hold each other tightly swaying side to side along with the beat. Katrina rests her head on Dana's shoulders. The song is ironic. The singer sings a song by Jon B. called *Love Hurts*. Dana feels the emotion to the words that the singer sings;

Sometimes love can feel
Like the closest thing to heaven

Dana remembers how it feels when he was in love. Everything seems to be serene; everyday is spring time and the sun always shined.

Sometimes love can feel
Like you've been run over by a car

Love can make your angry, when love fails after you have tried and tried. You made all the compromise and the sacrifices, and you climbed the highest mountains.

Yes it can it's the strangest thing I know
Make you feel warm when you feel cold
And if you down on happiness
You better get used to the taste of sadness
Cause love can sure hurt sometimes

Dana also knows that sometimes love can be turbulent; unsteady and unpredictable.-where you love and hate at the same time. So many fillings are stirring around in Dana at this moment. He is wishing it is River that he is holding in his arms right now. Dana smiles when Katrina looks up at him. He kisses her gently on the lips. Katrina is a good woman. She doesn't give Dana any drama, just good loving and a warm meal. She is intelligent, but as he looks up and glances in another direction, the one thing that Katrina isn't is River.

As River watches Dana and Katrina, she too has mixed emotions. She remembers dancing with Dana. She remembers how he holds her close and smiles at her when she would look him in the eyes. How did she dance with Dave and think of Dana? The singer on the stage said it best:

"Love hurts and it don't, love don't always work, love ain't all it seems, it feels good, but it stings, love hurts and don't."

The best love is the worst love, because the lover would never meet the other's expectations. It was Dana that broke River's heart. He didn't meet her expectations because it was he that let her down.   River looks at her watch as sees that her promised hour is up.

"Uncle, my time has come."

Reuben pretends to pout, but he takes River's hands and kisses them.

"Thanks for coming baby, have a safe trip back." Reuben says with a chuckle.

He leans over and kisses her on the forehead.

"See you in two weeks, tell Grandma I love her."

As River walks out, Dana watches her leave. This is it. His work is done. No more reasons to stay to oversee construction to the building in hopes that River might show. The club is finished. He doubts that he may accidentally run into her. Will it be another fifteen years? The singer continues to sing,

You know that you're alive
Because you feel so much pain

Dana is in pain now. His heart has fallen to live permanently in his stomach. He's head is pounding and his body is aching.

And when you think you can't survive
But your make it anyway
When it feels too good to stop
But it hurts too much to say,
It feels too good enough to stop
But it hurts too much to stay
Then you know

The singer sings; then sings it again almost as if he is crying out from his own heart ache:
Then you know, you ought to know
that love hurts and it don't.

Reuben watches from a distance, he sees Dana's countenance fall. Reuben wishes that he can go over and talk to him, to cheer him up. Reuben can tell that Dana loves River. Nevertheless, after the song is over Dana and Katrina walk back to the bar, Reuben sets a drink in front of Dana, then nods at him. Dana gives Reuben a small grin.

RIVER SITS IN THE TAXI as it drives her to the airport. Her thoughts go back to the time when Dana and she were dating. They were lying in the bed, snuggling and cuddling under the covers. The room was hot and humid from the passion that filled the air. River gets up to open the window and to look at the beautiful view outside. The indigo colored sky made the gray moon looked like a big silver ball in the heavens.

"What are you looking at?" Dana asked her.

"The sky," she answered back. "Look the moon looks like it's glowing. Come see it,"

Reluctantly, Dana climbs out of bed and stands besides River. He chuckles. The sky looks ordinary. He wondered why River saw such beauty.

"River, it's just a sky," Dana replied.

"It's more than just the sky," River said. "Look at how the clouds and the moon play peek-a-boo, and look at those stars, looks like a dust of diamonds."

Dana wrapped his arm around River,

"It's just the simple things that make you smile."

"I don't need diamonds," River said. "As long as I have diamonds in the sky, I'm okay, unlike you."

River walked back to the bed.

"Unlike me," Dana asked. "What do you mean unlike me? Dana walked to River.

"You need a lot to satisfy you," River said.

"No," Dana said. He sat down next to River, "I don't need much. I would like a good job, a nice home and car, and every night good sex, but I don't need much." He joked.

River laughed.

166

"Seriously, what I do need is to see you smile. River, there is something about your smile. After a hard day, just seeing your smile, I'm good."

Hearing those words was like hearing a captivating melody in her ears. Many men said those words to her before but the way that Dana said them, it's like a love song that he dedicated only to her. River wanted to tell him that she loved him that night that she would love only him. Her heart and soul can be his if he wanted them. River looked Dana in the eyes and she saw that he loved her. She was the moon and he was the sky, and as long as he loved her, she will shine like the silver ball up in the heavens. But it wasn't too long after that night, that Dana told her that he didn't want to date her anymore. River wanted to scream.

How dare you get me to trust you and you walk away? How dare you make love to me, taking my body in depths and leave me feeling vacant and empty. I was willing to give you my soul, you had my heart. How dare you? I know you love me. I know you care about me. Every time I look into your eyes, I can see that you love me. I can feel you.

"MA'AM," THE TAXI DRIVER said.

River looks at him.

"We're at the airport."

She grins. She pays the driver and gets out of the car and walks through the airport. As she walks to her gate, she thinks about Dana Wilson. He is a joke and so is his goofy girlfriend. He is sorry for whatever resentment that she has towards him. Was that goofy girlfriend around when he was sorry? River isn't blind. She saw how he looked at her tonight.

Please, Dana tell me that she has a brain. River thought to herself.

She has to admit that the woman is beautiful with her amber colored eyes. River can tell that she is not Dana's type unless she is candy in the day and company at night.

Oh, how the mighty have fallen.

CHAPTER FIFTEEN

DANA ENTERS HIS HOME. It is two in the morning. He is drunk, tired, and depressed. As Katrina takes a shower, Dana grabs a bottle of beer from the refrigerator, sits down on the couch and turns the television on. There is nothing on but poor rated B movies and infomercials. He is extremely tired and worn out. It is hot and humid in the living room but he refuses to open the window. He is not in the mood to get hypnotized by the imaginary lilies. He doesn't want any reminders of River. He thinks that maybe it's a good idea for him not to go to Reuben's club; fearing that he might run into River. Dana is starting to resent Jim Christie as well; Christies is where he first saw River after fifteen years.

Sit back and let fate happen. – Dana replays Jim's words in his head.

What does Jim know about fate, how many times has he run into an ex-girlfriend? Dana questions, as he messages his temples.

Katrina comes out of the bathroom smelling like Dove body wash, pomegranate and lemon verbena. She looks good in her tiny silk bathrobe. She sits next to Dana. Within the past month, Katrina has managed to have a few clothes at Dana's, and she does the grocery shopping. She wants him to be her husband and she wants to have at least four of his children; two boys and two girls. Dana Jr. whom they will call D.J., the other three she will let him name. She will obtain this goal. Every goal that Katrina has set, she has received.

Dana looks at a woman that made herself his girlfriend. How did she become his girlfriend? She is not his girlfriend. Katrina is just a woman who has managed to attach herself on to him and looks very good sitting in that bathrobe. He quickly glances at her thick thighs, but his heart is aching too much for him to want sex.

"You're quiet tonight," she says in a soft tone.

"Long night," he replies.

Katrina smiles,

"One would think that tonight was your opening night, instead of Reuben's," she replies.

"In a way it was. This is the biggest project that I've done." Dana says.

"Well now that Reuben's Room is finished. I can have your undivided attention on my firm." Katrina leans over and kisses him. "Maybe, you can actually get some sleep." Katrina says between kisses. "Reuben really put you to work. All those sleepless nights. I promise my firm won't be so detailed."

Dana grins. It wasn't his high maintenance client that kept him up at night, but his ice cold niece. Katrina positioned herself on to the couch to massage Dana's shoulders. He tilts his head back receiving the touch and sighs. Why is River so heavy on his mind? If River was not a factor, he would be happy with Katrina. Here is a woman that apparently loves him, a woman that is a good woman. Whenever Katrina looks at Dana, she smiles. She is happy being with him. And she is here soothing him, comforting him, after a long and hard night of emotional agony. Katrina leans in to kiss the back of his neck. Her kisses and touches feel nice, but he is not in the mood for sex. He could have the sex with Katrina and think of River like he usually does, but right now at this moment it would be pointless because she is *not* River; this fact continues to depress him.

Katrina senses that Dana is not in the mood, but that doesn't stop her advances. She is in the mood and she wants him to be, too.

"I was shocked to see River Daniels tonight," Katrina replies. "She is on a book tour and she manages a special trip just for an opening."

"I guess," Dana said as he sipped his beer.

"River looked beautiful tonight," Katrina chuckled. "She was almost over dressed, with those diamonds and that designer dress. Do you think she came to show off?"

"Show off what?" Dana asks.

"You know her celebrity status?" Katrina answers. "Who comes to make a stop to Pittsburgh in the middle of their book tour just to say hi; famous people."

"What do you mean by that?" Dana asks.

"She looked like a million dollars, like she was going to a movie premiere; you know, Hollywood." She says with a chuckle.

Katrina stops massaging Dana's shoulders and sits close to him on the couch.

"And that was just for an hour appearance. That's what celebrities do."

"That's not River," Dana comments.

"Oh?" Katrina questions.

"No," Dana answers.

"How do you know?" Katrina asks trying to hide her suspicions.

Dana senses her paranoia. He takes in a deep breath.

"Reuben and River are very close. They're more like brother and sister than uncle and niece. She knew how important this club is for Reuben so she came out to be supportive."

"Or to make sure that her money was invested well."

"How do you know about that?" Dana asks.

"It's not secret," Katrina chuckles in a mocking way. "I know she practically paid for that club. Reuben's Room didn't look like some old juke joint."

"Katrina why do you care?" Dana questioned.

Katrina shrugs her shoulders then looks at Dana wondering if there is any information

"Well, if she did come to make sure her investment was well spent, I won't blame her. River worked hard for her success." Dana said.

"Is that right?" Katrina questions suspiciously.

"Yeah, River doesn't flaunt her money. River is humble,"

"Is she?" Katrina asks. "How do you know so much about River?"

"She's a client, Kat, I got to know a few things about her." Dana answers evasively.

Katrina is in attorney mode. She remembers the nervous chuckles and looks that Rueben and Dana shared. The way Dana was looking at River tonight.

"Did you get to know her like you have gotten to know me?" she questions.

Dana is on stand. He is the defendant who appears to be very guilty. Her job is to make sure that he does not serve jail time, but things do not look positive. The way Dana looked at River tonight shows that he is guilty of something. The way Reuben acts shows that he was some kind of accomplice.

"What?" Dana asks caught off guard by the attorney's question.

That is not a question that he had been prepped for.

"I'm not blind, Dana, I saw the way you were looking at her tonight."

In lawyer talk; "Just answer the question Mr. Wilson."

"Looking at her?" Dana said in a form of a question.

"Yes," Katrina said. "Is there something about you and River that I don't know about?"

Dana's heart froze. He doesn't know what to say or do. Are his feelings for River that obvious? He tried his best to play cool when he saw River tonight. Should he tell Katrina that River and he dated many, many, many years ago and that maybe it is fate that she somehow was back in his life again. Or, should he just ease Katrina's insecurities by telling her that River is a client and just like Reuben, he and River became friends. If he tells Katrina the truth, maybe she get mad and leave him and this is what Jim meant that fate will intervene. The idea is pleasing to him.

"River and I were old acquaintances," Dana answers.

"How old?" Katrina asks.

"We were friends,"

"Good friends?"

"She and I used to talk," he replies to her in a blasé manner.

"So you dated?" Katrina questioned interrogating. "How serious?"

"Back in the day when we were kids," Dana answered evasively.

"You didn't answer my question," Katrina said looking at Dana.

Dana looks away. To Katrina, his eyes say that they were serious.

"Were you going to tell me?" she asks.

"No."

"Why not?" Katrina asks offended.

"Because it was over a decade ago," Dana says with a laugh. "Why are you paranoid?"

Katrina takes a deep breath.

"The way you were looking at her tonight says that something was going on with you two." Katrina confesses.

She suddenly feels foolish.

Katrina waits for him to speak. As she waits, she wonders about Dana and River. Was it just a decade ago, and now they're old friends? When they were together did he make strong passionate love to River? Dana has never made slow passionate love to Katrina. There isn't much tenderness. Whenever they have sex, it's as if he is releasing off steam. He would come home from work; see her at her and simply take her. After dinner, as she washes the dishes, he grabs her in his arms. She shrieks with excitement and within moments they are on his couch. Katrina loves when she would be in the shower, Dana would come in to join her and under the hot water, she calls out his name. The spontaneous love making is exciting to Katrina. She is very satisfied. She looks at Dana hoping that he will satisfy her right now.

Dana feels bad about he feels regarding Katrina and River. Katrina hasn't done anything wrong. He is wrong by leading her on. Is he leading her on? He never made a vowel of commitment. They are consenting adults. They enjoy each other's company. Maybe this can go somewhere, maybe not. Dana should not be afraid to tell Katrina that he once dated

River Daniels. However, Dana knows that no matter how he tries to rationalize his semi-normal relationship with Katrina, this relationship is not normal, because he does not have the backbone to tell Katrina that he does not want a relationship with her. Whenever they do have sex, he is thinking of River.

Dana sits his bottle of beer on the table and leans forward to kiss Katrina.

"I didn't bring it up cause it doesn't matter. River was back in the day, nothing significant."

Dana kisses her on the cheek.

"It's okay," she said, melting in his hands.

She is not going to let up on her women's intuition.

Tonight Katrina saw more than just a look of old acquaintances. She saw the look of secret lovers who tried to avoid eye contact in fear that someone might find out their secret.

"Were you in love with her?" Katrina asked.

"What?"

"Did you love her?"

"I cannot believe I am having this conversation." Dana starts to pace the floor. "Katrina, I dated a lot of women in this city, and if you are going to question me about every girlfriend, then we cannot be together. What if I told you that I had a problem with you defending some client because he was your ex-boyfriend?"

"Dana, you were just looking at her as if-,"

"She looked good!" Dana confesses. "For six months, she wore nothing but pantsuits and tonight, she looked nice. I am a man, Kat, if I see a nice looking woman, I'm going to look."

"Dana, I don't mean to come off insecure," Katrina replies. "It's just that I am crazy about you. These past couple of months have been wonderful, and I don't want to waste my time if I am not wanted."

Dana grins and walks back to the couch and sits back down. He caresses her face.

"Katrina, I want you," Dana told her softly. "You don't have anything to worry about with River and me. Like I said, she and I were years ago. It was just a business investment."

Dana leans in and begins to kiss her passionately. Within moments they lay on the couch making love. Instead of the hard rapid passion, he moves slow, not because he wants to be passionate, but because he is still drunk and doesn't have the energy to move fast. However as Katrina receives him, she is enjoying his slow movements. She does need the slow passionate love making. She looks up at him and he looks back at her.

Tears form into her eyes.

"I love you," she whispers.

The ruling is for the defendant.

THE NEW ASSIGNED BODYGUARD greets River as she walks in the L.A. hotel. The registration desk has been expecting her. They introduce the bellboy and then he leads her to her suite. Dave had arrived hours earlier to make sure that everything for River is in order. He unpacked her luggage, and set up the small office in the suite. Since the incident in Miami, Dave has not been looking for the mysterious woman, because he now knows that she is a figment of River's imagination. What he does look for are the signs that might lead River to seeing her. What is going on in River's mind when she thinks that she sees the girl? Dave knows that the hallucinations are due to stress. So he makes is going to make sure that River gets plenty of rest.

She walks in her suite. Dave greets her with a smile and a big hug.

"How was the opening?" Dave asks.

"It was really nice," she tells him.

Dave steps back and looks at River. She is still wearing the dress she wore to Reuben's Room.

"You look beautiful," Dave says to her smiling.

"Thank you, kind sir," River says, giving Dave a curtsy.

"Everything is set up for you. You're unpacked and I set up your lap top."

"Thanks, I'm going to change." River says.

River walks in her room to change her clothes. Dave had hung her suits and arranges her shoes in perfect order. River grins. Quickly, she steps out of her dress and in to the shower. The hot water is relaxing and soothing. River tilts her head back and lets the water fall over her head. River wants to wash away tonight. She washes her hair; wash away the amber colored eyes that stared at her.   River can sit next to Dave and forget about tonight. After her shower, she puts on old pair of sweat pants and a T-shirt and joins Dave in the living room.

"What does the club look like?" Dave asks.

"Like a grand museum." River answers. "Even my grandmother was there,"

"Sounds like you invested well."

"Yep, the place was packed." She tells him. "What time is the signing?"

"Ten in the morning," he told her. "Was the architect there?"

"Why?"

"Some architects go to their buildings' opening day." Dave replies.

River shrugs. She doesn't want to think about the architect and his toys.

"Well it sounds like you had an eventful evening," Dave says.

He notices River yawning.

"Tired?"

"No, not really, just a little jet lag. It's only midnight here, when I left Reuben's it was after one in the morning. I felt like I went back in time."

"Maybe you should get some rest," Dave suggests.

"I'm not ready to sleep," she said. "I got sleep on the plane."

Together they watch television. Without realizing it, River rests her head on Dave's shoulders and within moments, she falls asleep. Dave shifts his arm so that River's head rests upon his chest. He leans back on the couch and he goes to sleep.

DANA AWAKENS TO THE smell of breakfast and a throbbing headache. He showers and dresses and finds Katrina in the kitchen. He has grown accustomed to this routine, to be well fed in the morning and well loved at night. Katrina looks nice in her cream colored business suit and her long hair pulled back into a pony tail.

"Good morning," she says smiling

"Good morning," Dana replies.

As he sits down at the table, Katrina place a cup of coffee and two aspirin in front of him.

"Thank you," Dana says, taking the medication.

"How are you feeling?" she asks.

Dana sips his coffee.

"I'll be all right."

"You slept fitfully again last night," Katrina informs him.

"Really?" Dana asks.

"I thought those sleepless nights would stop after Reuben's club was finished."

Dana sips his coffee again as Katrina sits a full plate in front of him.

"Katrina, you're going to make me fat," Dana replies.

"Well you know what they say, the way to a man's heart," she says with a wink.

Dana grins.

"About last night," Katrina began. "I wanted to apologize,"

"No need," Dana says.

"I'm not the insecure or the jealous type. I don't know what came over me." She says. "I think I had too much to drink,"

"Yeah," he said with a chuckle. "I had too much myself."

"So, we're okay?"

"Yeah, we're okay," Dana says.

Katrina finally sits down. She slowly inhales then exhales,

"Um, my parents are coming in this weekend. I thought that it would be nice to go out to dinner."

"Your parents?" Dana asks.

"Yes," Katrina answers, looking at him with hopeful eyes.

Dana doesn't want to meet her parents. How can he look her mother and father in the eyes knowing that every time he sleeps with his daughter he is thinking of someone else, and has no intention of promising Katrina anything?

"My father is coming here for business and mom is coming to shop," Katrina informs. "So they won't be here long. So how's Sunday, five o'clock?

"Sure."

Dana can meet them and then break up with her in a month.

Katrina smiles, then begins to eat her breakfast. Her man is about to meet her family. Once her mother is charmed by his smile and personality and her father is impressed that Dana has his own business, it would be a matter of months that they will be married.

SHE IS DREAMING. SHE is at Reuben's Room promising her presence for the hour. As music plays in the background, she sits at the bar eating her free hot wings and complimentary Long Island Ice Tea. Soon a very beautiful woman with sparkling amber colored eyes sits down besides River, talking excessively to her. River smiles and grins, and nods her head listening to this beauty ramble on and on. River wants her to leave. She doesn't have the heart to be rude.

River's eyes scan the room watching people dancing with one another; they dance slowly and seductively. Appearing from nowhere is Dana. He approaches River and stands in front of her table. He doesn't sit down, but stands still like a statue staring at River. Uncomfortable, but refusing to appear unruffled, River looks across the bar and sees Reuben talking with a few customers. She wants to get his attention so he can remove Dana and his beautiful friend, but he is in his own world, enjoying the successful night of his club opening. Then, River sees her personal friend who has seen it fit to shadow her within the past few months. She waves at River. Dana turns toward the pretty girl and waves at her.

"You know her?" River asks Dana.

"Yeah," Dana says as if River should know that he knows the girl.

"Who is she?" River asked. "She has been bothering me for months,"

"What do you mean, who is she?" Dana asks. "You know who she is," he begins to laugh at her.

"No, I don't," River says.

"Are you serious?" Dana asks.

Dana starts to laugh at her. River stands up, pushes Dana out of the way and walks to the girl. She looks familiar, very recognizable. She must be someone that River has known, but she cannot put her finger on it. River hears her name being called.

"River-," they called out, "River."

She feels her body jump and suddenly her surroundings change. She looks around and sees that she is back in her hotel suite, lying on the couch and Dave is standing over her. River tries to compose herself.

"I didn't mean to startle you," he says with a grin.

"I saw her," River says sitting up.

"What?"

"I saw her," River said again. "The girl who has been stalking me,"

River gets up from the couch and begins to pace the floor.

"You may think I am nuts, but I saw her." River continues to say.

"When?"

"While I was dreaming,"

"Did she say anything to you," Dave asks.

"No, but when I walked up towards her, I got a good look."

"What did she look like?" Dave asks.

"Okay, we got the pretty black girl, and with short hair part, but she had beautiful, beautiful brown eyes."

"You got yourself a real villain there," Dave jokes.

"I know that I know her, it's only a matter of finding out what her name is,"

"Who else was in the dream?"

"Reuben, I was at Reuben's club." River answered. "But he wasn't paying me any attention,"

"Do you think he might know who she is?"

"I doubt it," River says.

"Was there someone else in the dream that may have known who she was?"

River thinks and then remembers that Dana knew who she was and he was shocked to find out that River did not. She stops pacing and looks at Dave. She doesn't want to tell him anything about Dana Wilson, as far as she is concerned he was just the architect.

"No," she answers becoming suddenly distant.

Dave reads the sudden detachment. He walks to her wanting to pull out of her whatever it is she is keeping from him. River sees that he's reading her. She looks at the clock.

"I'm going to get dressed, do me a favor and make sure that our car is ready."

"River-,"

She doesn't respond. She walks to her room. She freshens up and dresses in her usual attire, a black business suit, her hair pinned in a bun and her wire rimmed glasses are on. She is back into her comfort zone.

DAVE AND THE BODYGUARD lead River out of the hotel and off to another two weeks of signing books, doing radio and television interviews and sightseeing. To Dave, much has happened within the past few weeks. He is almost afraid to think about the next two weeks. Regardless of what is to come, Dave is going to make sure that these two weeks for River are stress free.

Like the other book stores, River receives a warm welcome from the owner, telling her that she had access to everything coffee, the telephone, the fax machine. Customers are lined up to have their book signed by Dr. River Daniels.

AFTER THE DAY, RIVER decides to stay in and order room service and try to get some writing done. She's been having writer's block since she began this book tour. Dave is relived that she decided to stay in. She should definitely get some rest and maybe figure out what connection this mystery woman has to River's subconscious. Is she a person that River once knew and is subconsciously thinking about? Or is she a just a figment of River's imagination, if so, what would cause the hallucinations? The description: a pretty black girl, with short hair, and beautiful brown eyes, to Dave that is not much of a description. Does she have any facial markings, like a beauty mark?

While River chats on her cell phone with Mr. Bush, Dave orders room service. He doesn't asking River what she wants, she is easy to please. He ordered baked chicken breast, with flavored rice and a bottle of white wine.

"Dave," River calls for him after her conversation with Mr. Bush. "Can you believe that I have an interview on a late night talk show?"

"Oh yeah?"

"Yes," she said smiling. "it was last minute. It's tomorrow, but somehow Mr. Bush managed to get me an interview. He said that the host is a fan and would love to interview me,"

"Sounds cool, Riv,"

"Sounds crazy," River said sitting next to Dave. "What does it look like, me, a doctor of education going on one of those silly talk shows discussing my books."

"You were on the talk show in New York," Dave said.

"That's different," River said. "That show is more educational, a self-esteem show to encourage the world to stay in school, never give up your dreams."

"Mr. Bush, got us tickets to a play, *Destiny's Room*," River said.

"Is that a chick play? Because I'd rather go see the Lakers' game,"

"Didn't you watch them lose while we were in New York?" River jokes.

"You're funny," Dave comments with a smile.

River grins and then rests her head on Dave's shoulder. He lifts up his arm so she can rest her head on his chest. For a moment he holds her.

"You tired?" he asks.

"No, not really," she says. "You know this past month with me hasn't been easy. I just want to thank you for being here,"

"You're welcome," he said. "We had a few minor setbacks, but nothing that good friends couldn't handle."

"Since Miami, and other than this morning, you haven't mentioned our little friend." River said.

Dave doesn't respond. River sits up and looks at him with her piercing brown eyes,

"You don't think she's real, do you?" River asks.

Dave doesn't know what to say concerning their little friend.

"Tell me the truth," River demands.

He nods.

"I believe that you do see her, but she is someone that only you see."

"So you think I am seeing things," River asks.

Dave nods his head.

"Then who am I seeing?" she asks.

"I don't know," Dave told her, "That is something that you need to figure out. Try to remember when she first appeared and what was going on in your life. You have to tie all the pieces together and then you will get your answer. But what I do know is that you're over worked. You're on a book tour; you went back to Pittsburgh to see your uncle's night club opening, which by the way his club was a major investment, then out to California for two weeks. Also you teach just about every English subject, write for a local magazine, you look after your grandmother, and the icing on the cake, you're an author."

"So I am seeing her because I am over worked,"

Dave shrugs his shoulders indicating that her suggestion may be the answer.

"Someone in your dream knew who she was?"

River looks away. To Dave that means yes, but he knows that she is not going to answer.

"Let's change the subject," she suggests

"No," Dave says.

He takes his hand and gently glides her head so she can face him.

"You're fighting. Whatever it is your fighting is only keeping you from finding out who she is. There is more to this dream than what you're telling me."

She looks away again.

"River,"

"I was dreaming about Reuben's opening," she began.

"So your mind was still going off from last night," Dana analyzed. "Was the club crowded?"

"Yes," River answered. "People were dancing, dirty dancing, ya know."

"So you think your subconscious is still reliving what happened between us?" Dave asks nervously.

"Us," River questions.

"You and me dancing,"

"Oh," River said suddenly remembering dancing with Dave.

He is almost insulted when he sees that she has forgotten their almost romantic evening.

"Do you think that maybe that night had more of an effect than what you think?" Dave asks.

"No." River quickly answers shaking her head.

"River, tell me something. Were you thinking of me when we were together?"

"Dave, we weren't together, we just kissed." River said in a carefree manor.

"It was more than just a kiss. You were relaxed in my arms, dancing with me, feeling the groove, It seemed like you wanted to kiss me, that you enjoyed kissing me-,"

"Dave, I don't want to talk about us in Miami," River snaps. "It was nothing,"

"Okay," Dave said, not taking the rejection personally. "but just remember, the longer you hide behind whatever it is that you're hiding from, the worst things will become. You're not that far from a mental ward."

"Excuse me?" River asks offended.

"You heard me," Dave said. "River, you need rest and a real social life."

River sighs. She never thought of herself as being a person with having hallucinations, those people are crazy.

"Dave, I'm fine, other than this girl. Did you ever think that you don't see her because she is *that* good of not making herself seen?"

"Okay, River," Dave said in a surrendering type of way.

There is a knock at the door. It is room service. They eat dinner and talk about other matters throughout the night.

CHAPTER SIXTEEN

KATRINA TOLD DANA TO meet her and her parents, Jack and Myra Robinson, at the Olive Garden around six. He is running late. Dana is never late and now meeting her parents, he's late. Katrina fidgets nervously while she looks over her menu.

"Relax, Trina," Myra said to her daughter with a smile.

Katrina grins then sipped her wine.

"Dana is usually never late," Katrina explains.

"I'm sure that there is a good explanation," Jack says forgivingly with a grin. "Everything is fine."

Although a successful business man, Jack Robinson is a patient man. He stands tall, over six feet. Although his size is intimidating, once getting to know him everyone realizes that he is a very friendly man. Myra is just as patient. She is a beautiful woman, with the same light brown eyes that Katrina inherited. As they continue to wait for Dana, Katrina and Jack debate over politics. Myra remains neutral on their conversation. They sip wine, laugh and enjoy the conversation. Within ten minutes Dana walks in, escorted to their table by the hostess.

"He's here," Katrina stands up to greet Dana.

Quickly they exchange a small affectionate kiss. Jack and Myra stand.

"I'm so sorry I'm late, I got held up at the office," He extends his hand to Jack and Myra, "I'm Dana Wilson."

"Very nice to meet you," Jack replied shaking Dana's hand. "I'm Jack Robinson and this is my wife Myra,"

"Nice to meet you," Myra smiles.

As soon as everyone sits down, the waiter who has been already introduced as Donnie approaches the table. The Robinsons had asked him to wait until Dana arrived.

"What can I get you to drink?" the waiter asks Dana.

"Just a coke," Dana replied. "Did everyone order?"

"Not yet," Jack said. "will you need some time?" asked Donnie.

"Awe no," Dana replied, then looked at the waiter. "Chicken scampi,"

The waiter looks at Jack.

"I will have the Seafood Alfredo," he said.

"Shrimp primavera," Katrina adds.

"And for me the Cheese Ravioli," Myra requests.

"Another glass of Straccali?" the waiter asks, looking at Jack.

Jack nods with a grin.

"Another glass of white zinfandel?" Donnie offers both Katrina and Myra.

"Yes," Myra answers for both Katrina and she.

The waiter grins, collected the menus and then leaves.

"So Dana, tells us a little about yourself," Jack suggests.

"Well, I am originally from Pittsburgh. A military man, the navy, and as of now, I own my own architect firm.

"Daddy, he is building my firm," Katrina announces proudly. "He also just finished building one of the newest clubs in Pittsburgh. Remember I showed you,"

"Yes, very impressive work," Jack replies.

"Thank you," Dana replies.

"Katrina is so excited about her firm," Myra says to Dana. "Ever since she was a little girl, she wanted to be a lawyer; always debating fact and truth."

"Is that so?" Dana asks with a chuckle.

"Yes, in school, she didn't run for president, but she aided the president. Once the school president was almost forced to resign because she was failing algebra, Katrina went before the school principal and defended him saying the teacher was not teaching well, and had three other students as witnesses. The school was forced to consider the teacher teaching techniques."

"Are you serious?" Dana asks laughing.

"Oh, yes." Myra says laughing.

Dana laughs, amused at Katrina's early law career.

"Dana, that is not true," Katrina says with a laugh.

"Trina," Myra coaxed.

"Mom, Deidra was my friend and Mr. Baker was tough and confusing." Katrina defends with a coy smile.

"Right," Jack chuckles with a wink. "Mr. Baker was intimidated by a thirteen year old girl,"

Laughter goes forth throughout the table.

Donnie returns with their drinks, salad and bread sticks.

"Katrina tells me that you're a business man yourself," Dana says to Jack.

"I am retired, but I do end up running a few errands,"

"Don't be fooled," Myra said. "My husband works from sun up till sun down,"

Jack chuckles.

"It is hard to leave the board room, but trust me, I am retired."

Dana nods his head hearing what Jack was saying.

"I love what I do. I wouldn't know how to retire."

"You'll know when it is time," Jack replies.

DANA IS HAVING A good time laughing and talking with Katrina's parents. There is no pressure. They are as easy to talk to as Katrina. As he smiles and laughs, he feels bad because it is very evident that his parents are fond of him and he is growing less fond of Katrina. It is only a matter of time when he breaks up with her. Dana plans on doing it after her firm is finished.

Katrina sees that her mother has been won over by Dana's charm and she sees how impressed her father is with him. As they eat dessert, Katrina begins to imagine the restaurant as a large banquet hall full of family and friends who have come to celebrate the union of Dana and Katrina Wilson. Katrina would be wearing an elegant white gown looking far more elegant than River Daniels.

"Katrina," Jack said, startling Katrina's thoughts.

"Uh, yes sir-," Katrina said smiling.

"I said that is time to leave, honey," Jack said.

"Oh, yes, okay," Katrina summons the waiter, "Check please,"

"I am going to the ladies room," Myra replies.

"I'll come with you, Mom,"

Together both women walk into the rest room. Katrina is relieved to see the stalls empty.

"So, Mom, what do you think?

"He is a very nice man," Myra said.

Katrina smiled brightly,

"I think he's the one,"

Although Myra is smiling, Katrina sees doubt in her mother's eyes. Myra is not sharing the same joy that Katrina is feeling.

"Mom,"

"We'll talk later-,"

"No, Mom,"

Myra doesn't want to discuss her daughter's love life in a public restroom, but she sees the urgency that her daughter needed to know what she is thinking.

"You're in love, aren't you?" Myra asks.

Katrina nods her head with a small smile. Myra gently pushes her daughter's hair off her shoulder.

"He's not," Myra says.

Katrina eyes questions her mother's statement.

"Baby, I can see that he's very fond of you, but baby, he does not love you."

"Mom, how can you tell that after one meeting?"

"Sweetie, first of all he came late. He should have called. In the days of cell phones and texting, he would have called. The way he looks at you, he looks at you as a dear friend, not as his woman."

"We've been dating a few months. He's been real busy with the building of that club and the firm."

"And you are building up your firm and working with your clients. Yes you two are both busy. Katrina honey, you're a defense attorney, you are trained to defend the guilty until proven innocent. You are not going to find innocence with him. His crime is not loving you the way you love him."

Katrina sighs. She knows that her mother is right. Katrina is hoping that one day Dana would wake up and see her for the first time and fall in love with her. She began to remember how Dana looked at River.

"Focus on your priorities, and if it is meant to be, then it will happen. Don't push or fight and play hard to get a little, and see what happens."

Katrina smiles and hugs her mother.

THE WOMEN RETURN FROM the restroom and see Dana and Jack waiting.

"I'm going to take my parents back to their hotel," Katrina says to Dana. "I'll call you later,"

"Okay," Dana told her, "Mr. and Mrs. Robinson, it was very nice meeting you,"

"Same here, son," Jack said, shaking Dana's hand.

SHE IS DEEP IN her book, reading every page as if she is living with the characters. She is involved with their lives. As she walks with them down the abandoned back road she hears the owl sings its song during the night. As she sits in her backyard, she is unaware of her surroundings. The only surroundings she is aware of are those of the imaginary lives that she is reading about. She doesn't hear River sneaking up behind her. It takes just one small tap on the shoulder for her to jump out of her skin and back into reality. She turns around and sees her dear friend.

"You silly thing!" she exclaims trying to catch her breath and gather her composure.

She hugs River.

"When did you get back into town?"

"Yesterday," River said. "I missed you, Miss Jenny,"

Jennifer and River hug each other again tightly as if they haven't seen each other in years. Although River enjoyed Dave's company, she missed Jenny.

"How was your trip?" Jennifer asks.

"Very, very, nice," River says. "I have presents."

"River you didn't have to get me anything," Jennifer replies.

River only shrugged her shoulders,

"Let's open a bottle of white zinfandel, put some chicken breasts on the grill, and make a day of it." Jennifer suggests.

River nods smiling.

While Jennifer preps the barbeque grill, River gets the gifts that she brought for Jennifer out from her car. As the grill heats up, Jennifer puts jazz music on, then watches as River brings in her gifts.

"I heard that you came back in town for Reuben's opening," Jennifer said. "Didn't bother to stop in to say hello to your old friend Jenny,"

"I was only here for an hour, a promised visit to Reuben. Then I was on the plane back to California,"

"I am just teasing you," Jennifer replies. "Talk to me, did you see exotic sights, meet any handsome men?"

As Jennifer pours two glasses of wine, River thinks for a moment. The exotic sights; there was the exotic beauty in the tight dress. The handsome men; there was the Italian man with the eyes the colors of indigo, who told her that he loved her in Miami. And then there was the pretty girl that seemed to be everywhere for the past six months.

"None, nothing crazy, just work, work, work," River says.

She watches as Jennifer places chicken breasts on the grill.

"What are you reading?" River asks.

"Just an old mystery thriller," Jennifer answers. "Maybe we can read it together. I have an extra copy. I can wait for you to catch up."

River nods as she sips the wine.

"Now," Jennifer begins. "I never got a chance to tell you that my son had a very nice time with you that night."

"Oh, don't start, Jenny, please," River groans, yet smiling.

Jennifer pretends not to hear River.

"Oh, I can see it now, Mr. and Mrs. Robert Murdock and their four beautiful children. RJ, Tia, the adventurous one; Isaiah, and my pride Bunny, she would be Grandma's little angel."

River looks at Jennifer, then shakes her head.

"You are crazy!" River states.

Jenny nods her head in agreement.

"River, I promise you that I would not be one of those nagging mother-in-laws."

"You're acting like one now!"

Jennifer laughs.

Jennifer smiles and proceeds to barbeque and listen to River fill her in on the past six weeks. They talk about literature, drinking, and have a good time.

CHAPTER SEVENTEEN

IT'S ANOTHER GRAND OPENING for Wilson's Architect Firm. Katrina's law firm is complete. Katrina's staff includes four litigators and three paralegals. Today is the day. It is all about her, not Reuben, not River, -her. She has her own firm. Like Reuben's Room, the firm is crowded with family members, clients and investors toasting the event. Dana and a few members of his dream team are also present. Katrina remembers not seeing anyone from his architect firm at Reuben's Room. Dana is not standing beside her, or smiling with her, or being the supportive boyfriend. Katrina knows that Dana's mind would not be on the concept of this big opening, but she hopes that he may stand beside her while pictures are being taken. Dana and his dream team go from room to room, making sure that everything is intact.

Beginning with the reception area, there are many offices which include Katrina's office and four offices for her other litigators. There is an office for her paralegals, a library full of research materials from previous cases and studies. There is a conference room, which is a large room where their minds can meet for agreements.

As many friends and family congratulate Katrina, she can't get her mother's words out of her mind. For two weeks she just focuses on her clients and her new firm. Katrina didn't go to Dana's house to cook and they barely had sex. She was hoping that Dana would encourage her to come to his house, but he didn't. Is he the unattainable goal? The one thing that she cannot have or has he been under stress with the building of the club and her firm; two major projects back to back. He is just one man; not the only man. Katrina does not need him. She is the successful defense attorney that graduated Summa Cum Laude, she was up for partner only after two years of working for a major New York Firm, and she has just started her own law firm. Katrina is beautiful and intelligent. However, the more she talks herself out of not needing or wanting Dana, the more she needs and wants Dana. Katrina's mind is plagued with thoughts.

Does he even know what my favorite color is? What is my favorite movie? My favorite book, it was one of River's but should I even like River anymore? They way he looked at her that night. River seemed so..., accomplished, so untouchable. Did she notice my man looking at her that way, that night? That club, that club is beautiful, and that was her money. I have money, but not enough to do a club like that.

EVERYONE HAS LEFT, family, friends, co-workers, and boyfriends, Katrina stays in her office going over paper work. Dana and she did not make plans and she is not ready to go home. She focuses her energy on her work. Michael Richards one of the litigators enters her office. Michael is a handsome African-American man that stands at an even six feet; with his round wired-rimmed glasses he resembles Langston Hughes. Michael is a high maintenance man, the type of man that gets manicures and pedicures, but he is all man. He is what men like Dana would call pretty boys and Michael is quite fond of Katrina.

"Penny for your thoughts," Michael asks, disturbing Katrina from her thoughts.

She looks up from her work and smiles at her friend.

"Do you think that this firm will make it?" she asks.

Katrina knows that her firm will succeed. However, she does not want to admit that she may have lost at something.

"You know that this firm will survive," Michael answers. "What's the real problem, it's the grand opening and your smile is not genuine."

"I have a lot on my mind," Katrina replies.

"About the architect?" he asks with a smug smile. "Let me tell you something, Kat, you're wasting your time."

"What?" she asked.

"He's not the one," He told her, "He doesn't even look at you,"

"He's busy looking over the place, making sure-,"

"Making sure of what?" Michael interrupted. "That the ceiling doesn't fall? That wouldn't make him a good architect if he has to do that. Good architects don't have a grand opening and then double check the place. They do all that before they tell you that the place is finished. He's avoiding you."

Katrina's mind went back to Dana's actions at Reuben's club. Checking out the structure of the place was his excuse. Was that his excuse so he could stare at River? She now hates River.

"He's not the one, babe." Michael tells her.

"You sound like my mother," she says.

"Your mother," Michael asks with a chuckle.

"Yeah, Dana and I have been dating for a few months," Katrina confessed. "I can't help but to feel deeply for him. I just have the feeling that he is using me to buy him time in case someone better comes along,"

"Have you spoken with him about this?"

"Sort of," Katrina said as she gets up from her seat.

She walks around the desk and sits on the edge. Michael sits beside her.

"He says that he is crazy about me, but I got this feeling that his mind is elsewhere."

"Like what?"

"For one he is a work-a-holic," Katrina told him. "but so am I,"

"Do you think there is someone else?"

Katrina's mind flashes back to the night at Reuben's Room and River Daniels. She remembers how Dana looked at River. She remembers how he told her that she was his ex-girlfriend. However the love making they shared that night proved that River and he are over.

"I don't think there is someone else, but-,"

"But,"

"You know there isn't anyone else, but there is-,"

"No, either there is or there isn't," Michael said.

Katrina shrugged her shoulders. "My mom says that she can see that he is not in love with me. That he cares, but not love."

"Listen to your mother," Michael told her.

"I know, but don't you think that with him working on both that club and this firm, that he's just too busy to-,"

Katrina stopped talking when she saw that Michael was shaking his head.

"He can be as busy all he wants, if he loves you, work will not come in between. His work is done, yours is just beginning. You just opened up a firm now you're going to be too busy. So who makes the first move to establish the relationship? If it is not established by now, then it will never be. You know that you cannot change a man."

"So what do I do?"

"Find a new man," Michael said bluntly.

"Just break up with him," Katrina asked. "Just like that,"

"Either that or get hurt,"

She lets out a sigh. Michael leans in, then kisses Katrina on the cheek. She grins, then looks at him. Katrina sees something in his eyes.

"I'm stepping way over the line, but I like you," Michael said to her softly. Katrina looks shocked. "I won't make this weird even if you're not interested, but consider me."

And on the note, Michael slowly walks out of her office, leaving Katrina with a curious mind, wondering what to do next.

RIVER SITS IN KENNEDY'S OFFICE going over the adventures in New York, Miami, and California, and as he sips coffee she asks for her next assignment.

"Rest," Mr. Bush says her.

"Mr. Bush, I don't want to rest," River says smiling. "I have too much energy,"

Kennedy hands River information on the next issue for the *Bush Factor*. She smiles with delight at the fact of having a new agenda.

The sound of loud thunder claps in the sky startling River and Kennedy.

"The hurricane is coming this way," he says to her. "The weather man said that we will be getting hit from Hurricane Jason from the south. You need to be getting home,"

She nods her head looking over the assignment for the next article.

"I mean it River, get home." Kennedy says sternly.

"You should have this by the end of the week." She said still looking at the assignment.

Kennedy sighs. He knows that River is not listening to his instructions.

"River, look at me," Kennedy commands.

River looks up confused by Kennedy sudden demanding tone.

"Okay, now listen to me," Kennedy begins. "You just had a busy six weeks, do not push yourself."

"Yeah, okay," she says.

Although River hears Kennedy's words, she doesn't take them in.

"Okay, see ya later, Mr. Bush." River says.

Immediately she walks out of Bush Publications. The rain is falling hard, but River ignores it and drives to her grandmother's.

SHIRLEY IS HAPPY TO see her granddaughter. River unloads boxes of presents which include clothes, shoes, coats and jewelry.

"You spoil me," Shirley says smiling. "Baby, I don't need all this stuff."

"It's not about needing," River says placing a one thousand dollar cashmere long white coat on her grandmother. "It is about having, and I want you to have all this stuff. Besides, who are you to tell Grandpa's angel no?"

"Now, River, don't bring your grandfather in this!" Shirley said smiling.

Shirley looks at the ceiling.

"I can't tell her no,"

"Grandma, stop talking to the ceiling," River admonishes.

"Reuben has been at his club working his tail off," Shirley replies.

Shirley walks towards the window and sees the rain falling.

"I'll stop by to see him later." River says. "Listen, I really have to run, I got a lot of work to do."

"River, I want you to get out of this rain," Shirley warns.

"I will see you on Sunday, Grandma,"

Shirley walks River to the door. River dashes into the rain and quickly gets into her car and drives home. Within the past two hours smoky gray clouds have hovered in the sky. The rain falls hard, pouring out from the heavens and lightning dances rapidly while the thunder loudly claps. The atmosphere looks terrifying but River drives along the highway as if the rain is non-existing. This is Pittsburgh, and Pittsburgh is known for its unpredictable weather for the blizzards in the middle of March and the sunny weather in December. Considering that it is hurricane season, the rain is only the result of the tropical storm down south. She is not a stranger to bad weather.

River picks up her cell phone and calls the University to arrange her schedule for the fall semester. As she made small talk with a few members of her staff her car begins to swerve and begins to hydroplane; there is water in her breaks. She begins to pump her breaks but no luck and soon there is a loud pop and River's car slides off the road and into a tree. River lays helplessly with her face in the air bag.

SHE HEARS THE KNOCKING on the window. As she comes to, she begins to make sense of what just happened. River lifts her head slowly and squints her eyes to see who is knocking on the window.

"What the...," she asked herself.

Dana is standing outside with an umbrella in his hand knocking on the window. River cannot believe that he is standing outside her car knocking on her window. Is she dreaming? Is he really outside knocking on her window? Eventually she lets the window down.

Dana is surprise to see River.

"Oh, my.., River are you all right?" he asks.

"Yes," she said.

"River you're bleeding!"

River touches her head and feels blood.

"I'm okay,"

"I saw the car go off the road. I had no idea that it was you. We need to get you to a hospital-,"

"No, I'm fine," she says quickly.

"Your tire is flat, and the front end of your car is smashed, I think this car is totaled."

Immediately she gets out of the car. She stumbles a little but quickly regains her composure. Soaked with rain, she tries to make a call with her cell phone but sees that her battery is dead. Quickly she looks in her car for her charger, but doesn't see it. Quickly she moves to trunk to look for her cell phone charger. River notices that Dana keeps following her.

"What do you want?" she snaps.

"I'm just trying to see if you're all right," Dana replies.

"I'm okay, just trying to find my charger,"

"Is there some place I can take you?"

"You can go," she said. "Once I find my charger, I will be okay,"

"River let me take you home," he offers.

Thunder clapped loudly startling River.

"I live an hour away," she tells him. "Seriously, you can leave."

"River, all the main roads are closed," Dana tells her. "Look, I live a half a mile from here, I can take you to my-,"

"No thank you," River says quickly.

Dana is growing irritated with River. She is not letting him help her. She is being so spiteful.

"River, what are you going to do?" Dana asked. "Stay out here in the rain. Your car is ruined, your cell phone is dead, you're stuck out here."

River shoots Dana a scornful look.

"You can come over my house, use my phone and get whatever help you need."

River doesn't want to be forced into a situation of relying on Dana. However she is soaked from the rain. She looks at her car and sees that it is totally totaled. River is too far away from her grandmother or Reuben's to crash there. The university is also too far away and she doesn't know if Jennifer is home. Going to Bush Publications is on the main road which, per Dana; is closed.

Stupid Pittsburgh weather, she says to herself.

When the rain lets up, she plans of moving to a place with no rain, where the main roads are always open, and no Dana Wilson. The idea of going to his house is frightening. What if she gets there and she is greeted by that exotic beauty that does not shut up.

"River come on, let me help," Dana requests.

She sighs.

River grabs the things from her car, her business case and her lap top. Dana leads her to his car and helps her get settled in. He wonders if this is fate knocking on his door again. Just the odds of running into her after all these years, and again, what are the odds of him running into her on the road in the storm. River feels like she sold her soul to the devil. She is allowing the enemy to help her. The mile ride seems like an hour. They sit quietly; no one trying to speak.

AS THEY ENTER THE house, River stands still looking around the perfectly neat and organized house.

"There is a phone over there by the sofa, feel free to call whomever you need."

She nods her head and takes in a deep breath. Dana goes in his bedroom to change his clothes. He is in shock that River Daniels, the writer is in his house, and he is very shocked that River Daniels the ex-girlfriend is in his home. Katrina will not be here, she claims that she has tons of work to do with her client and her colleague Michael Richards is sitting in as second chair in a particular case. This suits Dana just fine, because maybe with River here there might be a chance that he and she can talk and be civilized. After he changes into a pair of jeans and a t-shirt, he grabs a pair of sweats pants and sweat shirt for River. He returns to the living room and sees that she is still standing in the same spot that he left her.

"Did you make your phone calls?" Dana asks.

"I-, can't move," she stammers from being cold.

"Oh, okay," he said setting the clothes down. "I'll turn on the heat. Let me take your coat."

"No," she said taking in deep breath. "Just give me a minute."

"Um, I brought you some sweats so you can change your clothes."

"Oh, no thank you," she stammers.

"River, you'll get pneumonia if you stay in those wet clothes," Dana warns her sternly.

River looks at Dana with her ice cold eyes and she sighs. She is cold and wet. Reluctantly, very reluctantly, she gives in and takes the clothes. Dana told her to change in the bathroom. Slowly River walks to the bathroom and begins to change clothes. The thought of wearing his clothes and having his scent absorbing its way into her skin is frightening her. As she changes, she looks around the neat bathroom, everything is blue and white. River begins to remember how much Dana loves the color blue. She looks around and sees that there is nothing that indicates that Katrina lives there. There isn't an extra wash cloth hanging on the towel rack, only one toothbrush inside the little cup. River lets her wet pantsuit hang on the hanger in the bathroom, shoves her trouser socks into her boots. River is now dressed in Dana's clothes. She is practically swimming in Dana's clothes.

When she comes out she is hit with the enticing smell of hazelnut cappuccino. River places her boots by the door.

"I never understood how you women wore those heels," Dana comments.

River grins politely then walks to the phone. She calls everyone who she thinks to call. Dave's phone goes straight to voicemail. She knew he is in the middle of teaching class. Jennifer is not home and Mr. Bush is in a meeting. River knows that Shirley had unplugged the phone, her superstitions of talking on the phone when it rains. Reuben is missing in action. Dana turns on the weather channel. The pretty weather girl said that storms are severe and it would be best to stay in safe place. The hurricane, known as Hurricane Jason is brewing along the east coast from South Carolina, and that Pittsburgh, Baltimore, and all of the other cities along the coast will get hit with terrible winds and rains. River tries to call everyone again.

"Here," Dana says as he hands her a cup of cappuccino.

"Thanks."

River sips the drink and the sweet taste of hazelnut tickles her cheeks and begins to warm her body. She loves hazelnut cappuccino. He had fixed it just how she likes it with a bit of sugar and hint of cinnamon.

"Just how I like it, thank you," River said. "How did you know?"

Dana grins at her. His smiles said that he remembers and he never forgot. River quickly looks away. He is still coy with his charm.

"Well, I might as well get to work," River says.

She grabs her lap top and sets it up on the table. She begins to email Dave and Mr. Bush telling them what happened and if they could come get her. She leaves Dana's phone number so they could call her. Then she begins to work on her research for *The Bush Factor.*

"Would you like a sandwich?" Dana asks.

"No thank you," she answers, not looking up from her work.

TWO HOURS PASS. RIVER types away on her lap top as Dana pretends to not pay attention. Her beauty is still captivating. She doesn't wear makeup and her hair is worn down, pushed back from her face. Dana cannot get over the long hair. With her hair down, she looks soft and innocent.

"You working on a lesson?" Dana asks.

"No," she responds.

"Another best seller?"

"No,"

"Would you like more cappuccino?"

River shoots Dana a look telling him to be quiet. He is distracting her. River remembers how Dana used to disturb her when she would try to write.

The telephone rings. Quickly Dana answers the phone, but it is no one who River is expecting, it's someone from his dream team. Dana makes quick small talk, then hangs up on the phone. River begins to feel edgy. She lets out a long sigh, then walks to the window. Dana sees felt her frustration. He is insulted. He has shown hospitality, invites her into his home and shares his clothes and coffee. She is ungrateful.

"You know, I'm not so bad," he comments.

"Excuse me?" she asked.

"I'm not so bad. Staying here is not killing you,"

"No, it's not killing me, but this is putting a big hindrance on my plans," she states.

"Well push comes to shove I can take you home." Dana said. "But the weather man said that power lines are down, trees all over the place."

The telephone rings again. Dana answers the phone. It is no one for River. It is Katrina, telling Dana that she will not be stopping by to give a home cooked meal and a warm night under the sheets. The rain has put a damper in their plans and she is stuck at the office with Michael. Dana is not stupid, he knows that Michael is moving on his woman. However, all this is fine with Dana, because the woman that he really wants in his home is already here.

As Dana hangs up the phone, he watches River walk back to the window.

He wants to talk to her, ask if she ever thinks about him; because only God knows how he thinks about her. He wants to hug her, hold her and caress her. Dana wants to put his fingers through her long hair. Dana wants to kiss her full lips.

Dana watches as River returns to her seat.

"How long have you been teaching?" he asked.

"A few years,"

"How do you manage teaching when you write so much?"

"I manage somehow, I guess," she says.

She reads over her article, hoping that Dana will get the hint and stop talking.

"Can I ask you another question?" Dana asks.

"Shoot,"

"Do you smile?"

"What?" the question caught River off guard.

She looks at Dana.

"I remember that you had this beautiful smile." Dana says to her.

River doesn't respond. She returns to her work.

"Or you just don't smile at ex-boyfriends," Dana says.

River looks at Dana with her cold eyes. He sees that he has hit, not just touched, but hit a sensitive issue. River can respond to the statement with something derogatory or she can cut him down to the little man that he really is but she knows that it will be pointless to stoop down to his level. Dana feels bad about making the statement.

"Sorry," he said. "That was not cool,"

River doesn't respond. She looks back at her work and pretends that he is not there or does not exist.

"Wow, I see how you teach everything. You don't talk,"

"I beg your pardon," she asks shooting her icy eyes at him.

"You're hard to talk to," Dana said. "The River I knew, was never hard to talk to,"

"I'm not the River you knew," she states to him.

"No, the River I knew used to smile, she loved to laugh, she loved life, and she was beautiful." Dana said. "This River, the one that is here now, is cold, angry, very disciplined, however one that hasn't changed."

"What," she asks frustrated.

"You're still beautiful," he said softly.

River looks away.

"Let's not dwell in the past," she says him.

"I'm not dwelling in the past. I am just stating the facts." He said. "If I didn't know you then, I wouldn't be able to tell you that you are the same person."

"Dana stop," River snap.

Dana continues,

"You're not...," he trailed off. "my River," he finishes in a soft tone hoping that she didn't hear him; she did.

River gets up and walks to the window. The sky is the color of smoky gray. It is a lovely but haunting image, but the image that is really haunting is the pretty girl standing in a distance.

How did she find me?, River asks herself.

She closes her eyes and looks away.

"Dana, can we close the curtains?" River asks.

"Sure," Dana said, walking to her.

He stands next to her looking into her dark brown eyes. They look like blocks of ice. "Are you okay?" he asks.

"Yes," she answers looking away.

River walks back to her table.

"I just don't need fans-,"

"Fans," Dana chuckles walking back to his seat.

"Yes, I have fans. I'm River Daniels."

"Oh right," Dana says with a chuckle.

"Don't be so amused, Mr. Wilson," River said with a sexy, yet coy smirk on her face. "Even your girlfriend is a fan,"

Dana laughs at her remark. River sits down.

"Okay, okay, Ms. River," Dana surrenders.

"How did you meet her?" River asks.

"She's a client. I had built her law firm." he answered. "She's a defense attorney."

River nods her head.

"I'm hungry," Dana said. "Would you like something to eat?"

River shakes her head.

"Oh, come on, you have to be starving. I got sea food, shrimp, and crab legs. I remembered your sea food fetish."

"Oh my," River replied stuns. "You remembered so much about me?"

"That's because you're unforgettable."

River grins bashfully.

"What's that? Is that a smile?" Dana teases.

"I am finishing my work," She says. "Let me know when the food is ready."

Dana walks into the kitchen and begins to fix dinner. He hit a soft spot with River.

AFTER DINNER, RIVER HELPS Dana with the dishes she returns to her lap top with a fresh cup of cappuccino. The telephone rings, Dana answers it.

"Yes, she's here." Dana says and then hands River the phone.

"Hello," River said smiling. "Hi, Jennifer, yes, I'm okay, but my car is totaled."

River is so excited to hear from someone on the outside. She hands Dana the phone and he gives Jennifer directions to his house. Jennifer says that she would be there to pick River up in thirty-minutes. River looks out of the window, it stopped raining. Dana turns on the weather channel, and it informs that the main roads are clear.

Quickly River runs to Dana's bathroom to change back into her clothes. After being there for five hours, her clothes are nearly dry. She neatly folds his clothes and then leaves them where she had sat. Dana is sorry to see her go, but he knows that this is best. At least he got her to smile.

RIVER HEARS THE HORN HONK. She peeks out of the window and sees Jennifer's car. River gathers up her things and heads out the door. She turns to Dana. They look each other in the eyes. At this moment, he realizes that he is in love with her, more than he should be. Her eyes spoke of strength and power. He wishes that they were on better terms because he wants to kiss her.

"Thanks a lot," she says with a grin.

"Any time," he says smiling.

River walks out of the house and gets in Jennifer's car, and she drives away.

"Are you all right?" Jennifer asks.

"Yes,"

"Who what that?" Jennifer asks.

"An old friend,"

CHAPTER EIGHTEEN

A MONTH HAS PASSED since the horrific storm. The fall semester has not begun yet and there is nothing to submit to Mr. Bush; not a book or article. She needs a book. But River has writer's block. Instead of hiding out in her home or sitting in her grandmother's back yard, River goes to Christie's to work on some writing. She is tucked away in a booth in the furthest corner of the restaurant tapping away rapidly on her lap top.

After she sets up her lap top, River walks to the bar to order her food. On her way to the bar, she sees Dana. Hoping that he doesn't see her, she tries to move fast, but he sees her.

"Hey, how are you?" he says smiling.

"I'm well," she said putting on a fake smile yet pleasant smile.

She looks in another direction hoping that he wouldn't try to make conversation.

"Did you get your car taken care of?"

"Ended up getting a new one, but thanks for asking," she answers politely.

Suddenly she feels a sharp pain in her chest.

"Good," Dana said. "I'm glad that everything worked out,"

She grins politely, and rubs the pain that is in her chest. River takes in a deep breath, looks over at the bar tender.

"A dozen of hot wings, ranch dressing, fries, and a Long Island Ice Tea." River orders. "Can you bring my food over to the booth, please?"

"Sure thing," The bar tender says.

River attempts to walk away.

"See ya later?" Dana says.

He sticks out his hand for her to shake.

"Um, yeah," River says as the sharp pains increase.

Ignoring the pain in her chest, River shakes Dana's hand, but the pains in her chest are tremendous. She tries to take a deep breath but she can't, she is struggling for air.

"Are you okay?" Dana questions, seeing the struggle.

River reaches out for him, Dana grabs on to her as she loses her balance. Her legs give way and Dana holds her as they both fall to the floor.

"I'm having chest pains," she said, almost inaudible.

"Okay, okay," Dana said soothingly. "Jim!"

Chaos begins to erupt among those who are close by. Jim quickly runs out from the back and sees Dana and River on the floor.

"I think she's having a heart attack," Dana exclaims.

"I'll call an ambulance." Jim volunteers then quickly left.

Dana looks at River as he is holding her in his arms.

"River," he said. "River, you're going to be okay,"

"Dave," she whispers. "Call Dave,"

THE AMBULANCE COMES AND takes control of the situation. Nervously Dana watches as EMS workers prep River for the ride. Dana calls Reuben on his cell phone and leaves a message on the voice mail. It's time to go to hospital, Dana rides alongside River. River's chest is aching, she feels people probing and poking at her. Several times she attempts to get up but the paramedics stop her.

"River, relax, honey," she hears someone say.

"Dave," she whispers again.

"You're going to be okay, River." Another says.

FINALLY SHE IS ABLE to breathe. River takes a deep breath and finds herself walking in a garden. The garden has a rich and healthy green lawn and off in a distance there are tall gorgeous trees. River hears the sound of water running. She looks in the direction of the sound and sees a waterfall. The water is clear and sparkles like crystal and diamonds. River looks up and sees the transparent sky. The clouds look like white pillows. River smiles as she looks down at herself and sees that she is wearing a white pant suit.

"Heaven," she said. "I've died and gone to heaven,"

River walks further along through the garden.

"Hello," she called out. "Is there anyone here?"

"Hello," she said with a small voice.

Slowly coming from behind an apple tree is a petite and beautiful woman. Her skin the color of ivory, she has long black hair. She is also wearing a white gown.

"I'm River Daniels," she introduces.

"I know,"

"What's your name?" River asks.

The woman looks away bashfully.

River begins to walk through the garden. The woman trails her slowly. This is a quiet place; no one to bother her. River can write or read and no one will pester her. There are no uncles to hunt her down for money. There are no ex-boyfriends to bump into. River looks around for the pretty girl and she is not here.

"You're looking for her, aren't you?" the woman asks.

River looks at the woman.

"The girl that has been following you,"

River doesn't reply. Her eyes look away and she focuses on the bushes that are full of berries.

"Where am I?" River finally spoke. "Am I in heaven?"

"No,"

"I know that this isn't hell," River says with a chuckle.

The woman smiles.

"Where am I?" River questions.

River looks at the woman, her icy eyes piercing through her.

"Your eyes, there's no light," the woman said. "Your past has made them dark. She wants to live."

NERVOUSLY DANA PACES THE hospital floor. He watches the nurses and doctors come and go -ignoring his presence. No one has told him anything concerning River. He has been waiting for over two hours for some information. All this is devastating. River is too young to have a heart attack. She is only thirty-seven years old. Why is a thirty-seven year old having a heart attack? Stress causes heart attacks. She does fifty million things, teaches every subject, writes every book, and then goes on book tours. She makes large investments in night clubs and runs into former lovers. Dana begins to wonder why he didn't say something to her when she was at his house. Why didn't he try to resolve any issues that were left unsettled? Dana wishes that he never built Reuben's club. He only built that club to prove that he was over River. He knew that he was not over her. She wills always be a permanent figure in his heart. He thought that he escape the sweet memories of her, but instead every time he smells lilies, or goes to Reuben's Room or goes to Christie's he is reminded of his one true love. He should have told her that he loves her, that he will always love her.

 "Dana," Reuben calls out.

 Dana turns around and sees Reuben and Shirley rushing in.

 "How is she?" Shirley asked.

 "No one said anything," Dana answers.

 "What happened?" Reuben asks.

 "I saw at her at Christie's, and we said hi. I attempted to shake her hand and the next thing I know she was collapsing."

 "Reuben," Shirley said crying, holding on to Reuben, "Not our angel."

 "Momma," Reuben says holding his mother. "Come sit down,"

 Reuben leads his mother to an empty seat. At seventy-six, Shirley is in considerable good health, there are no physical ailments or pain, but Reuben knows that if he has to bury his niece he will have to bury his mother.

 "Did they say anything about this being a heart attack?" Reuben asks Dana.

 "I've been told nothing," Dana replies. "The last thing that River said was to call Dave."

 "Her friend, Reuben," Shirley said.

 Reuben nods his head remembering who Dave was.

 "Who's Dave," Dana asks hoping that Dave is not too important to her.

 "Her co-worker," Reuben answers.

As Dana let out a secret sigh of relief, the doctors comes forward to report on River's condition.

"Mr. Wilson," the doctor begins.

"Yes," Dana replies as Reuben and Shirley walk to the doctor. "Doctor, this is Reuben and Shirley Massie; River's uncle and grandmother."

"Nice to meet you both," the doctor says, shaking their hands.

"River, is she-," Shirley said.

"River is going to be fine," the doctor says.

Sighs of relief fill the air. Shirley hugs Reuben and cries.

"What happened?"

"River suffered from Takotsubo cardiomyopathy," the doctor replied, he saw the bewildered looks on their faces. "Also known as transient apical ballooning syndrome, stress-induced cardiomyopathy,"

River's family hears the word stress, and immediately realizes what has caused her break down. The doctor continues to explain her condition.

"This is a type of non-ischemic cardiomyopathy in which there is a sudden temporary weakening of the myocardium, the muscle of the heart. Also, her blood pressure is high, too high for a woman her age. She is anemic, which is a contradiction to the high blood pressure, but and she has a slight case of potassium deficiency. However, with how her blood pressure is, it is amazing that this was only an anxiety attack. Is she under a lot of stress?"

"Yes," Dana, Reuben and Shirley said in unison.

"Technically, River had something like an anxiety attack?" Reuben asks.

The doctor nods his head.

"River is going to need a lot of rest; the next time she might not be so lucky."

Tears steam down Shirley's cheeks.

"Can we see her, Doctor," she asks.

"Yes, but now she is sleeping." The doctor informs. "Maybe, you guys should go in one at a time."

"Okay, Momma, you first,"

"Okay,"

"Follow me, Mrs. Massie," The doctor replies.

Reuben watches as the doctor lead his mother down the hall. He turns toward Dana who looks tired and worn out.

"Thanks for getting her here," Reuben says.

Dana grins, then sits down.

"You okay?" Reuben asks.

"Yeah," Dana answers.

Reuben sits down in the empty chair next to Dana. Reuben looks at Dana and wonders why he is torturing himself and just tell River how he feels.

"You still love her," Reuben said.

Dana looks over at Reuben shocked at his question. "What?"

"Don't play me, man." Reuben says looking at the small round table in front him. "I can see it all over your face, especially when she is around. Remember when you asked if this was fate or coincidence?" Dana nods. "Well this is no coincidence, this is fate."

"River hates my guts," Dana says.

"She just mad," Reuben replies, "You know how women get when they're mad. Once I forgot Mother's Day, I was twenty-one years old. Momma cried, told me how she labored twenty-five hours and I temporarily paralyzed her, all that guilty drama.-,"

"Your sweet, momma," Dana asks.

"My sweet momma," Reuben said with a chuckle. "laid on the guilty drama."

The two of them chuckle and pound their fists.

"Look," Reuben began. "Just talk to River,"

"So what do I do, just go up to here and say, 'River, I love you'?" Dana asks.

"Yep," Reuben said. "Just tell her how you feel and give that thick honey her walking papers. How did you hook up with her anyway?"

"I designed and built her law firm,"

"Oh man," Reuben groans playfully. "You got yourself a thick and smart sista,"

"I like her, she's a good woman. A little clingy though. But she is good to me, whenever she spends the night, we have good sex and I wake up to a hot breakfast."

"Hmmm," Reuben says closing his eyes. "Them are the best ones, baby. She talking marriage yet?"

"Nope," Dana said. "She's not hard to please. No kids, she's ain't never asked for money,"

"Yeah baby," Reuben says with his eyes still closed. "You got yourself a good one. A lot of brothas wish that they had someone like her. But," his eyes open and he looks over at Dana. "Do you love her?"

"No," Dana said. "I'm in love with your niece,"

"Seriously," Reuben replies. "you in love with your girl."

"No," Dana answered.

"Then drop her," Reuben says him.

Dana sighs.

"What if River doesn't love me, what if she doesn't feel the same."

Reuben sighs and shrugs his shoulders.

SHIRLEY CRIES AS SHE looks upon River laying peacefully in bed. There is an I.V. needle in her right arm. The doctor said she is only sleeping and she will wake up at any moment. She knows that River is over worked. She knows that River is over stressed, but for some reason Shirley feels as if she is to blame. She encourages River, told her how proud she is of her accomplishments; that her grandfather would be so proud of his angel. Shirley blames herself for not being firm enough in telling River that she is working too hard. So now her beloved, her husband's angel, is lying helplessly in the hospital, lying still as if she is dead. Shirley leans forward and whispers in River's ear.

"River, Grandma is here. I love you Angel; you just rest."

Shirley looks up at the heavens and speaks to her dead husband.

"I'm sorry, my love." She sobs. "I promised you and Imani that I would take care of your angel,"

Reuben overhears his mother apology to her dead husband. He hears her sobbing as his niece lies on the bed. He enters the room. Shirley turns towards Reuben, her face is wet from tears.

"Momma," Reuben says with concern.

"Imani and your father would be so upset with me," she cries.

"Come here," he says.

Reuben takes his mother in his arms and holds her as she sobs.

"It's not your fault, Momma, you know this."

Reuben walks her out of the room. He sits her down in the vacant seat and kneels in front of her.

"River is over worked," Reuben says. "Don't do this to yourself."

Shirley takes in a deep breath.

"She is sleeping so peacefully," Shirley cries. "She looks like an angel, doesn't she Ruby,"

"Momma, come on, don't cry," Reuben comforts.

"Where did we go wrong?" she asks.

"We didn't go wrong, Momma," Reuben told her. "River is a work-a-holic; that is just her nature."

"When did she change?" says a voice from behind.

Shirley and Reuben turn around and see Dana. He grins and sits down.

"I mean when we were dating, she was carefree, and now she is by the book." Dana told her.

"After you two broke up, she enrolled in school, community college full time and worked part-time on the weekends. River just buckled down in school and during her free time, she started writing again." Shirley says.

"When I got out of jail," Reuben begins. "and came back to Pittsburgh she was wearing these dark suits, slack, high heel boots and her glasses. River hated to wear her glasses."

Reuben said as he shakes his head. "This is my fault, I drove her crazy with the club."

"No baby, like you said, it's no one's fault," Shirley says finally gathering her composure. "River is over worked, just like you said. Now it is our time to make sure that she relaxes and stops trying to do everything."

Reuben sighs and gets up and walks into River's room. He sits down in the empty chair and looks at his niece. Tears welled up in his eyes. He did this, he drove her to this. *Stupid Club*, he says to himself. *Why River?*

He feels horrible about how much he pestered her; constantly bugging her, nagging her, over petty and insignificant details that have made Reuben's Room the number one hot spot since its opening. So now while he is banking on her major investment, she lays helplessly as if she is in a coma.

Meanwhile Dana and Shirley sit outside waiting. He glances at Shirley, he is amazed that after all these years that Miss. Shirley is doing well.

"I didn't think you remembered me," Dana replies.

She smiles at him.

"Oh yes, I remember you."

"The man that broke River's heart," Dana comments.

"No, you were the one who treated her right. Of all the simple headed and stupid boyfriends, you were good to her. You just wanted to move on, that's all."

Dana grins.

"Can I get you some coffee?" Dana offers.

"Yes, please," Shirley answers as she reaches for her purse. Dana stops her.

"No, no, I got it." Dana stands up and walks away.

AN HOUR PASSES AND, Dave arrives at the hospital. Shirley and Dana are sitting outside River's room while Reuben sat at her bedside. A nurse leads Dave to River's room. Shirley looks up and smiles at Dave.

"Dave," Shirley says standing up.

She greets him with a grin. Dave and Shirley hug each other.

"I came as soon as I got Reuben's message," Dave says. "What is going on?"

"She had an anxiety attack, a bad one." Shirley reports as she and Dave sat down. "The doctor said that she will be fine but she will need a lot of rest. She is asleep right now."

Dave nods his head. He sighs as he begins to think about the recent book tour, the imaginary stalker. She is definitely under stress.

"Let me introduce you," Shirley says. "Dave, this is Dana Wilson, he is a friend of Reuben's. He was there when River got sick. Dana, this is River's friend, Dave Marouni."

The two men shake hands.

"When she went down, she told me to call you," Dana reports.

Dave nods at Dana indicating a thank you.

"Um, I am going to the hospital chapel. Call me if anything changes." Dana says.

Dana walks into a small chapel. Soft therapeutic type music plays in the background. A large white cross hangs in the center of a wall in front of the chapel. Lit candles and flowers are placed throughout the room. Dana takes a seat on the pew and sighs. He felt so guilty and worthless, so alone and unwanted.

What am I staying, for? He asks himself. *River doesn't need me here,*

However as much as Dana thinks about going home, he doesn't want to go home. He sits back in the seat, closes his eyes and begins to pray.

"Jesus, forgive me, forgive me for using an innocent person and not dealing with my issues with River. Forgive me for not being the man I know that I need to be. Please God, let River be okay, so Reuben and her grandmother can have peace of mind. If River is well, I promise I will not let another opportunity pass without me telling her how I feel and leading Katrina on, Amen,"

TWO DAYS PASS SINCE River's anxiety and still, she slept peacefully, showing no signs of waking up. The doctors inform River's family that her sleeping is normal. That all her vitals are good and that all she is doing is just sleeping. While Reuben, Shirley, and Dave all took turns sitting in the room with River, hoping and praying that she would wake up at any minute, Dana sat outside her room or in the chapel. Shirley notices that everyone has spent time in the room except Dana.

"Why don't you go check on River," Shirley suggests.

"Um, I don't-," Dana replied.

"It's okay," Shirley says to him with a comforting grin, "Reuben and I will be in the cafeteria,"

"I have to make a few phone calls," Dave imputes. "Someone should be here in case River wakes up,"

Dana looks at Rueben. Rueben nods his head indicating that it is a good idea. Dana takes in a deep breath. Slowly he walks in River's room. His heart is pounding rapidly in his chest as he opens the door. She looks like Sleeping Beauty waiting for her prince to come wake her up with a kiss. Her long hair lies over her shoulders and her hands are at her waist. Dana wants to lean over to kiss her. Instead he walks to the vacant chair, sits down, and covers his face.

What if she wakes up and sees me? Maybe I should leave.

Just as Dana thinks of getting up, Dave enters in. He grins at Dana. Dana wonders who Dave is to River.

Does he know about me? Does he know that I am the reason that River is here? Dave hands Dana a cup of coffee.

"Thanks," Dana says.

"Sure," Dana replies.

"Have you known River long?" Dana asks.

"Almost twenty years," Dave answers.

Dana begins to wonder why he hasn't heard of Dave.

Dave looks at River lying still upon the bed. Gently he sits down on the edge and caresses her forehead, then cups the side of her face. Slowly, she inhales and exhales, then turns her head toward Dave. She takes a deep breath, then slowly opens her eyes. As she looks up at him, he smiles at her.

"Good morning," he says to her softly.

Dana quickly stands up in amazement. Who is this handsome prince that has awakened Sleeping Beauty?

"Go get the doctor," Dave says to Dana, not taking his eyes off River.

Dana quickly leaves to get a doctor.

"You gave us quite a scare," Dave says to River.

Dave smiles at her. She looks up him. Her eyes are still heavy and she wants to go back to sleep; she manages to give him a weak grin.

Immediately Shirley and Reuben enter the room. Dave moves from the bed as Shirley rushes to River's side. She holds River in her arms and weeps.

"Thank you Jesus," she praises. "Thank you God,"

"River," Reuben said in a soft voice.

Shirley moves to the side. River looks up at Reuben. Tears form in Shirley's eyes.

"Hey Niece,"

The doctor comes in and everyone steps aside but don't leave the room.

"How are you feeling, River," the doctor asks.

She nods her head weakly.

"Momma, come on let the doctor check River," Reuben says to Shirley.

Dave and Dana follow Reuben and Shirley out of the room while the doctor can looks River over.

"I am so happy," Shirley cries.

She looks up at the ceiling and calls out to her husband and daughter.

"Our angel is going to be all right," Shirley cries.

Rueben takes his mother in his arms and holds her, and for a moment she cries. Then Shirley looks at Dave and Dana.

"Oh gosh, I am so sorry," Shirley says burying, her face in Reuben's chests.

"What for?" both men ask with a chuckle.

"We're carrying on, never mind that fact that you are just as happy as we are." Shirley answered.

Shirley looks at Dana, "Dana, thank you so much for being here with us."

Dana grins and then nods his head.

"Once River is released I am taking her to my parent's cabin," Dave announces.

"Oh Dave thank you, but River can stay with me," Shirley replies.

"No, too many distractions," Dave says shaking his head. "She gets involved in too many projects."

"Too many projects?" Reuben asked with a chuckle.

"Yes, your club for starters," Dave comments.

"My club? What does my club have to do with her getting sick?"

"It's one of her many tasks. River teaches at not one but at two schools, six different classes, writes for a local magazine and she's a bestselling author. River is overworked and with her here around you people, she is going to feel obligated to want to do something," Dave explains.

"So what does your parent's cabin have that my mother's house does not?" Reuben questions. "My mother can take care of River,"

"I'm not saying that she can't," Dave states. "Mrs. Massie, River loves you very much but with her in the city there is too much at her reach. Her jobs and I, again I emphasize that with a 's', with her at my cabin, there is nothing that can tempt her, she can rest."

"How long will she be gone?" Shirley asks.

"Whenever the doctor says that she is out of the woods," Dave answers. "You said yourself that next time she might not be so lucky and those tears of joy, Mrs. Massie will be tears of sorrow."

The doctor came out of River's room.

"River is going to be fine." the doctor reports. "However she is extremely exhausted physically. You had mentioned that she is over worked, but I am sensing emotional fatigue as well.

The anxiety attack can be triggered by emotional stress, such as the death of a loved one for example. The condition is also known as broken heart syndrome."

No one notices that Dana let out a sigh.

"When can we take her home?" Shirley asks.

"I want to keep her here at least a week just to get her strength up." the doctor answers.

"Can we go back in?" Shirley asks.

"Sure, I will be back in a few hours to check on her."

Everyone watches as the doctor leaves. Shirley lets out a long sigh, then looks at Dave.

"I've cancelled her classes for the semester," Dave announces.

"Who are you to run River's life?" Reuben snaps.

Rueben attempts to approach Dave; Shirley holds him back.

"Reuben," Shirley admonishes.

"Let me tell you something," Dave says. "There is a lot more than River just being over worked. You know this as much as I know. And we all know that they are more emotional than anything, heart ache, pain, grief,"

Reuben quickly shoots Dana a glance.

"She *must rest,* nothing can trigger her again, not until she's well again. You, Uncle Reuben need to back off. Now I am not asking you, I am telling you. When she is released, I am taking her with me."

"Okay," Shirley gives in.

She has her arm around Reuben to keep him charging after Dave. She looks at Reuben,

"Ruby, take me home so I can change."

"We'll be back," Reuben said through his teeth and staring hard at Dave.

"I'll be here," Dave said not being intimidated by Reuben.

Dave watches as Rueben, Shirley and Dana leave. He walks back into River's room. He sits down on the edge of her bed. She looks up at him and grins.

"What happened?" she asks weakly.

"You had an anxiety attack," Dave answers. "You're stressed out."

River sighs.

"I'm tired," she says.

"The doctors said that you are exhausted," Dave informs. "As soon as you're released I'm taking to you to my parents' cabin and you are going to rest."

"I'm resting now," she says.

"You are recovering now," Dave says.

River rolls her eyes and she tries to sit up, but she is too weak.

"River, I am serious." Dave scolded.

"I'm not going to argue with you," she says with a grin, then closes her eyes.

"Get some sleep," Dave says to her.

He kisses her on the forehead and sits down in the vacant chair.

CHAPTER NINETEEN

THE LOUD POUNDING WAKES Dana. He was sound asleep on his couch. He sits up trying to grasp reality, wondering what is going on. Dana is tired and worn. He also hasn't eaten in days. When he came home from the hospital he didn't bother to shower or shave. Reluctantly he gets up to answer the door; Katrina is standing before him.

"Hi," she says.

"Hey," he says. "Come in,"

Katrina walks in Dana shuts the door. He walks in the kitchen and fixes himself a pot of coffee. While he is in the kitchen, Katrina sits down in the living room. She looks around hoping to find any traces of another woman. There is no smell of perfume lingering. Maybe he is working hard on a new building and didn't want to be bothered. He didn't answer his telephone and his cell was turned off. After Dana preps his coffee he goes to the bathroom to freshen up. When he comes back, Dana finds Katrina sitting in the same spot. He sits down on the couch beside her. He looked over at her.

"Um, I haven't heard from you," she said

"I got caught up with a few things,"

"I called your office, and they said that you haven't been in for a few days." Katrina replies.

She looks at him and sees that he is bleary eyed.

"Are you okay?" she asks.

He nods his head slowly. She sees the doubt in his eyes,

"I drove by but I didn't see your car?" Katrina mentions.

"I was away," is his response.

"Away," Katrina asked, "Where is away,"

"A friend of mine was in the hospital," he answers. "I stayed until I knew that everything was all right. It looked like it was a heart attack, but she had an anxiety attack, but everything is going to all right."

"She," Katrina asked. *So there is another woman.*

"Yeah,"

"Who is *she?*" Katrina asked.

Dana waits for a moment before answering. Should he tell Katrina that *she* is *River?* Katrina was so insecure that night at Reuben's club. Dana remembers his vow and the promise that he made to God.

The look in Dana's eyes told her who *she* was. Katrina doesn't show emotion to her discovery.

"How is she?" Katrina asked.

"She's fine," Dana answered. "I saw her at Christie's a few days ago. She and I were talking and before you know it she was clutching on to me, having chest pains."

"Oh my," Katrina replied stunned.

"We naturally thought that it was a heart attack, but it was just an anxiety attack,"

"This took two days to figure out?"

"No, she slept for two days. We all stayed until she woke up."

"We,"

"Reuben and her grandmother and some guy she works with," Dana answers.

"I'm glad that she is all right," Katrina said. "but with her family there, why did you feel that you had to stay?"

"Because, Kat, I was there when it started. Plus she and I are-,"

"What?"

"Cool, that's my girl, I wanted to make sure that she is okay,"

"I'm your girl," Katrina snaps. "I am your girl,"

Dana is shocked at her temper. Katrina takes a deep breath and tries to regain her composure.

"You could have called." She said.

"Katrina, my focus was on River, I'm sorry."

"River," Katrina said her name as if it was something disgusting.

"Kat, don't be insecure," he says closing his eyes.

"It's not being insecure, it's about respect!" Katrina says to him. "You didn't tell me that you two dated. You disappear for two days not telling me because you were at the hospital when you didn't need to be."

"How are you going to tell me where I need to be?" Dana asks irritated with Katrina.

"Because her family was there," Katrina said. "They didn't need you,"

"She is my friend," Dana said.

"Is she? How come you never mentioned her before I knew that you knew her?" Katrina asked. "You mentioned, Reuben, you mentioned the guys from work, but there was never a mention of River; none! Then I figured out who she was at Reuben's, *then* you tell me that about you two."

Dana doesn't reply. He looks at Katrina. She doesn't deserve to be misguided. Dana begins to tell Katrina everything about River and him. He tells the same story that he told Reuben that day at Christie's. Dana told her that he did love her then; that he was a coward to not have told her. Dana confesses that he doesn't know if this strange reunion is fate or coincidence. He told Katrina how River looks at him, as if she wants his blood, but every time he looks at her, he realizes that he still loves her. Dana tells Katrina about the old River, the free spirited person that loved life, and that danced at every song and laughed at the silliest things. He told her about this River, the unrecognizable River, the stoic and cool River. As Katrina listens, her heart is breaking because every time Dana mentions River's name there is light in his bleary eyes.

Dana looks at Katrina,

"I'm sorry," he says.

Katrina nods her head. She stands up and slowly walks out of the door. Dana lets out a sigh. He leaned back on the couch and tried to catch his breath. His chest is aching. After a moment he gathers himself together. Without thinking, Dana walked to the window and opened it, welcoming the scent of the imaginary lilies.

DAVE FINDS SHIRLEY IN the chapel. She is reading her Bible. Dave sits down beside her.

"Hi," he says to her smiling.

"Hi baby," she replies back smiling.

"You're not mad at me," he asks.

"No," Shirley says with a chuckle. "I don't like you taking my baby away from me, but it's what she needs. River is blessed to have a friend like you. You'll have to forgive Reuben, he is very protective of his niece."

Dave grins. Shirley looks over at Dave.

"You love her, don't you?"

"River," he began, "She and I have history. She is my best friend," Dave answers.

"Answer my question," Shirley says with sternly.

Dave takes in a deep breath and then looks over at Shirley. Her eyes are trusting.

"Yes, ma'am," Dave confessed. "but River doesn't feel the same,"

"Stupid child," Shirley mumbles.

"What?" Dave asks with a chuckle.

"Nothing baby," Shirley says then closes her Bible.

A picture fell from the pages and on to the floor. Dave bends over to pick it up. He glances at the photo and then looks at it again. It is a picture of a pretty girl. She is smiling in the photo, as if she was laughing at a joke. She has the prettiest brown eyes, there is so much light in her eyes. What really catches his eyes is her hair style; she had a cute short pixie style haircut. This picture looks like a vague description of the pretty girl that River has been seeing.

"Isn't she beautiful," Shirley asks smiling. "River was so beautiful,"

"River?" Dave asks.

"Yeah, that was River when she was younger,"

Dave now realizes why he couldn't see her and River could. Everything is making sense. This pretty girl was once alive and full of life. Something killed her carefree and beautiful existence creating the River that world has come to know. Dave realizes why River is not able to recognize herself. The old River is dead. The new River buried the old River and buried away the memories that once established the characters of the old River. The hallucinations of the old River means that something from River's past is causing this strange resurrection, haunting this new River. So what is from the past?

Dave cannot believe that he is not able to recognize the old River. With the description and now this picture, it has been over fifteen years since he saw that River. He remembers how she looked but he never thought to put two and two together.

"I keep this picture because I miss this River," Shirley says. "This River was funny, silly, that River in there-,"

"She's sick," Dave says.

Shirley nods her head.

CHAPTER TWENTY

DAVE SLOWLY DRIVES ALONG the long drive way that leads to the cabin. As River sits in the passenger seat, she looks out the window and admires the picturesque scenery. Words cannot describe the beauty. The sky is the color of baby blue, the bright yellow sun is high in the sky, and the trees are still in full bloom waving their green leaves. With the cabin being in the north, the air is much cooler than it would be in Pittsburgh. River grins when she sees snow covering the peeks of the mountains.

River looks at Dave. Where will she be without him? Dave has taken her away from everyone and everything, the pretty girl that has been haunting her can't find her. He is going to take care of her until she is well again.

RIVER FOLLOWS DAVE INSIDE the cabin. Inside the air is stale. As Dave opens the windows to let fresh air flow through the cabin, River tours the house. There are four bedrooms, two bathrooms, a large eat in kitchen. In the kitchen there is a back door that leads to a patio deck. The living room is large with a large bay window. There are a couch, two love seats, coffee and end tables, and a recliner. Also, in there is a fire place in front on the living room.

"This is nice," River says.

"This is what you need," Dave says to her.

River takes in a deep breath.

"No cell phone," Dave says. "No fax machines, nothing but your lap top so you can write and books so you can read."

"How long are we staying?" River asks.

"As long as we it need to," Dave replies.

"We,"

Dave continues to moves around the living room. He fluffs pillows and pulls the curtains back from the window.

"Yes we, - you and me." Dave turns to face River. "I am not letting you out of my sight until you are better."

"Until I'm better?" River questions.

She is offended by his statement.

"Dave, you talk like I am sick," she states.

"You are," Dave states, looking at River.

She doesn't respond.

"I'm going to get the luggage." Dave informs. "Choose any of the bedrooms that you want."

Dave walks out of the cabin. River sighs and continues to walk around the cabin.

Sick, I'm not sick, she said to herself. *Tired, over worked, but not sick. Sick people need psychiatric help or medical help. Dave is a doctor; Ph.D in education, not medical and he is not a psychiatrist. He is someone who thinks he knows me. What does he know? Dave doesn't know anything. He doesn't understand anything. And now here he was keeping me a prisoner. Does he think that the serenity of this cabin will make all the pain go away? Does he think that he can fix what is broken with me when I don't know how to fix things? I am okay, just over worked. So I won't teach as many subjects; that will give me more time with my writing. My writing is somewhat therapeutic. But where will I be if I can't teach; if I don't teach? I would be nowhere, alone in my thoughts and not thinking about things has kept me safe for this long. Why is Dave taking my safety away from me?*

"Did you pick a room?" He asks startling River from his thoughts.

River looks at Dave holding her luggage.

"Dave, what about your work?" she asks.

Dave carries the suitcases past River not answering her question.

"Which room, River?" he asks walking down the hall.

"It doesn't matter," she answers following him.

Dave goes in a bed room. He sets the luggage down, turns the lamp on and opens the windows. He turns and looks at River.

"What if this retreat takes all semester?" River asks.

Dave shrugs. She looks away nervously.

"I will go crazy if I am-,"

"If you're not what?" he interrupts.

"Not busy," she says, feeling like a child being scolded.

Dave can see that she is getting overwhelmed. He walks to her and gently wraps his arms around her, pulling her in to him.

"River," he says softly, "You could have died. Do you understand the severity in that?"

"Dave, you don't die from an anxiety attack," she says pulling away from him. "I just got a little-,"

"A little what?" he interrogates.

"Nothing," she sighs.

River folds her arms across her chest.

"No, not nothing; talk to me," Dave coaxes.

River takes in a deep breath then exhales.

"This is nice, this is real nice and everything. It's quiet, away from the world, but I don't need this. I can have peace and quiet in my own home."

"No," he said shaking his head.

Dave cups his hands on the side of her face.

"Trust me," he said in soft tone. "I won't hurt you, you know that,"

She nods her head as tears fall from her eyes. River quickly wipes them away.

"You're safe here, okay." Dave says.

THE NEXT DAY, DAVE finds River sitting outside on the deck watching the sunrise. The hour is not quite seven am. She has a cup of coffee in her hands. She looks relaxed in her pine green colored sweat suit. There is sharp cool breeze flowing threatening the day that has been predicted to be at least eighty degrees. River doesn't mind that sharp breeze. The cool air is comforting to her. River hears Dave walk onto the deck.

"Good morning, dear." She jokes.

"Good morning, sweetheart." he jokes back.

He leans down and kisses the top of her head, and then sits down in the chair next to her. River's attention never left the sunrise.

"How did you sleep?" he asks.

River shrugs.

"What's on your mind?" Dave asks.

"A lot of things," she answers.

"Elaborate," he orders softly.

"Why did I have an anxiety attack?" she asks.

Dave looks at the same sunrise. He takes in a deep breath then looks over at River.

"When I left for Vegas," he begins. "You were twenty years old. You brought energy everywhere you went; it was both annoying and enjoyable. Every day was a party to you. Seven years later, you are now this person that is solemn and serious. Life is about business with you. Everything is serious to you. I have yet to see that smile. I regret being annoyed by that energy. I know that a lot has happened to you within those years."

River doesn't respond.

"River, talk to me, tell me what happened."

River finally looks away from the sky and looks at her coffee cup to take a sip.

"Where do I start?" she says with a chuckle.

"At the beginning," Dave says. "Come on,"

Dave stands up and holds his hand out to River. She takes his hand and together they walk inside. They enter the kitchen. River sits down as Dave refreshes her cup of coffee and fixes a cup for himself. Together they walk into the living room. They sit down on the couch. River begins to tell him how she was always in love. Dating was adventurous to her. Who will she love next? Who would make her heart skip a beat? Who would make her heart sing or soar? But with love came a price.

"They wanted more than what I was willing to give," she said.

"You know what those guys wanted, River," Dave comments with a chuckle.

She nods her head.

"I know," she said. "And I managed to bounce back; bounced high enough to fly again. But in the midst of my flying, my grandfather dies. He was my king. I was his angel. He never called me River, he called me Angel."

River looks away as she begins to remember her grandfather. She takes in a deep breath. Dave patiently waits for her.

"My grandpa loved me, only me. I mean, he loved my mom and my uncles, and Reuben. Reuben kept him laughing. But me, I was special. I had him wrapped around my finger and he loved being wrapped. I would snuggle up with him, rest my head on his large chest and fall asleep to the sound of his heartbeat. It was a rhythm only for me, my own personal heartbeat. He would say, 'Angel, give me a squeeze.' I wrapped my arms around him and squeeze him as hard as I could; thinking I was really squeezing him. My mom said from the moment I was born, he was in love."

River looks at Dave, tears are in her eyes, and she takes in a deep breath and continues.

"My grandfather had issues. He wasn't very nice to his first wife, my grandma Betty, my mom's mom. He was really mean, abusive and just nasty. No one knew or understood why. They finally split; divorced. Years later he met my grandma Shirley. I don't know how but she made him a better man, he wanted to be a better father, so he reconciled with his children; my mom and her brothers. He made amends with my grandma Betty. By the time I was born, he was a changed man. I guess with Rueben and me, he was given a second chance to be a better father not a better father reconciled. Life was good. However he had heart disease, and he died one afternoon in his sleep. Kings don't die Dave. They live forever, but my grandpa, my king, died."

She stops talking, covers her face and cries. Dave puts his arms around her and holds her. Dave remembers when River's grandfather died. It was during the time when they worked together at the Mexican Restaurant. River uncovers her face and looks at Dave. She takes in a deep breath and continues.

"I had never experienced that much pain." She cried. "My heart broke,"

River takes a deep breath.

"Because my grandfather made his piece with those he hurt. He is in a better place. I believe that, but it just-,"

"Hurts," Dave says, holding her.

River nods and continues.

"I focused on school, work, writing, and the adventures of dating. By now, you had left for Vegas. The dating got more intense. I was dating more experienced men, men too mature for me. And one thing led to another and well," she stopped talking for a moment. "I wanted to be mature. I wanted to have a boyfriend, someone you can talk to, laugh with, at the end of the night, make love to and wake up in each other's arms. All that seemed normal in relationships. But he just wanted me whenever it was convenient. I couldn't talk with him, because he didn't listen or care. I couldn't laugh with him, because his game wasn't funny and the love making, he just did what he wanted to me and left me alone at night,"

"River, why did you put up with that?" Dave questioned.

River shrugs her shoulders.

"I had a boyfriend,"

"Having a boyfriend was that important to you?" Dave questions.

"Not necessarily important, but I wanted a relationship that was longer that three months. I wanted someone in my life-,"

"Never mind self-respect just long as you had a boyfriend," Dave questions.

River shrugs her shoulders. Dave looks at her wondering why this woman allowed some man to use her.

"How long did it take you to realize that he was using you?"

"After a year and a half, I was twenty-two. Considering that he only came around once a month or so, I once again got my priorities in order. I focused on my writing, school, work, and my mom. She had been diagnosed with breast cancer; I took care of her. I got my driver's license. I met up with other writers, went on conferences. I didn't wait around for him to call me. Once he saw that I was moving on, he began to chase me. He was coming around with that coy sinister grin.

"Did you give in?" Dave asks.

"Yeah, but I was real cold about it," River said. "Whenever I would go over his place, I purposely didn't talk. He noticed that I was quiet. Whenever he would say something, I didn't respond. I acted as if I didn't care. Whenever he came by my place I acted as if he wasn't there. When it came down to sex, I said things like: 'let's get this over with,' and when he was finished, I'd tell him to leave. As sick and twisted as this was, I was not quite ready to leave him, he was in my blood."

"First lovers usually are," Dave comments.

"Whenever someone asked if I had a boyfriend, I would say: 'Not one worth bragging about,'."

"Again I ask you, why didn't you break up with him?"

"Believe it or not, I saw redeeming qualities," River said with a shrug. "When things were good, he was funny when he did make me laugh. Whenever he was not ignoring me; he made me special. Whenever he actually looked at me, he saw me. I hoped that one day, he would wake up and see me and love me. I decided to give him six months. By then it would be two years for us, and if he didn't get his act together then I knew that it was never going to be. In the meanwhile, my mother's condition worsened. Her breast cancer had spread into her lungs. At night, I cried worrying about her. I wanted someone to hold me, but no one was there. No sympathetic boyfriend, no best friend, no one. But then one day, there was some one-,"

River stopped talking.

"When I met you-," Dave begins.

"She was just diagnosed." River replies. "She had the surgery, the doctors removed her breast. She took the chemo and it appeared that she was in remission,"

"How long did she have it?" he asked.

"Three years," River answered. "After her mastectomy she was doing well; really well, but-," River stops talking.

River takes a deep breath.

"My mom never got a chance to go into remission. After the chemo; she appeared to be recovering well, but when my grandfather died, the cancer came back. Then she was taking radiation but nothing seemed to work. It was like the more treatments she took, the more advanced her cancer got."

River shakes her head; still feeling the struggle. She watched her mother suffer.

"She died when I was twenty-two," River said softly.

She wipes the tears away from her eyes.

"Where was this-that boyfriend?" Dave asks.

"The last three weeks of her life. She was in the hospital. To my surprise he was giving me the attention that I had been waiting for. It was if he finally had looked at me."

"Really," Dave asked surprised.

River nods.

"There was a reason. He only came to the apartment because my mom was not around. My mom couldn't stand him, and with her not around he felt better about being with me. But you want to know the sick part of all this. While she lied dying in the hospital, he felt content to lie in her home; no respect. Not once did he offer to take me to see her, or to buy flowers as a get well gesture. He looked at it as if we can have sex in every room of the house,"

"River, please tell me that you didn't-,"

"No, of course not," River replied.

"When did you finally let him go?"

"Technically, six weeks before my mom died. I met this guy. We sort of dated. I wouldn't say that I dated him behind Jerry's back, this new guy and I weren't technically serious. Slowly, we became friends. He was sweet, all of the qualities of a good boyfriend. He kept me distracted, not from my priorities, but from the lack of regarding Jerry. He was there for me when I needed a friend to talk to regarding my mom. I trusted him, there was peace with him."

"What happened to him?"

River looks around the room. She notices that Dave and she had talked all morning. She is now tired.

"I'm tired," she says to him.

Dave nods his head accepting that she doesn't want to talk any more.

"Let me fix you something to eat," he says.

River grins. Dave goes in the kitchen.

Heartache, he says to himself.

There is no break to heal from heartache. If it wasn't love that was breaking her heart it was death.

RIVER AWAKES AND FINDS Dave in the living room. He had fallen asleep watching television. He looks so peaceful sleeping in the dark brown easy chair. River grins at her oldest and dearest friend. Maybe that is what she should write about; friendship. A group of friends who grow up together and grow old together and although this concept has been done before, it hasn't been done her way. Creating characters was never a problem. In fact character development is easy for her. Like most writers, her characters are based from people she knows. However this time, these characters will be from those that she loves. The main character will be a young woman, with four good friends in her life. One is a friend who is old enough to be her mother, but they love each other like sisters. The next friend is going to be a friend that is old enough to be her grandfather. He is wise and gives her good advice. The next friend is someone very dear to her, someone whom she loves and trusts. He has the qualities of being a best friend as well as the main character's lover. He cares deeply for her. When looking into his eyes it's like looking at precious stones; there is a sense of serenity whenever she looks into his eyes. No matter the kind of storms that surrounds her, looking into his eyes put her into a peaceful meadow. The last good friend has double connection to the main character. He is a member of the family. He is neurotic, demanding, but loyal and faithful. His hyper strung demeanor is both comical and irritating.

As River writes, she realizes that the people in her life are more than just her friends- they are family. Her family will do anything for River. Is she as good of a friend as her friends are for her? Her best friend sits in another room. He has taken time away from his job to take care of her. If Dave was in trouble would she take time away from one of her many jobs?

As she writes, River doesn't notice Dave standing in the door way watching her. As she types away on her lap top he smiles. He is happy that she is writing. He doesn't want to disturb her. Instead he prepares dinner.

THE SCENT OF THE steak and baked potato beckons River. She stops writing and follows the enticing smell into kitchen. They smile at each other. He wraps his arms around her and kisses the top of her head.

"You spoil me," she says, enjoying his embrace.

She sees the vegetables on the stove.

"Awe Dave," she whines.

"Yes, steamed broccoli and cauliflower," he says as she frowns, "Don't make a face; this is good for you,"

She walks to the table and smiles. There is a tossed salad in the center and red wine is one ice and candles have been lit. The scenery gives the illusion of a romantic dinner. River knows that Dave is creating a relaxing atmosphere.

"You are too good to me," she says.

"I care about you," he replies.

"Still?" she asks sitting down.

"What do you mean still?" he asks with a chuckle.

He turns around to face her. She looks away before she answers.

"I shot you down,"

"You rejected me as your boyfriend, not as your friend."

"What's wrong with me? Why can I not love a guy as good as you, but love men that use me?"

"The good guy never wins," Dave replies. "I cannot believe that there has been no one that you loved and they loved you back?"

"I thought so," she answers. "I mean, I really thought so. With the new guy, I knew he loved me. I could see it in his eyes. Whenever he looked at me, it was as if I was the only one, I wasn't just his girl but his friend. And the way he touched me, he was gentle. I was never hungry because he was my food. I was never thirsty because he was refreshing. His smile was my light and in his arms I was secure. I felt safe. When he exhaled, I inhaled."

"What happened?" Dave asks.

"He got tired of me," River replies. "Like the rest of them. It came out of nowhere, out of the blue. It was if someone ripped my heart out, leaving my soul empty. I thought I was going to die."

"You did die," Dave said to her.

"Here we go with this dead philosophy," River says rolling her eyes.

"What was his name?"

River gets up from the table. She opens the oven to check on the steak.

"Well done?" River asks.

"Yeah," Dave tells her as he uncorks the wine and pours River and himself a glass. "What was the guy's name?" he waits for an answer while she sips her wine. "It wasn't Jerry?"

"No," River answers.

Dave is perceptive of River's evasive demeanor.

"Tell me more about your mom,"

"What about her?" River asks.

"What was she like?"

"My mom was amazing," River told him proudly. "She was tall and beautiful. A black beauty, you know. She had skin the color of mahogany. Her eyes were the color of onyx. Her smile was beyond bright. If you didn't smile when she smiled, you were a lost cause."

"Sounds like you," Dave compliments.

River shakes her head.

"I am nothing like my mother," River says.

Dave hands her a glass of wine.

"My mom had style, like Jackie O slash Diana Ross style,"

"That's a combination," Dave chuckles.

"Yeah, but she made it work," River says. "My mother was very passionate, she was life. Even when she was sick, she still laughed. She still captured the essence of life. She had cancer, the cancer didn't have her."

River takes a deep breath to fight the tears from forming up in her eyes.

"River," Dave calls her name.

She looks at him with her eyes full of tears.

"Let it out," he coaxes.

River sighs with a smile. The tears fall from her eyes. River quickly wipes them away.

"Anyway, my mom was very cool. She was class." River says.

It is quiet for a while. Dave didn't know what to say. She looks up at him with a weak grin. He wraps his arms around her. River buries her head in his chest. She takes in a deep breath. River pulls away.

"I had family for support. Both my grandmothers; my grandma Betty, and my grandma Shirley, they made sure that I was okay. But the person I needed the most was Reuben. He didn't come for my mom."

"Why?"

River shrugs her shoulders.

"Reuben was not in a good place mentally at the time. He was hanging with the wrong crowd. It still kills him that he was not mentally there," River replies. "A year after my mom died he went to jail for two years. During those two years, Reuben got his life together. After Reuben got out of jail he got his life back together. He went back to school and got his Master's in business. That's why I didn't mind helping him with the club, he really changed. Not being there for my mom really bothered him. My mom has been dead for fifteen years and he still apologizes.

"Do you forgive him?"

"Of course I do," River says with a grin. "Four months after my mom died, my grandma Betty died; she also had cancer. In my opinion, she died of a broken heart."

"This guy that you loved was he there with you during all this?"

"He was there, when my mom died. He broke up with me two months after she died, four days before Christmas,"

THE STEAKS AND THE steamed vegetables are ready. River goes to the bathroom to freshen up. Just as she finishes washing her hands, River lifts up her eyes and looks in the mirror and suddenly she is startled by an image smiling at her. It's the girl; the pretty girl that has been stalking her for months.

River screams and rams her hands into the mirror, glass shatters everywhere.

Alarmed, Dave runs into the bathroom. He finds River screaming and scurrying around as if she is looking for something.

"River!" he exclaims.

"Dave, she's here!" River screams.

River tosses shower curtain in hopes of finding the pretty girl in the tub.

"I saw her!"

Dave knows who River is talking about. He tries to grab River in his arms, but she moves too fast and she is too hysterical. She violently pushes Dave aside and quickly River runs out of the bathroom and down the hall.

"Call the police!" she screams.

Dave follows her.

"River!" he calls out.

Dave follows her in his bedroom. He shuts and locks the door.

"What are you doing?" River asks petrified.

Quickly Dana grabs River and pulls her into his arms. She tries to fight him off, but he is too strong. The more she struggles to break free, the tighter his hold gets. He begins to think what caused River to see that girl. They were in the kitchen sitting around and talking; talking about the past. What in River's past is triggering the hallucinations?

"Dave, please go get her," she cries.

"River, shhh," he coaxes.

"Dave she-," River cries.

"Okay, okay," he coaxes her in a soft tone. "I need you to calm down."

Dave slowly rocks her in his arms. He his hold is tight, he's not let her go.

"Look, look baby, we're safe." Dave says. "No one is here but you and me." Dave says.

MOMENTS PASS UNTIL RIVER begins to settle down. Dave still holds her in his arms.

Slowly, River moves her head, trying to take a peek.

"Look at me," Dave demands softly.

Dave loosens his grip enough for River to look into his eyes. The sapphires are calming. He looks deep into her eyes to make sure that she is okay. She is still trembling and breathing heavy and tears fall from her eyes.

"You're safe, baby," he says softly yet sternly. "I promise; you're safe."

She nods but Dave can see that she is still frightened. She rests her head on Dave's chest. As long as he holds her she is safe. She starts crying again.

"I'm seeing things again," she said crying. "I'm sorry,"

"It's okay," Dave said. "Come here, let me look at you,"

Dave loosens his hold but he strongly holds on to River's wrist. He needs to exam her hands and to keep his hold on her.

"Did you hurt yourself?" he asks.

Together River and Dave look down at her hands; she is bleeding. Dave finally lets River go so he can leave to get a warm cloth to clean her hands off, but she grabs on to him.

"Don't go, please," she pleads crying.

Without taking his eyes from her, Dave nods his head. He takes off his shirt and wraps her hands. Dave leads her to the bed and they sit down.

"I saw her Dave, I did," River sobs.

She begins to get hysterical and antsy.

"Hey, hey, shhh, I know," he says as he calming her down. "River look at me,"

River looks at Dave, fear is still in her eyes.

"You're okay," Dave encouraged.

River nods her head but she is still scared.

Dave takes in a deep breath.

"River, she is someone from your past." Dave answers.

"Who?" River questions.

Her eyes are shifty. Growing nervous and anxious, there is agony on her face.

"You," he said slowly.

A minute passes before River responds.

"What," she asks confused.

"River baby, this girl is you, fifteen maybe sixteen years ago. Since then you have changed. Something made you change and it was pain. Heartbreak, disappointment, grief, and it killed you-the old River. And this River-you now, you created."

"I don't understand," River says shaking her head as tears fall down.

"I can't be more clear, baby." Dave says with a chuckle.

"You have to," she snaps, growing hysterical. "I can't-, Dave, look at me."

"Okay, okay," Dave says, holding on to her. "Relax,"

River slowly inhales.

"River," Dave begins. "you used to be so carefree, free spirited, open minded-,"

"I don't want to hear about me being carefree!" River snaps.

"River," Dave admonishes. "Listen."

River takes a deep breath.

"River, she is not a stalker. You are hallucinating an image of your old self; the old carefree self. From the events that happened in your past, you had an emotional breakdown. You emotionally killed yourself and you created the you now. The busy you, the work-a- holic you, the very disciplined you.

She is the symbol of repressed memories. Today you talked about your past. You let out the pain and frustration that has been built up. What were you thinking about when you saw her?"

River shakes her head and shrugged her shoulders.

"Think River," Dave says sternly. "You were thinking about the people that had hurt you. Think back when you first saw her, did someone or something from your past show up that you haven't dealt with?"

River thought for a moment and then gasps as if she is both startled and horrified. Two words: Dana Wilson. River springs from Dave's arms and nervously begins to pace the floor.

"River," Dave calls her name nervously.

She doesn't respond.

"River, talk to me," Dave coaxes nervously.

Dave stands up ready for her to have another panic attack.

"River," he says her name.

River is lost in thought. How could she not have comprehended this? As much as she dealt with Dana in the past few months, she never would have put the two together. Hallucination of her old self is a result of Dana Wilson? Why? Because that break up was the straw that broke the camel's back.

"River," Dave calls her name sternly.

Finally River looks at Dave. His sapphire colored eyes relax her.

"I can believe I didn't know who she was; who I was." She says. "What do I do now?"

"Resolve whatever issues that you have."

River looks away.

Go talk to Dana, no way, she thinks to herself. She looks at her hands that are still wrapped in Dave's shirt. She looks at Dave. He approaches her and unwraps the shirt from her hands and looks them over. Dave leads her into the bathroom. Carefully they walk over the broken glass and he begins to clean her cuts. He runs water over them and then cleans them with peroxide.

"These cuts are not deep. We'll wrap your hands tonight and check them in the morning." He says to her.

"I can clean up the mess," she says to him.

"Don't worry about it." He tells her with a smile and caresses her face. "Let's eat dinner,"

River shakes her head.

"I'm not hungry," she says.

"You're eating," Dave states sternly. "Go sit at the table and wait for me."

AFTER DINNER, RIVER AND DAVE quietly sit on the patio deck, and stare at the stars, and finish off the wine.

"Dave, how did you know who she was?"

"At the hospital, your grandmother showed me an old picture of you. I almost forgot what you looked like back then. The short hair, those pretty brown eyes, it was the perfect description. I figured that something was triggering your thoughts for you to see her."

"Dana Wilson," she confesses.

"What?" Dave asks, not understanding.

As she sips her glass of wine, Dave looks over at River.

"The architect," River says. "We dated fifteen years ago."

"What?" Dave asked, still not comprehending.

"The architect that built Reuben's club," River replied. "We dated, fifteen years ago; he was the one I loved. The one who loved me; that I thought loved me."

"He was at the hospital?" Dave asks.

River nods. Dave's eyes grow to the size of quarters. River finishes her glass of wine then refreshes her glass.

"Every time I would bring up the architect you got fidgety." Dave says.

River nods her head and tells Dave about Dana, about their reunion when she first saw him at Christie's.

"Do you think that maybe you two-,"

"No," River said with a chuckle. "It was over a decade,"

"Yeah, but there is a reason why he's back in your life, how else would you explain the hallucinations?"

"Just like you said, to bring resolution to the past."

TWO WEEKS OF THE CABIN and River has cabin fever. She feels well enough to go home. She has taken walks along the trail in the woods, slept in, worked on her new book. In the evenings, Dave and she drink wine, eat steak, and cuddle by the fire place.

"I will have a doctor come out here to check you out, before I say that you are out of the woods." He tells her sternly one particular night.

Together they sit in the living room sitting on the couch.

"I feel good, I promise." She complains. "Dave, come on, I am getting cabin fever."

Dave doesn't respond to her statement.

"When did you go back to school?" he asks.

The subject of Dana resurrects. River sighs.

"River," Dave coaxes sternly.

"After the break up," she answers. "I went back to school. I went full time, starting out at community college. I made my focus and prioritized on school and my writing. I studied hard, can't be rejected by good grade. My relationships came through my books, the plot or the characters wouldn't disappoint; I was safe. My writing, nothing or no one could hurt me-again."

"You made a conscious decision not to date?" Dave asks.

"Yes, I was not going to be heartbroken again. I didn't think about guys anymore as someone to date. They were classmates, professors, colleagues. Kissing you that night in Miami was the first time I kissed a guy since Dana."

"River, that was fifteen years ago!" Dave said.

River shrugs her shoulders.

"When I saw you after I came back to Vegas, the first thing I noticed about you was that your appearance had changed. You used to wear stylish clothes,"

"I still do," River says with a chuckle.

"As a business woman yes, very Jackie O, but the old River was more Carrie Bradshaw,"

"Carrie Bradshaw," River laughs. "I guess I changed the way I looked because I didn't want anyone to notice me. If I dress business minded then people will see that I am about business, not for entertaining. I am serious, so I dress like a serious person. I dealt with serious people."

"So you never got urges to-,"

"Not really, I was so focused on work and writing, by the time I got to bed, I was beat. I had forgotten how it felt to be turned on. That night with you, dancing was nice but scary. I haven't been held in a long time."

"So now what?" Dave asks.

"Now what, what," River asks.

"Now that you know what the issues are and why, what are you going to do?" Dave asks.

"What do you mean?"

"No, River, you can't bury those memories. You cannot go on as if there hasn't been any hurt. You live through it, don't bury it or your little friend will never leave."

"I'll deal with things, but I can't be that River anymore."

"What's wrong with that River?" Dave asks.

"She was fickle, simple, and irresponsible. She didn't have standards. Do I need to go on?"

"Yes, because that River loved life, she loved to laugh, she was passionate. Baby, don't lose that passion. Yes, set your standards, have structure, but don't die."

"How do I live my life like the old River without losing all that I have?"

"Live, you don't have to teach everything, you don't have to write everything. You can take a summer vacation; fall in love."

"What if I get hurt?"

"That is the chance that you take."

River shrugs her shoulders and yawns. She finishes her glass of wine.

"You're tired," Dave says looking at her. "Maybe you should get some sleep,"

She nods her head but hesitates to move.

"What?" Dave asks, sensing that there is something that she needs.

"I don't want to sleep alone,"

Dave reaches out his arms to her and she lays her head on his chest. Together they lay across on the couch. Dave softly caresses her back.

"Where would I be without you," she asks, listening to the sound of his heartbeat.

"In a nut house," he answers with a chuckle.

River chuckles at his remark.

"Would you come visit me?"

"I'd never leave your side," he says.

CHAPTER TWENTY-ONE

ANOTHER TWO WEEKS PASS before the doctor and Dave clear River to return to civilization. She's been home for three days. The past several months seem like a few years. Her house is a mess. Papers, books and files are scattered throughout her rooms. How did she get so disorganized? When did she get so disorganized? Is it because she got sick?

Sick, River laughs at that concept. *What makes one sick; mentally sick to the point they need some kind of medication?* She questions. *Doctors prescribe pills that are supposed to make me feel better. Iron pills yes, because I am anemic, vitamins yes, who doesn't need a little boost to their body? But pills to help her cope emotionally?* River shakes her head at the thought that she is sick.

I'm not sick, stressed- maybe; over worked- possibly.

As she puts away books back on the shelves and organizes files and paper work, River continues to rationalize with herself.

I had an emotional moment. She says to herself. *So my stalker turns out to be a reflection of myself when I was young, just mild hallucinations that had me somewhat mental. Who isn't a little bit crazy? With my loony uncle, ignorant students, and-and Dana. Okay, I realize why I had a "moment",* she uses air quotes. *Now that I realized that I had a moment, I can get back to life.*

She realizes that she may have some issues from the past that she hasn't quite resolved, but that doesn't make her sick; it makes her human. Considering that Dave has cancelled her classes for the fall semester, she has nothing but time on her hands.

Have nothing to do will drive me crazy, -she says to herself.

River looks at herself in the mirror. She looks at the structure of her face. River can't remember what she looks like when she was younger. Was that pretty girl really her or just a representative that was supposed to mean her?

The pretty girl's image is in the mirror. The image startles River, but River doesn't run. She takes a deep breath and looks at the image.

"You're here because I have to deal with Dana." River says out loud to the image.

River looks at the image strangely because staring at River is the younger version and that River mirrors the new River.

How are you mirroring me? River asks, afraid to move her lips.

River closes her eyes and focuses on the reason why the girl is there; one word: Dana. His name makes her shiver. River thought that he was out of her system. There was closure that day at his house. She was able to have dinner with him, eat seafood and drink cappuccino.

Why am I still looking at you? River asks the image in the mirror.

Again, thinking the words, not audibly saying them.

River takes in a deep breath and then walks away from the mirror. The quickly she returns, only to find the girl still there; mirroring her. River shakes her head. She leaves the mirror again and looks around her house; all clean, organized.

So now what? –she asks herself,

She walks through her living room looking at the photos that are hung on the wall. There is a photo of her mom, her maternal grandmother, and her grandfather. River smiles at the photos, and blows them a kiss.

"You don't think I'm sick, do you?" She asks the photos. She laughs.

"Yeah, I'm sick, talking to photos of dead people. Just like Grandma Shirley talking to the ceiling."

She takes in a deep breath and realizes that she has to make sure that Dana is behind her.

River makes a decision.

DANA HAD DECIDED TO take the day to work from home. He returned calls to clients, arranged meeting engagements, and worked on new designs. If a member from his dream team needed to speak with him, they would call, fax or send an email. With all that has happened within the past few months, Dana wants to be away from the office. The concept of River, her family, the concept of Katrina, Dana feels as if he lost his way. He has not been himself in the past few months. He doesn't use women as a means to an end. He doesn't smell imaginary flowers. He too needs to get his life back on track; focus on his business. These past several months have been a pandemonium of confusion. Dana wonders if he was going to have some kind of anxiety attack. However, needs to get back into his work. If River was the past, then leave her there. The next woman he dates; he wouldn't lead her on the way he did Katrina.

AS MUCH AS HE tries to forget her, it is a pleasant surprise to see standing outside his door. He was not expecting any one to stop by his home, especially not River. Dana doesn't know what to say. He can see that she is doing well; she looks serious and very somber as she stands before him. She wears black wide leg slacks, a brown button up shirt. Her hair is pulled back in a bun and she wears glasses on her face. She wears her four inch high heeled boots-in the summer time; only River. However, in spite of her stoic appearance, she looks good. The last time Dana had seen her she was lying in a hospital bed, her body weakened by stress.

"River, hi," he says.

"Hello," River replies.

"Ah, come in." Dana steps aside so River can enter inside.

As she enters, River is still amazed at how neat and organized his home is.

"Can, I get you something to drink?" he asks approaching her.

"Um, no thank you," she answers.

Her eyes set strongly on him.

"Ah have a seat, please." Dana says, suddenly nervous.

Dana slowly inhales and then exhales as he waits for River to take a seat on the couch. He doesn't know if he should sit next to her, her cold eyes are intimidating.

Why am I afraid of this woman, he asks himself.

As nervous as he was feeling, Dana is happy that she is here. He sits down on the opposite end of the couch.

"How are you feeling?" he asks.

"Well, thank you." River answers. "Um, I never got a chance to thank you for getting me to the hospital and for calling my family, thank you."

Her cold eyes are now soft; Dana smiles. He wants to touch her hands.

"Of course," he told her to her.

"Dana, there's a reason why I'm here," River replied. "I have something to say,"

"Okay," Dana leans forward.

River takes in a deep breath. She needs to find the right words to tell him that the pretty girl that is stalking her mind is his fault.

"Um, for some time, I have been depressed- for a few years actually. And the thing is I didn't know that I was depressed because I thought that I was a living what I thought was a perfectly normal life. I was not taking any anti-depressants or anything like that. I was not seeing a psychiatrist. So here I was thinking all is well. Yeah, I was a work-a-holic," she uses air quotes for that word, "but I was only a work-a-holic because unconsciously, I was depressed. Now a few months ago, I was being stalked by my subconscious and it was all your fault."

"Excuse me?" Dana asked, confused.

"Since I ran into you at Christie's and you started working on Reuben's club. I saw this this girl, this pretty girl with short hair, pixie cut, and I thought that she was stalker; some crazed fan, but it turns out to be me. I was hallucinating that girl; it was me from the past, repressed memories."

"Okay, where does this being my fault come in?"

"If I hadn't run into you that day, I would never have seen her."

"So it's my fault that you trippin'?" Dana asks skeptically.

"Yes,"

Dana shakes his head and chuckles.

River has gone mad.-he thinks to himself.

"Okay," Dana takes in a deep breath. "You seeing things is not my fault, it's your fault from repressing those memories in the first place. I didn't have anything to do with that."

"Yes, you did." River strongly states. "You are the reason why I suppressed them,"

"Because I broke up with you,"

"Now we're getting somewhere!" River replies.

Dana takes in another deep breath.

"River, you buggin' over something that was fifteen years ago; *fifteen years*! Girl, I don't know how many people I've been with in those fifteen years."

"Yeah, I know and one of them is one of my fans," River states very coolly.

Her eyes are cold shooting darts into Dana.

"That is beside the point." Dana snaps. "I could have been married and had least five kids within those fifteen years."

"Then why didn't you?" River questions.

Because none of them was you, Dana thinks to himself, but his reply was;

"Why didn't you get married?" he asks.

"Because I was mad at you for dumping me," River snaps back.

"River, you walk around all puffed up mad at me as if I did you so wrong. You act like I was a terrible boyfriend, as if I hit you or cheated on you. I was good to you."

"That's the whole point!" River exclaims.

River stands up. She is breathing hard. She tries to catch her breath. Slowly, she takes in a deep breath.

"That's the point, you were good to me and I was good to you. I was a good girlfriend, I didn't want or ask for anything and then out of the blue you just dump me, with no explanation. Just dump me as if I was trash. I loved you, I loved you so much."

Tears forms in River's eyes. She takes in another deep breath.

"Anyway, like I said." She said in a cool tone. "I was depressed, but it was unknown to me. Before I met you I dated several guys and they all ended up breaking my heart. All of them treated me as if I was nothing, but then you come along. You, someone like you would notice someone like me. Dana, you were the one that mattered. Seeing you that day at Christie's, all those memories came flooding back, I had to deal with them. The fact that I came here on my own today, shows my growth. That's all I have to say."

River turns around and walks to the door, but Dana quickly gets up and stops her. He knows now for sure that *this* is fate.

"River wait," Dana says.

River stops walking but she doesn't turn around. He wants to grab her and hold her but he doesn't.

"I loved you too," he confesses. "I loved you more than you will *ever* understand, but at the same time I couldn't do anything for you. I was not at a right place financially-,"

"I didn't need you to buy me anything," she says still not facing him. "I just needed you,"

"But for how long?"

River's face is wet from tears.

"Forever," she says.

The word cut deep like a knife in his chest.

"You leaving me was the straw that broke the camel's back. With you there were no gray skies. You made me laugh. You were my sweet love song. When you left, *she*, that River died leaving what you see today, this River. I've forgotten about love, about everything. I had forgotten what I had looked like. I didn't know that *she* was me."

"Just thinking that she was a stalker," Dana replies softly.

"Yes," River says.

She quickly wipes the tears from her face.

She turns around to face him; her cold eyes staring in to his.

"But like you said, I was *trippin'*, so I am going to trip out of here."

River turns around to leave, but again Dana stops her.

"I never stopped," Dana says.

"Never stopped what?" River asks now wishing that she never came.

"Loving you," he answers. "Like I said, I dated many, but there was something missing."

"What?"

"You," Dana said. "River they didn't have your charm, your personality, your smile. You had the prettiest smile." Dana places his hand on River's shoulder. "River, don't let me talk to your back."

River slowly turns around to face him. Her face is wet again with tears.

"I'm sorry," he confesses. "Letting you go was the biggest mistake in my life. Since that day at Christie's I've been thinking of you,"

"What about your girlfriend?" River asks.

"She's gone," Dana told her. "She was in the way,"

"In the way," River asked. Dana nodded. "In the way of what?"

"Fate," Dana tells her.

"Fate,"

"It's not a coincidence that we met up after all these years," Dana asks.

"Dana, I don't believe in fate," River tells him.

"Then you should. Why else would your subconscious be bothering you?"

"To deal with things,"

"Me," Dana said. "You have to deal with me and now you're here,"

"Fine, I've dealt with you," River states. "I said what I came here to say so now I have to go,"

"Okay, but before you go answer this one question,"

"What?" she snaps.

Dana waits a moment before he asks the question that he has wanted to ask for months. He looks deep into River's eyes, hoping to get past the icy stare.

"Do you still love me?"

River looks away. She takes in a deep breath. If she says no, then she knows that she would be lying to him and to herself and when she leaves his house, her friend would reappear. And if she says yes, then the doors will be opened and she is not ready to go through them. Dana takes a step closer to her. River takes a step back from him, not realizing that she is backing herself in to a corner. Tears fall from her eyes and down her cheeks.

Dana moves in closer. He cups her face in his palms. His touch alone sends chills through her body. Tears continue to stream down her face, Dana wipes them away.

"Don't cry," Dana says softly. "River, I'm so sorry, I should have never let you go."

The sound of his voice is like music, the sweet love song that he had once provided. Those words struck River's heart. Feeling warm; the ice that surrounds her heart is melting. River takes in a deep breath. He knows that she still loves him. River's hair falls from the bun and cascades down on to Dana's hands. At this moment, he wants to kiss her. She looks up at him and those icy eyes are no longer cold.

For a moment they just look into each other's eyes. River is being re-introduced to those brown eyes that captivated her. Finally Dana leans in to kiss her. He starts slowly, with a soft peck on her top lip then he kissed her bottom lip and then he kisses them her slowly and passionately. As nervous as she is, she is willing to allow Dana to kiss her.

For a long time, they kiss each other, both of them not wanting the other to stop. It feels good to be in each other's arms again. River opens her eyes to make sure that it is Dana that she is kissing. Dana stops kissing her long enough to pick her up in his arms and carry her into his room. He gently places her down on the bed. She looks up at him nervously.

"What's the matter," he asks kneeling down at her.
"I haven't done this in some time." She says then looks away shyly. "Not since you,"
Dana grins. He kisses her gently on the lips.
"Then we can pick up where we left off."

THEY MAKE LOVE AS if they had been together for years; moving instinctively with one another. Nothing seems foreign or strange. River misses the intimacy, someone holding her, loving her, kissing and caressing her. The same man that killed her is the same man that is reviving her. Dana keeps looking down at her, making sure that it is really River that he is making love to.

AFTERWARDS, THEY LIE IN each other's arms, holding one another and looking into each other's eyes. Dana leans in to kiss her gain.
"I love you," he said. "I love you so much,"
Afraid to move because neither of them wants to let the other go, Dana looks at River. He takes his finger and outlines her face.
"What are you doing?" she asks.
"Studying," he tells her.
"Studying," he says.
"Yes, you still look the same. Those same brown eyes, that smile. I'm just making sure that it's really you."
"It's me, just older," she jokes.
"Everything is still the same." Dana says, "your scent."
"My scent?" River asks with a chuckle.
"Yeah, the perfume you use. It has a floral scent, what is it?"
"Soap," River answers sarcastically.
"Soap," Dana replies, "Okay, but the only thing is different is how long your hair is."
River grins and then takes in a deep breath. Dana senses that something is on her mind.
"What are you thinking about?"
"Nothing," she says smiling. "I'm okay,"

"Yeah,"
"I don't want to close my eyes," she says.
"Why?"
"If I open them and you're not here; and this is just a fantasy-,"
"No," Dana says.
He leans forward to kiss her.
"This is very much real." Dana says. "Close them,"
River closes her eyes.
"Open them." Dana says.
She opens her eyes. He is smiling at her.
"I'm still here," he says.
She closes her eyes again; falling asleep in Dana's arms

RIVER OPENS HER EYES to the moon light shining its light through the window of the dark room. She wonders where she is but she is quickly reminded seeing the body that is sleeping beside her. Dana is sleeping soundly. They had reunited their love. She smiles as she thinks about how he told her that he loved her and that he will always love her. Suddenly she is struck with a case of fear.

What did I just do? She asked herself. *I just had sex, good old fashion sex for the first time in fifteen years. I did not come here to have sex. I came here to tell Dana that it was his fault that I was so called trippin'.*

Tonight was not supposed to happen.

She got distracted with his smooth words and soft hands and now she is lying naked in his bed, her body still tingling from his touch and powerful passion. Her body is not supposed to be throbbing with desire. Her heart was beating rapidly. She is afraid to move and even more afraid to stay.

Slowly and very carefully she slips out of bed and quickly gets dressed and quickly escapes from Dana's home. Once she is inside her car she drives quickly back to the safety of her home.

INSIDE HER HOUSE, SHE shuts and locks the door. Quickly she gets undressed and takes a shower allowing the hot water to wash away his scent, his smell, and his touch. Trembling, River tries to catch her breath and to calm her nerves down and hope to erase the past few hours.

Tonight should not have happened, she scolds herself.

How did she let her guard down? Why was she not able to resist Dana's kisses and touch?

DANA WAKES UP TO the sunlight shining through the same window that the moon light had shown through just a few hours ago. Before he opens his eyes, he smiles remembering everything. His true love has come back into his life. They had made love; sweet love. Still not opening his eyes, Dana reaches over in hopes of holding River in his arms, hoping to make love again, but as he reaches; he feels nothing but space. Dana doesn't want to open his eyes but he does; River is gone. He sits up and finds her gone. He grows nervous, maybe she got dressed and is fixing him breakfast like Katrina did, but there isn't the scent of bacon in the air or the smell of fresh coffee.

"River," he calls out.

There is no answer.

Dana gets up and put his pants on and looks for her. He knows that he is not dreaming about her because her scent is still lingering in the air and in his sheets. The fragrance is too strong for this to be just his imagination.

Why did she leave? He asks himself. *I thought that this is what she wanted.*

Dana doesn't understand. He told her that he loves her and she told him that she loves him so why would she leave? Quickly Dana showers and gets dressed. He is going to find her and he is not going to let her go again. It is a good thing that he knows where she works because he is going to the university to find her.

AS DAVE WALKS DOWN the hall of the university to his office, he hears River's voice. He didn't hear anything about her coming back to work. He peeks in her office and finds her talking to her faithful assistant Bonnie. River looks up and sees Dave and smiles at him.

"Good morning, Dr. Marouni," River says.

"Dr. Daniels, good morning," Dave said, entering inside. "Bonnie, hello,"

"Hi Dave," Bonnie said. "It's good to have River back, isn't it?"

Dave nods his head while keeping his eyes on River.

"Ah, Bonnie, that will be all," River says looking at Dave.

Bonnie smiles and leaves.

"I didn't know that you were coming back," Dave replies as he hugs River.

"Because I knew that you would object to me coming back so soon." River replies. "I talked with the Dean and I was able to get into fall schedule."

"So you're doing a full load?" Dave questions.

"No, just two classes this semester, and I didn't sign up for the history courses at the community college. I'm taking it easy Dr. Marouni."

Dave nods approvingly and then winks at River. She grins.

"I haven't heard from you since we came back," he says.

River nods her head.

"I ah, needed to clear my head," she tells him, then takes a deep breath.

She fights the images of Dana from the night before. Dave senses that she is hiding something.

"Anything you want to tell me?" Dave questions.

"Nope," River says taking in a deep breath.

Dave subtly looks River over.

"How are you feeling?" he asks.

"Good," she answers.

Dave looks at her trying to read her evasive demeanor.

"Dave, I only have two classes." River says.

She feels like pleading for his permission to come back to work.

"Okay, Riv, don't overdo it." Dave warns.

River crosses her heart and puts her right hand up.

"How's the writing?" He asks.

"It's coming," River answers.

Together they hug each other again.

"What's different about you?" he asks her. "You have this glow,"

River shrugs her shoulders.

"Don't know; rest," she answers.

"Excuse me, River there is a gentleman here to see you," Bonnie says.

"Send him in," River replies.

Bonnie leaves. Entering is the last person River thought would be in her office; Dana Wilson. Her composure is cool, but inside her body jumps as if she sees a ghost and her heart is now racing.

Now is the time for an anxiety attack, she says to herself.

Dave knows his friend too well. He is able to read past the cool composure and he notices the alarmed look in her eyes. River takes a deep breath. Dana looks at Dave, remembering the smooth Casanova from the hospital; the prince who was able to wake the sleeping beauty.

"Hi," Dave replied shaking Dana's hand. "Nice to see you again,"

"Yes," Dana said. "Uh, River, can I talk with you for a minute,"

"Well, I ah-, well Dave and I...," River stammers nervously, glancing at Dave.

Dave looks at River hoping to find shelter in his sapphire eyes, but he only smiles. He leans in and kisses River on the cheek.

"Call me later, okay," Dave says.

River grins and nods her head.

Dave walks away and shuts the door behind him. River can't move. She doesn't know if she should look at Dana or find something to do at her desk; hoping to brush him off.

Eventually she manages to take a few steps back and sits down on the edge of her desk.

"I've missed you this morning," Dana finally says.

"Ah, yeah, I start classes next week, so um-,"

Dana nods his head,

"Oh, so, ah, do you want to have lunch-,"

"I don't think I can, I have meetings today." She says.

"Dinner-,"

"Dinner, well, ah," River stammers, "I have to check my schedule-,"

"River," Dana stops her. "What's the matter?

"Nothing,"

"Are you sure?" he asks.

River waits before she answers.

"No, I'm not sure, last night-,"

"Don't tell me that you have regrets because last night was beautiful,"

"Last night should not have happened." She replies bluntly.

"What?" Dana asks surprised; almost insulted.

"Listen," River began, "I'm sorry, I didn't come over for that. I lost focus, I only came by because-,"

"Fate," Dana says. "Fate, River, fate brought you to me," Dana approaches her. "Last night meant that we were beginning to heal from the past,"

"I just came over to talk," River said.

"And we did," Dana agreed "And I told you that I still love you and you love me,"

River looks away. Dana walks closer to her. He is close enough to caress her face. He holds her face in his hands. As she closes her eyes to absorb his touch, tears falls slowly down her cheeks.

"River talk to me,"

"I can't do this," she whispers.

"Do, what?" he asks.

River doesn't answer. She looks at him with tears in her eyes.

"I'll do whatever it takes as long as I have you." Dana says.

River looks away but he takes his hand and gently glides her face to look at him.

"Tonight, you and I will have a nice dinner and we'll talk, okay."

River takes in a deep breath and reluctantly nods her head.

Dana grins, then gently kisses her on the lips.

CHAPTER TWENTY-TWO

DANA TOLD RIVER THAT he would pick her up at seven o'clock. Although she is excited, she hesitates to get ready. Instead of preparing for her date, River works on her book and organized lesson plans and she also did research for the *Bush Factor*. At six-thirty she decided to get ready.

SHE STANDS IN FRONT of the mirror examining herself. She can't believe that she is going out on a date, a real date; not some kind of business meeting. They would talk about what they expect out of whatever what is going to happen.

If I date you, then I want things to go this way, she says to herself. *And if you date me, then things can go that way.*

River decides to wear a pair of black wide leg slacks, a navy blue button up shirt. She decides to wear her hair down and she doesn't wear her glasses. For River preparing for a date didn't take long. River begins to remember how she would spend hours primping and preparing for a date. She would take a bath in scented oils and her makeup would be flawless, but this time; no makeup or scented oils; just a hot shower.

Her heart pounds when she hears the doorbell ring. She looks at her clock, it reads 6:57 pm; he is early. She waits a moment before she answers the door. River takes in a deep breath, then answers the door.

"Hi," she said.

"Hey," he said smiling to her.

"Come in," River said stepping aside.

"Our reservation is not for another hour so I thought we could talk or something," Dana said as he leans in to kiss River on the cheek.

He looks at her surroundings. He is impressed with her home. River's home is beautiful. The rich gold and maroon colors look as if royalty lives there instead of a writer.

"Would you like some coffee while we wait?" River asks.

"Sure,"

River leads Dana to her kitchen. He sits down while River prepares the coffee. Once the coffee is prepared, she pours two cups and place one in front of Dana.

"Would you like cream and sugar?" she asks.

"No, black is fine," he answers.

River sits down at the table. "

My coffee is strong, but Dave's is the best."

The charming prince, Dana comments to himself.

He wonders if there is more to their friendship. Was he more than just a work friend?

"I would show you around, but some areas are somewhat of a mess," River replies. "I had some work to do. Sometimes, Bonnie comes over and helps me to get organized before each semester. Besides there isn't much to see, except my office and the library that Dave built."

"A library?" Dana asks.

River nods her head matter of fact like.

"Would you like to see?"

"Sure," Dana says.

Caring coffee mugs, River leads him into the library that Dave created. He stands in awe at the large room filled with books.

"Have you read all these books?" he asks.

"Yeah," she answers with a chuckle. "Sometimes I would teach from them, if there was a book that I am particular to."

"The University lets you teach from a book you like?" Dana asks.

"I have to get it approved by the school board, if there is some kind of lesson in the story,"

"Like what?"

"*The Bluest Eyes,* by Toni Morrison, well that books deals with self-esteem, how a parent sees a child. A parent can look at a child and see their clothes wrinkled and fixated on that, but a kid, they need to see approval in their parent's eyes. So if a kid sees the irritated look in their parents' eyes and hears them fussing over a wrinkled shirt, in the kids eyes, they don't measure up, but in the parents' eyes they are making sure their kid looks good."

"Wow," Dana replies.

River shrugs and bashfully looks away.

"Toni Morrison if my favorite writer," River replies smiling. "The rest of the books are down stairs, those are the extra books that Dave and I couldn't fit in the library."

"There are more?" Dana asks surprised.

River nods her head.

Dana is amazed that one person lives in this large home. Her home is beautiful, not flashy. He can tell that nothing in here is cheap, but she lives humbly.

"Your home is nice," he compliments.

River shrugs her shoulders nonchalantly.

"It's okay, I'm not really at home to actually enjoy it," she chuckles.

"Why did you stay in Pittsburgh?" Dana asks.

"My family I guess; my grandmother, Reuben. After I got my Masters, I got hired at the University, and then at the community college; focused on getting my doctrine, and just never considered leaving."

"What do you do in your spare time?" Dana asks.

"I don't have spare time," River says with a chuckle. "I'm either writing a book, teaching, or writing for *The Bush Factor*. However considering recent events, I am only allowed to teach two classes. I am going to be so bored."

Dana laughs. River grins bashfully.

"Tell me about being an architect," she says.

"Fun, I mean really fun." Dana said with a grin. "Sometimes I feel like a little kid who gets to draw all day, designing buildings. One day, I would like to recreate Pittsburgh, ya know, restore some of the old buildings."

"Reuben's club is beautiful," River compliments.

"Thank you," Dana smiles. "That means a lot from you,"

"Was his club your biggest project?" River asks.

Dana nods. They return to the kitchen and sit down.

"Um, can I ask you another question, a personal question?" River asks.

"Your girlfriend, what did you see in her?"

Dana starts to laugh.

"Oh, man, well," he hesitated. "It was something that just happened."

"Just happened?" River inquires suspiciously.

"Yeah," Dana said. "Katrina was cool,"

"Did you love her?"

"I tried, she was a good woman, but like I said, she got in the way,"

River looks away. Dana gently places his hands on River's hand.

"River," he said softly. "For months I wondered if running into you was fate or coincidence. Like you, I was remembering things too, about us. It took a long time to get over you-what I thought was over you. But no matter how many women I dated something was missing, and that was you. They didn't have your fire. I still love you."

River grins, then removes her hand from Dana's, and notices that his coffee is now low.

"Would you like more coffee?"

"No," he says looking at her.

River looks away. She looks at her watch,

"We'd better get going,"

Dana nods his head, feeling the tension in the room.

DANA DRIVES TO THE restaurant and parks the car. He looks at River and smile.

"What?" she asks.

"I'm just happy that you're here, that we're here."

River grins. Together Dana and she enter the restaurant. As they approach the hostess station, River is greeted by the host.

"Good evening, Dr. Daniels, we have your usual table available."

River looks at Dana.

"We're here for the reservations for Wilson,"
The host looks down at his ledger and grins.
"Ah yes, right this way,"
River and Dana follow the host to a small private table for two. They sit down and listen to the host recite the evening soups and specials.
"Dr. Daniels, would you like your usual drink?"
"Yes, that will be fine," River answers.
The host nods his head then looks at Dana,
"What can I tell the server to get for you?"
"Whatever she is having," Dana answers.
The host nods his head,
"Luke, will be your server tonight," the host informs them and then leaves.
River glances at Dana, then looks through her menu.
"You come here a lot?" he asks with a smirk on his face.
"I've been here a few times," she answers modestly.
The two share a chuckle.
"Actually, I come here at least once or twice a month, with Dave or my publisher."
Dave, there goes that name again.
"Um, let me ask you something," Dana asked. "You and Dave, ah- you two-,"
"No," River said with a laughs. "No, Dave is my friend, a dear friend, my best friend. He is a colleague, a mentor. Dave is very special to me."
Dana nods his head. He likes what he heard.
"He seems to be a cool guy."
"He's the best," River says looking at Dana.
The waiter approaches bringing the drinks. There is no need for formalities, because River knows the waiter.
"Give us a minute to look at the menu, Luke," River says politely.
Luke grins and quickly leaves.
"I'd like to make a toast," Dana says holding up his drink. "To fate and what is destined to come,"
River toasts with Dana.

AFTER DINNER, DANA TAKES River to the Point State Park, affectionately known as The Point. Together they walk along the field. Dana grows nervous walking along side River. He feels like he is on his first date in high school. He wants to hold her hand, but his hands are clammy. Dana can't understand why he is so nervous, just the night before he just made passionate love to her and now he is afraid to touch her. River is also feeling nervous because this is her first date in fifteen years. He is the man that she has once known, and now she was about to enter into a world that she left over a decade ago. She is allowing herself to get to know him again. River wonders if he has changed at all or was he the same sweet Dana; he man who captured her heart.

"What's on your mind?" he finally asks.

"A lot of things," she answers.

"Like what?" Dana asks.

"That is my first date in fifteen years and I really don't know what to say or do,"

"Just do what feels natural," Dana said.

River doesn't respond.

"Our break up must have been really bad for you to not want to date for so long."

River finds a vacant bench and sits down.

"You never thought about getting married or having children?" Dana asks, sitting down beside her.

"After you broke up with me, I couldn't be with another. If I couldn't have you, then I didn't want anyone."

He takes in a deep breath and tries to take in the concept of her living a life of solitude all because he was no longer around.

River continues.

"I focused my attention work, from school to writing. I centered my life on them. I didn't focus on my looks, threw my makeup away, and changed my wardrobe. I didn't want to look pretty or desirable. I didn't want men to come and flirt getting me off track."

"River, you are naturally beautiful. You couldn't hide your beauty if you tried." Dana replies. "I wished I was as focused as you were. Instead, I dated women trying to fill the void of not having you."

River looks at Dana. Although she was touched by his words, she doesn't show any emotion.

"I thought about you a lot." Dana confesses. "So many things reminded me of you. I remember when I saw your first book in the stores, I was really happy for you. Then when I saw you at Christie's, I had no idea that you were Reuben's niece,"

She listens to Dana, wondering if she willing to go down that road again.

"I wondered if *this* was fate but what confirmed my curiosity was you yesterday. When you almost left, I couldn't let you go, not without telling you how much I love you."

"Dana, I don't believe in fate," River states.

"Then why are we here?" Dana asks. "Fate brought us back together again. It was fate that caused us to be together last night. Think about it River, last night was your first time in fifteen years and it was with me, the last guy you made love to."

"If this is so right, then why does it feel so weird?"

"Because you haven't dated in so long."

Dana stands up and extends his hand to River. She takes his hand and he gently pulls her to him and he wraps his arms around her.

"I know that I am going to have to walk through flames to gain your trust again, but that is a walk that I am willing to go through."

CHAPTER TWENTY-THREE

"RIVER I WAS THINKING, that maybe we can go on vacation," Dana suggests to River one Friday evening.

Together they sit outside on the balcony at Dana's house.

It's been a month since they reconciled-the word that Dana uses. They spend Friday and Saturday evenings together. Dana is persistent. He emails her frequently throughout the day, calls her in the evening. The attention is flattering to River, but she is not quite sure how to handle everything. After fifteen years she is actually dating. After fifteen years she has a- boyfriend. That term sounds very juvenile. River doesn't think of that term. She tells herself that she is seeing someone. How does one date? They call each other on the phone, spend time together. River remembers that concept; she remembers it all too well. River remembers not getting work done, not getting writing done, not studying. When she was younger, she had all the time in the world, she enjoyed writing, but she didn't have an established writing career. She was in school but flunking out of community college, and as far as work, she was a hostess at a restaurant. Now she is a successful author and an excellent professor. How does she manage a dating life as well?

Dana has made many references of the old River. How she looks, how she dressed, her laugh. To Dana, this River seems too serious. During dinner, she would discuss work, not dreams and goals. Dana wants the old River; he misses that River. As they sit on the balcony, Dana looks at River. He wonders what's on her mind. What is she thinking? Knowing her, school or writing.

They haven't made love since that first time. River wants to wait until she's ready.

Ready for what? Dana asks himself.

It's not about the sex, but Dana wants the old River that used to lounge around waiting for him after a long day. He wants to hold her, fall asleep with her in his arms. River has yet to spend the night. Her reasons for leaving are she has to write or study for her lesson.

○

"A vacation?" she asked.
Dana nods.
He refills her glass of wine.
"You know, maybe this weekend."
"That's too sudden," River replies, sipping the glass.
"Sudden?" Dana questioned. "What is sudden about a vacation?"
"Because I have to work this weekend." she answers.
"You're working this weekend?" Dana asks doubtfully.
"Yes, I have to work on my article for Mr. Bush," River answers.
"River you're always working," Dana comments.
"I'm a writer," River said. "I don't get a break. Besides, I took enough of a vacation with this semi-medical leave."
Dana sighs.
"Don't sigh," she says. "
"River, I want to spend time with you." Dana said.
"We're spending time together now," River replies.
"No, more than Friday and Saturday nights, I want you more than via email."
"Dana, we need to take things slow. We just started dating, Dana, we're still getting to know each other,"
"River, we already know each other," Dana states. "I know you, you know me,"
Taking in a deep breath, she looks at Dana, then stands up and walks back into the house. Dana follows.
"River," Dana calls out after her.
"Dana, it's complicated,"
"Complicated?" he asked. "What is complicated about us? You and me-,"
"I haven't dated anyone in over ten years. No dates, no good night kiss, nothing. I am not going to rush something

because it's you. Plus, I don't know you. I know the Dana I dated years ago. I don't know this Dana."

"River, I'm the same person. You are the one on the other hand that is acting all weird and distant, stand-offish. The River from before would sing off key and not care, she would just enjoy that song. You would go outside in the rain and dance, not caring who sees you. No one saw that River coming, but whenever she did, her smile would light out the room, causing everyone to stop and take notice-,"

"I'm not her," River snaps. "I'm not that River. Dana I've changed, my whole life changed."

"You changed because of me,"

"Not just you," River said. "I changed for a lot of reasons, but my life now is not about being unpredictable. I'm not that River that sings and dances in the rain. I don't light up rooms. I am the River that reads books and writes them. I am the River that teaches. I am about structure. I need structure and discipline. I can't be that River you would want me to be, because she doesn't exist anymore. I told you this, us, is new, very new, the concept is new."

"River," Dana pleads.

"Dana, all my life I wanted to be a writer and in case my writing career didn't take off, I was able to teach, I am living the life I wanted. Now granted, I have become somewhat stand-offish, but I am living my dream."

"I don't want to disrupt the life you build," Dana said. "You are a very successful woman. I just want to be with you. I want to love you. I want to give you everything that I wanted to give you then. Then I couldn't commit, because of my pride. Now, I am putting the pride aside and letting you know that I love you-,"

"You loved the old me, you don't know the new me,"

"Okay, so let me get to know her. Let's do things together, for starters, let's start telling people-,"

"Not yet," River interrupted. "I still need time to soak all this in," she sighs. "I have to go,"

"Where are you going?" Dana asks. "Don't run,"

"I need to-," she hesitates. "I'll call you later,"

Quickly she grabs her car keys and walks out of the door. As she closes the door behind her she hears Dana say:

"I love you,"

River wanted to go back inside and tell him that she loves him too, but pride doesn't let her surrender. Instead she walks to her car and drives home. Nothing matters right now, because from this conversation she may be walking away from a beautiful relationship.

He wants to pick up where they left off. How can he pick up there? So much has happened in the past fifteen years; Presidents, wars, technology. He wants the unpredictable and energetic River. The girlfriend that had the electrifying smile and eyes that danced whenever she laughed. River however is slowly trying to get know herself again. She needs to know Dana as well as herself. This concept of dating is strange. Having a significant other in her life, to call her throughout the day, take her to dinner in the evening is strange, it's an unfamiliar concept.

Did River miss having someone special give her a good night kiss? Did she miss someone giving her flowers simply because that person was thinking of her? She didn't have a person's eyes to gaze into promising them her eternal love. What River had was her decision to never love again but that is because she had been hurt. How does she manage her career that she truly loves and have a successful relationship?

Dana wants to love her, the old her. River wants nothing to do with the old her.

RIVER SITS IN HER LIVING room that night, she cannot sleep. As she sits on her couch, she looks out the window staring at the outside thinking about the pretty girl. Is she gone for good?

Life is so complicated, she thought to herself. *Why did Dana have to come back into her life and why in the world did I sleep with him?*

Making love to him was emotional suicide. Life seems so much easier hiding. River needs to talk to someone, to a friend. Someone who would understand what she is feeling. She can talk to Jennifer, but as a widow her pain is somewhat different. River would call Dave, but after all that Dave has done for her within' the past few months, she doesn't want to burden him. Then River realizes the one person who knows what she may be going through; her beloved grandmother. Grandma Shirley is the one person who has been there for River since the very beginning. River decides to wait until the morning to talk with her Grandmother.

SHIRLEY IS HAPPY TO see River early Saturday morning. Shirley prepares breakfast, bacon, eggs, home fries, and coffee.

"Grandma, I don't need all this food,"

"You're too skinny," Shirley states.

River grins and watches as her grandmother prepares breakfast.

"What's the matter, baby?" Shirley asks.

River paces the floor as she tells her grandmother everything. She starts by telling her about the pretty girl who had been haunting her and what that girl represents. Then River informs her about Dana.

"Baby that's wonderful," Shirley exclaims.

"No grandma, this is not wonderful," River replied. "He wants that goofy River, not the mature and sophisticated River."

Shirley chuckles.

"Baby, sit down,"

River sits down at the kitchen table.

Breakfast is ready and she fixes River a hefty plate. River almost protests to the amount of food on her plate, but she doesn't. Instead she sips her coffee.

"Listen, your life has changed. You are not the same person you were when you were in your twenties. You have dramatically made a success out of yourself, as to oppose the child you were who always had their head in the clouds. But what I think that Dana wants is for you to be free. Don't think because you're not disciplined for a day that you are losing yourself. It is okay to run away for a week and just enjoy each other. It's okay to play hooky from work every now and then.

River, baby, don't fight love. River, you should have seen how nervous he was when you were in the hospital."

River closes her eyes and sighs. Shirley sits beside River.

"He might be mad at me now."

"No, baby," Shirley says as she softly caresses her face. "Tell him that you love him, it will be all right."

River grins then wraps her arms around Shirley.

"Grandma, I love you,"

"I love you too, Angel."

AFTER BREAKFAST, RIVER LEAVES her grandmother's house. She thinks about what Shirley said. Maybe Dana and she are meant to be. Maybe Dana and she can live happily ever after. Just them in a nice home, she will be reading and writing while he is sketching a new design for a building.

Without realizing it, River drives to Dana's house. She hesitates to get out of the car. How can he be so sure about his feelings? As she sits in the car, she is surprised to see the front door open. Slowly River gets out of the car and slowly walks to the door. She enters inside to find Dana standing on the other side.

"Hi," River said as she shut the door.

"Hi," he says. "I'm glad that you're here,"

"About yesterday," she begins, "I want to make sure that everything will be okay, because I don't have the energy to have another nervous breakdown or an anxiety attack,"

"River, I love you." Dana says with a grin.

"You don't know the new me," she replies softly.

"It doesn't matter," Dana said. "You, I love you."

Dana grins and gently pulls River into his arms. For a long time, they enjoy the embrace. After some time, she steps back.

"I have to go, I have to work."

"Okay," he says to her.

"I'll call you later," she says.

Dana nods his head. He leans in and kisses her. She smiles, then leaves.

A WEEK LATER DAVE and River decide to spend time together at his home. He orders Chinese food and they sit and talk. Through the past few weeks, he noticed that her demeanor has changed. He is curious to know if Dana Wilson is officially back in her life, but Dave gives River her space. When she is ready to share everything she will.

As they dine on shrimp fried rice and egg rolls. River is relaxed. She is laughing and smiling, a side of River that Dave had begged to see a few months ago while on the book tour. Has this new man brought life back into River?

"Rumor has it, that you didn't give homework this weekend," Dave jokes.

River casually shrugs her shoulders.

"Students are saying that old lady Daniels has gone soft." Dave continues to tease.

River chuckles.

"Well, per you and the rest of the world, I was told to take it easy." She replies to him. "The last thing I need in my life right now is you and the world nagging me on being over worked."

Dave nods his head and sips on a beer.

"So you're actually following the doctor's orders?" he asks suspiciously.

River nods. He looks at her suspiciously. River grins and looks away.

"River, I know you. I know when you're being coy, and I know when you're dodging."

"Dodging-," River replies.

"River-,"

"Dave, seriously," she laughs.

"Just out of curiosity, have you settled things with that architect?" he asks.

"Yes," she answers coolly.

Dave's sapphire blue eyes look at her intensely. She grins.

"We've been dating for a little over a month."

"Okay," Dave replies. "What led to this?"

River shrugs her shoulders.

"I went to talk with him after you and I came back from the cabin. One thing led to another and we realize that we still care for each other."

Dave nods his head approvingly.

"Are you happy?" he asks.

"I think so," she answers, taking a bite out of her egg roll.

"You think so?" Dave questions.

"The attention is nice. Dana wants to pick things up where we left off. I'm not that person. I don't think he gets it. If I lose sights of who I am now, will lose all that I have accomplished? Dave, I accomplished everything with hard work and discipline."

"You shut out the world," Dave replies.

"I know, I know, but looking at my life now, I am living my dream. Maybe not having a man in my life is what I needed to get what I wanted."

"You can honestly say that you were happy?" Dave asks skeptically.

River thinks.

"Yes," she answers. "I love teaching, I love writing. I love the nights I spend with Jennifer and I love spending time with you. How do I fit in a man?"

"If you want a man you make it work."

"He wants the old River, you know that goofy and fickle River."

"That River wasn't so bad," Dave replies.

"No, she wasn't but, this River, the me now, I like her. She's pretty cool."

"She is, but she was created because of pain,"

"Yes, and I have accepted that. I am dealing with the pain; the loss of love ones. But I still have to work and I enjoy what I do."

"Now that there is no more pain, will there be a new River?"

"You make me sound like a schizophrenic," River said with a chuckle.

"Well-," he teases.

River laughs.

"Okay, okay, all joking aside. Having a social life, not considering you spending time with me or Jennifer or your family, is okay, that old River that lost focus because she didn't have structure. You can have a balance. You can go to work, and have a man, it's about priorities. Work throughout the week and on the weekends, date, ya know what I mean."

River nods her head.

AFTER DINNER RIVER AND Dave sit on the couch. She is not ready to go home yet. Instead she rests her head on his chest and they talk.

"Life seems weird now," she says softly.

"Why do you say that?" Dave asks.

"Because things are so different from a year ago," she answers.

"Maybe you are evolving into another River," Dave replies.

River sits up and shakes her head.

"I don't need any more Rivers," she laughs.

Dave laughs.

"What do you need?" Dave asks.

River thinks for a moment.

"You," she says. "Right here, holding me, accepting me for all that I am."

"I'm right here," he says.

CHAPTER TWENTY-FOUR

IT HAS BEEN TOO long since they spent time together. River and Jennifer have missed each other tremendously. Since then, River has explained the sudden departure. Like a good friend, Jennifer listened to River as she explained everything.

"Suffering from a broken heart," Jennifer said.

River nodded her head.

"Did you know?" Jennifer asked.

"I knew that I was not going to allow myself to be distracted ever again," River answered.

"How did love distract you?" Jennifer asked.

River takes in a deep breath.

"It was the course of events, Jenny. I just died.

Jennifer looks at River with tears in her eyes. River is moved by Jennifer's compassion.

"You are so young to have experienced that much pain," Jennifer said as she quickly wiped the tears from her eyes.

"My dramatic change may have killed me, but I know one thing good came out of it." River said.

"What?" Jennifer asked.

"I would have never met you," River told her.

River's words caused Jennifer to gasp. Tears poured from Jennifer's eyes.

"You friendship means the world to me." Jennifer said.

They hug each other and resumed their weekly get together of food, international coffee, wine, and literature.

FAST FORWARD TO NOW. River and Dana have been together now for three months. All of her close and personal friends now know that Dana and she are back together. Dana has spent Thanksgiving and Christmas with River and her family. Within the three months, the doctor has allowed River to go back to work fulltime. River didn't waste time getting back to her demanding schedule. As far as her writing, that emotionless book is a bestseller and the one that she worked on while she was at the cabin with Dave is on its way to the book stores. Everything seems to be going well, except Dana's constant nagging about relaxing; not working so much, spending time with him. River spends Friday night with him, but considering her full time schedule, she feels like Dana is a duty, instead of a promising relationship.

O

TONIGHT, RIVER IS WITH Jennifer. Tonight they dine on shrimp, scallops and rice pilaf, and white wine. River's cell phone rings. She rolls her eyes when she sees who is calling.
"Is everything alright?" Jennifer asks.
River sighs and rolls her eyes. Jennifer chuckles.
"Trouble in paradise?" she asks.
River doesn't reply. She looks at Jennifer, shakes her head and sighs.
"I told him that it's literature night." River complains. "Shrimp, wine, and Zora."
Jennifer laughs.
Jennifer looks at River hoping that she would elaborate more on her relationship. She sees that River is deep in thought.
"What is on your mind?" Jennifer asks.
River waits a moment and then looks at Jennifer.
"Nothing," River said, refocusing her attention on Jennifer, she grins, then sip her wine.
Jennifer nods her head intuitively.
"Jennifer, let me ask you, when you were young, before you met your husband, you dated, right?"
"Not like this generation. I met people at dances. Every Friday and Saturday my friends and I went to fire halls. They would have dances there. I met nice people, men, women, and we socialized. There were a few boys I met that I liked and they liked me, but we didn't really date, some would come visit me at home. Some walked me home or to the soda shop."
"How did you know that Michael was the one?"

"Cause he told me," Jennifer said with a laugh. "He saw me at one of those dances and said, 'My name is Michael Murdox,' I introduced myself. He asked me to dance and later the evening he said to me, 'I'm going to marry you,' I laughed. 'You don't even know me,' but every weekend he somehow met me at a dance, and after a month, he put a ring on my finger, and said, 'You're Mike's girl, and you're going to be my wife,'."

"But how did you know, that *he,* was the one. He knew with you apparently, but you. How did you know?"

"Because he liked me, he made me laugh. He made me feel good. When we danced he didn't try to be fresh. He opened doors for me. Shook my father's hand, addressed my mother as ma'am. I liked that in a man. He took care of me." Jennifer smiled.

She looks at River,

"River," Jennifer coaxes.

"He's not allowing me to be me." River says.

"River when we met, you already had a guard up. I had no idea of what you had been through. Are you afraid of getting hurt again?"

River shakes her head.

"Afraid of losing focus on all that I have accomplished. What if I get so distracted? I enjoy my life. I am destined to a life of being lonely."

"There is a difference between being alone and lonely." Jennifer says.

Jennifer sips the wine.

"When Michael died, I thought I would die. To lose the love of your life, the pain is beyond; it still hurts. I didn't want to marry again not because no man would ever feel that void, but because I am enjoying my life; not as the Widow Murdox, but as someone who has more liberties than one who is married."

"What do I do?" River asks. "I have a man, but my man is not allowing me the life that I have grown accustomed to. I look forward to our nights. Dana is ringing my phone asking what I'm doing. I'm writing, or working, or-,"

"It sounds like you don't love him as much as you thought you did. That maybe all you needed was closure. But would you date if he was not around?"

"Maybe, I enjoy going out to dinner and a kiss good night," River grins, then sips her wine. "You know what he got me for Christmas, a white gold bangle bracelet."

"That's nice," Jennifer says.

"Dave brought me the collection of Leo Tolstory," River grins. "I don't want a bracelet. Leo; now-,"

Jennifer smiles.

"A bracelet is nice," Jennifer says.

"It is nice, but Tolstory, do you know what I can learn from him? The themes and the metaphors," River smiled. "Jenny, when was the last time you saw me with a bracelet? I can buy my own bracelet."

"You can buy your own Tolstory," Jennifer points out.

"Yes, but as a Christmas gift, get me what I want, not what you think I want."

"So Dave brought the obvious gift. I get it. Do you think you are in love with Dave?"

"No, but the old River would have worn that stupid bangle and spent my rent money on an outfit to match."

Jennifer laughs.

"The new River," River begins. "can't wait to get in to Leo with you, eat some hot wings, and drink red wine."

Jennifer smiles.

"Talk with your man," Jennifer encourages.

THE NEXT DAY DANA is with River at her home. Considering that River is not much of a cook. Dana prepares dinner for the two of them. River sips on a glass of red wine.

"How was your day?" he asks. "Whose life did you change with your teaching?"

"Everyone's," River answers. "I threatened to fail them if they didn't turn in their papers."

Dana laughs.

"Are you really a mean teacher?"

"I've been told that I am tough, but I can be fair,"

"So you are a mean teacher." Dana states with a laughs.

River shrugs her shoulders.

WHILE THEY EAT DINNER, Dana shares the adventures of his day at the architecture firm. After an hour or so, River found herself oddly comfortable with him. There isn't talk about the old River, or how she used to be. He talks with her as if he is enjoying this River. This River seems to have interested him. As she listens and laughs with Dana as he shares the woes about today's client, who is meticulous and anal, she found herself enjoying his company.

They affectionately touch one another, as if his hands belong on the small of her back, or her hand on his knee. Looking into each other's eyes and laughing is no longer unfamiliar forced. For the first time since they started dating again, River finally feels comfortable. Is Dana accepting this River?

She looks at Dana. He smiles.

"What?"

"I am wondering, is the offer for that vacation still on the table?" she asks.

"Of course," Dana says smiling. "What changed your mind?"

"I have a week before the spring semester begins, and maybe we can take some time away." She grins.

Dana leans in and kisses her; his River is back.

CHAPTER TWENTY-FIVE

THE AQUAMARINE COLORED OCEAN sparkles like diamonds. The white colored sand looks like plush wall to wall carpet. The sky is practically white and the sun looks like a crystal ball just hanging in the middle of the sky. This is the look of paradise. She stands on the balcony looking over the tropical island, while he looks throughout the suite. The last time she stood on a balcony, she was being stalked by her thoughts but now, she was spending a romantic weekend with her boyfriend, the boyfriend that triggered the hallucinations. River turns around and sees Dana tipping the bell boy. She turns back around to look at the view.

How did she get here, on a tropical island? Why is she not at home working on a tough assignment to give her students, or working on a book? As a matter of fact today is Sunday, why is she not devouring her grandmother's fried tilapia, homemade macaroni and cheese, mouth-watering buttered biscuits, and snap green beans? Why is her cell phone not ringing from Mr. Bush wanting an article for the *Bush Factor*? Why is she not on the internet looking up a new book for her and Jennifer to read and study? Why is she not at Christie's eating hot wings and writing? Because she has allowed love to come in and change her.

This River is not wearing a pant suit, but blue jeans and a t-shirt, something that she hasn't worn in years. This River is wearing her hair down instead of in a bun.

River would give anything to be sitting by her laptop typing another best seller, or grading papers with a sinister smile knowing she holds the students academics career in her hands. She gave in and is taking a vacation. She is regretting that she agreed to a vacation.

She loves Dana. There is no more denying that concept, but she doesn't want to lose herself and right now it seems that she was losing herself, giving up her life to please him. She has been giving in to please almost every man in her life, from Reuben's nagging about that silly club, to Dave, making her open up and sharing whatever feelings that are bottled inside. And now, Dana on this vacation,

"*Trust me, River*", Dana's words echo in her head. *I love you River.*"

She sighs and shakes her head.

It's is just a vacation, it is just one week, she says to herself. River is an organized person.

With her resourceful assistant, Bonnie Onesi, one week won't off set her agenda and everything will be in order when she gets back. Jennifer won't miss their weekly book meeting and Mr. Bush knows that River always delivers a good article before the deadline. Her writing- she doesn't have an idea right now. Maybe something on the island can inspire her. And Grandma will definitely fry more tilapia.

He wraps her arms around her, bringing her back from her thoughts.

"What is on your mind?" he asks, kissing the back of her neck.

"Nothing," she says taking a deep breath and inhaling the cool air.

"Liar," Dana says with a chuckle. "You're thinking about work, tormenting them poor students,"

River chuckles.

"No, just enjoying the scenery."

"Let's go to get something to eat."

"You grab a table. I'll catch up with you in a minute. I have a few phone calls to make,"

River turns around to face him.

"River, no work, okay?"

She crosses her heart with her index finger and raises her right hand.

"Scouts honor, I promise," she says.

Dana kisses her and then leaves the hotel suite.

DANA WATCHES RIVER WALK through the pool area. River doesn't notice the men staring at her. She wears her hair down. It hangs down her back. She wears a white boat neck long sleeve shirt and white wide leg pants. Her caramel colored skin shines under the crystal ball. The looks from the men don't faze her. Dana notices the men looking. He doesn't know if he should be offended or proud of his beautiful woman. He chuckles to himself, as the men ignore their girlfriends and wives. As for the women, some look at her with scornful eyes. Who this woman with the natural beauty?

"What are you smiling at?" River asks Dana as she sits down at the table.

"You," he said. "Every man is looking at you,"

She shrugs her shoulders and casually glances at her menu.

"Life of a star," he says.

"Oh please," River said. "I am no star."

"You don't think that people down here don't read,"

"Yeah, they read, but writers are not those celebrities. We can go to the grocery store to buy butter. We're not high profile,"

"Okay, Ms. Humble." Dana said. "Well, I am going to get some of this tropical fruit."

AS THEY EAT, RIVER and Dana plan the adventures they are going to do while on their vacation; scuba diving, sightseeing. The upcoming events seem exciting to Dana. Just he and his girl, enjoying their sweet vacation, but River has other plans. She is going to break up with Dana. All this was too much, he is disturbing her. No business calls on vacation, no working while looking at the tropical sun rise. River's hands are itching to grade a student's paper. Instead she is here looking at Dana inhale a melon pear. Then again if she ends things with Dana, will she be forced to deal with her, that pretty girl that haunted her for so many months? Will she be denying herself love and bury herself in her work? But she is not denying herself love; she'd rather be working right now. Everything seems normal back home.

Why isn't he worried about his business? He is a business owner, and how can he be here not wondering if everything is running smoothly at his firm. Is his staff that reliable? She been at his firm, his staff seemed responsible, but seriously, the boss has gone away to an island drinking Bahamas' Mamas.

In any event, River is going to get through this vacation, scuba dive, see the sights, have a couple of nights of good sex, and that should hold her over for the next fifteen years. By then she will be in her fifties and no man will want her, not Dana or the island men staring at her.

DANA AND RIVER GO on a scuba adventure with their tour guides Mark and Angie. As they dive into the water, River is captivated by the rainbow color from sea creatures. It looks like another world down below. The fish swim along, not paying attention to their intruders. The star fish sits comfortable along the floors. At this moment, River cannot have been happier, it is quiet, no one to bother her. She imagines herself as a mermaid living under the sea and only coming to land whenever she pleases. Dana observes as she swims; making new friends with colorful sea creatures. Dana is falling more and more in love with her. He thinks about building a beach house where they can come down and just enjoy life.

DINNER TIME, DANA AND River sit in an island restaurant.
"So are you enjoying yourself?" Dana asks.
"Yes," River said, eating shrimp cocktail.
She sips her wine,
"Now it's my turn. There are a few historical sites I want to see. Maybe we can go tomorrow, all right."
"Okay," Dana agreed willingly. "But in the meanwhile, let's have some quiet time, we can take a walk on the beach. There is something that I want to talk to you about."
River nods her head,
What in the world does he have to talk about? River says to herself.

THE NEXT DAY, RIVER and Dana go to a thrifty souvenir shop. She loads up on tacky collectables. Then River and Dana find the shops for the rich, filled with paintings and sculptures, clothes and jewelry.

"River, what are you going to do with all that stuff?" Dana asks.

"It's not for me. It's for Dave, Reuben, my gram and Jennifer, Jim, Mr. Bush,"

"Everyone but yourself,"

"What am I going to do with all this stuff?" River asks with a chuckle. "It makes me happy to know that I can give to my family and friends."

"For a moment, I thought you were becoming high maintenance,"

"Me, no, there isn't much to maintain with me," River told him. "Just give me my books and I am set,"

BACK AT THE HOTEL, River sets everything down that she bought down and collapses on the bed. Dana sits beside to her.

"You okay?" he asks taking off her shoes.

"Yeah, just bit tired."

"Yeah, well spending money can drain a person out," Dana teased. "What's it like?"

"What is what like?"

"Being rich?" Dana asked with a chuckle.

"Excused me?" she asked sitting up.

"You're a millionaire, right?"

"Is that any of your business?" River asks, offended.

"No," Dana said feeling silly. "I don't mean to get all in your bank account. I'm curious, not on how much you make, but your clout; success. We go out to dinner and the staff runs to you; they know you."

"That's because I'm a regular. It's nothing to do with my success."

"How many people buy their uncle a night club, maybe one; Oprah."

"Oprah," River replied. "Listen I am not in *Forbes* magazine or *Business Weekly*. I am successful; that is because of my work, I'm a work-a-holic, so I am told. Having money comes in handy because yeah, I can buy what I want, I can take care of my grandmother or invest in something for my uncle. But if I was stupid, then I am a rich fool. Knowledge is the one thing that matters to me."

"Would you have all this if you and I wouldn't have broken up?"

River looks away.

"Probably not, but my life now is something that I always have wanted, to be a successful author."

"So breaking up with you, do you think I did you a favor?" he asks.

"That is a question that needs not to be asked." River replied. "but you said that we're fate, maybe it was meant for us to break up, only to be back together. Considering that we're both changed peopled now."

"I haven't changed." Dana replies.

Is he questioning the new River again? If so, River doesn't have the energy to defend herself.

"I thought you like the new me," River said.

"I do," Dana said with a smile. "We're having fun," he leans in and kisses her. "I just don't want to be a priority, like your work. I don't want to be scheduled. As your man, I want to be a part of your life."

She grins.

"I want to lie down for a while," River said.

"Okay."

Together they lay down upon the bed and within moments, River drifts off into dream land. She dreams of the pretty girl. She is standing before River, they are face to face. River couldn't believe that she was once that brave to wear her hair that short. River circles around the girl making sure that she is who she claims to be.

"What's the matter?" the girl asks, smiling.

River doesn't respond; she continues to look at the girl. She stares long and hard in to the same brown eyes; those beautiful sparkling eyes.

"You don't believe I'm you." The pretty girl said.

"You were me," River corrects.

River stretches out her hand to touch the girl to see if she is real. She is able to touch her face and her arms. River then takes in a deep breath and exhales slowly.

"I'm real," the pretty one said.

"You're, you're so different." River replies.

"No, you're the one that is different." The girl says. "You changed because-,"

"I don't need a lecture," River interrupts sharply. "I've heard it from Dave, Grandma, and now my boy-,"

River catches herself.

"Boyfriend," the pretty one finishes River's sentence. "Dana is wonderful,"

River shrugs her shoulders.

"Oh, come on, don't act like that. Dana is still the same, sweet, caring, the man that listens, make us laugh,"

"He's a pest," River replies coolly.

"No," the pretty girl responds.

There is pain in her pretty eyes.

"Dana is everything we need." The pretty one says.

"He may have been everything that you needed, but for me. I am happy."

"I want to live." The pretty said almost pleading. "You killed me,"

"It was the best thing for us. If you lived, I would not be where I am today. Because of you, I was silly, fickle and just stupid. Now, I am rich, my boyfriend- our boyfriend, questions the value of my success,"

The pretty girl's eyes look distant as if she is looking at something. She looks back at River with a smile.

"Who would have thought, that I would be a successful author. I mean, I dreamed of it, but actually living my dream?" the old River says smiling.

"Wrong, I am living the dream," the new River corrects sternly. "You would have never made it. Now because of you, I am dating a man that I am not sure if I want to be with, but feel obligated because he was my past."

"We don't have to stay in the past, we can be now. Fate brought him back to us. We may have loved many, and many may have loved and left, but Dana was the one that came back."

"Do you know how long it took to get rid of you?" River says looking at her scornfully. "You were the reason why the many men we loved left. You are silly, naïve-,"

"I am missed," the old River says with arrogance. "Reuben misses me, Dave misses me and Dana wants me back, he doesn't want you."

"Whatever," River said rolling her eyes. "Reuben and Dave, love me. I am dependable, Because of me, I was able to make my uncle's dream come true. You would have never been able to do that. I am able to establish a legacy."

"For who, you have no children to leave anything to."

"But I can build schools, libraries. I can be the next Andrew Carnegie. My life will not go in vain. I am Dr. River Daniels. I can die now and have no regrets."

The pretty girl doesn't respond. River looks at her. Her eyes are intense and the icy glaze intimidates the pretty girl.

"It's best that you stay gone, if Dana is in our life or not."

River wakes up, it is dark; she's shaking. She hears music and laughter outside. A cool breeze comes in from the window.

"She's back," she says to herself.

For months, she has been gone, not forgotten about, but gone. River climbs out of bed and looks out of the window to see if she is outside. She isn't there. River lets out a sigh of relief. She turns on the light and sees a note on the night stand from Dana on the dresser saying that he is in the hotel lounge. Still trembling, River takes a shower to freshen up. She thinks about calling Dave. But she decides against it. After her shower, she gets dressed and finds Dana.

THE LOUNGE IS FULL of tourist and native islanders. There seems to be some kind of event. Balloons fill the room and there are pretty colorful ribbons along the tables, chairs and floors. Everyone one is dancing, drinking and having a good time. River chuckles at the clothing, the tourist and islanders are wearing loud and colorful clothing with big straw hats. River quickly glances around the room to see if the pretty girl is around. Now that she is back, she has a way of appearing in various places.

River grins when she sees Dana sitting at the bar talking to the bartender. He smiles when he sees her. Maybe Dana is not the enemy, he just wants her to relax and let her hair down and have fun and there is nothing wrong with that. One week away from the world is not a crime, a mild annoyance to someone so disciplined as River, but as much as he compromised for her, why not compromise for him?

"There she is," Dana says taking her hand.

He kisses her on the cheek.

"Hey you," River says.

River grins as she sits down on the bar stool besides Dana. She looks at the bartender,

"A Long Island please,"

The bartender nods his head and then fixes her drink.

"Feeling better?" he asks.

"What's going on here?" River nods her head to the colorful scenery.

"The hotel's thirty-fifth anniversary," the bartender says placing River's drink down in the front of her. "So a pig is being roasted, there have been contests, games, all kinds of events."

"So you've been roasting all evening?" River asks Dana with a chuckle.

"I got into some things," Dana replies laughing.

"Can I get you anything else," the bartender asks River.

She politely shakes her head no. Then Dana and the bartender look at each other. River's eye brow rises suspiciously.

"What?" River asks.

Dana chuckles, then sips his beer.

"Ms. Daniels, I am a fan of your work," the bartender begins.

"Is that so?" River asks.

"Yes, I have all of your books. I wanted to make your book signing in L.A., but time won't permit."

"Well, thank you for your support," River replies.

"If it is not too much, tomorrow, will you sign my books?"

"Of course," River replies.

"Thank you, the drink is on the house," the bartender replies, smiling.

The bartender leaves to attend to the other customers.

Dana smiles at her.

"What?"

"What? I told you, I am dating a celebrity," he says.

"Whatever," River said as she sips her drink. "Did you get him to say that?"

"No, he saw me with you when we first came here. Tonight, he wanted to ask, but considering that you are keeping a low profile-,"

"I'm not keeping a low profile." River chuckles, sipping her drink.

DANA WAITS UNTIL RIVER finishes her drink.

"Let's take a walk." he says to her.

Together River and Dana walk to a vacant area on the beach. They hold hands as they watch the ocean wave. There is a crescent moon in the sky and the stars are scattered aimlessly across the heavens.

"You having fun?" he asks.

"Yeah,"

"Don't act tough?" Dana said playfully pushing her. "You're having fun."

"Yeah, this is has been fun," River says.

They stop walking. Dana turns to face her.

"You know that I love you," River nods her head. "You know that I believe in my heart that we are meant to be." She nods again.

Then suddenly a rush of emotion fills her. Is he breaking up with her? Is this the purpose of the vacation to give a beautiful send off? This was her plan; this was not supposed to be his. Is her life style too much for him? Her being as successful as she is may be too much for him. Her demanding schedule may not be what he wants. He wants that old River, that goofy and silly River. River looks around to see if the pretty girl is here.

"Dana-,"

"River, wait. Let me talk," he says to her.

She takes in a deep breath. If this is it, then let it be. She can walk with her head held high. She tried love, she failed, but she won't die, not this time. River closes her eyes to hear the words: "It's over,"

But instead when she opens her eyes she sees Dana on one knee, holding a ring in his hands. She stands shocked, not able to breathe or move.

"River, marry me," he said.

She is not able to move. She doesn't know what to say or do. She is not prepared for a proposal. In a few days she is going break up with him and go back to a life of solitude and work and just a few moments ago she was prepared to get her heart broken, but instead of either plan, here is a man that is asking her for her life. Amused by her stunned and vacant expression, Dana slips the ring onto her finger. Dana stands up and cups her face in his palms and kisses her passionately.

"I love you," he said to her.

She still looks at him shocked and stunned. Dana laughs and hugs her. Standing behind him staring at the ocean, River sees her pretty little friend.

"Love brought him back!" the pretty girl yells out.

"Just think about it River," Dana whispers, "You and I living happily ever after, I can design a nice beach house here and we can come down her during the winter, you can write and teach the natives."

SHIRLEY SCREAMS WITH excitement! It Is Sunday, a week later, and everyone is at Shirley's for Sunday dinner. Reuben shakes Dana's hand and welcomed him to the family.

"Oh, it's going to be a wedding of the year!" Shirley exclaims. "No long engagements, I want you married and pregnant by the end of the year."

"Grandma," River admonishes.

"Oh, you have to River, the Lord is going to call me home soon,"

"Mama, stop talking about death," River admonishes again.

"I want some babies, girl! Reuben is an ultimate bachelor. Dana, I want some babies. Do you hear me? I want some babies."

"Oh yes, ma'am," Dana smiles, holding River.

THAT NIGHT AFTER GRANDMA'S, River kisses Dana goodnight and promised to call him later. She has to talk with Dave. She cannot wait until the morning when she can see him in school. She has to see him now.

She bangs loudly on the door. Dave finally answers the door, River walks inside.

"How was the Island?" Dave asks nervously.

She shows him her hand.

"I take it that you had a good time." She nods her head but she wasn't smiling. "What's the matter?"

Together they walk in the kitchen and sit down.

"I, ah, when we got down there, I made up my mind that I was going to break up with him."

"River-,"

"Don't River me," she says. "This is complicated, dating, compromising, understanding, trusting, it's too much for me to deal with at one time. I love him, I do, but every time I turn around he is right there in my face. Whenever I am trying to write or read, he's in my face; 'How you feeling, River? What's on your mind? Take a vacation with me, River,'."

Dave starts laughing.

"What are you laughing at?"

"You River, that is what a relationship is about."

"Dave, how do you manage a relationship and a full time career?"

"Stop scheduling your emotions,"

"I'm not scheduling my emotions, I do love him but-,"

"Do you want to marry him?" Dave asks.

River shrugged her shoulders.

"River, why did you say yes?"

"I didn't Dave," River exclaims.

She stands up and begins pacing the floor.

"He put the ring on my finger and then Grandma is talking about giving her great grand babies before she die, and now I am here in your kitchen. And then I saw her!"

"You saw *her*?" Dave asks.

River nods her head.

"I wasn't trying to bury any emotions or anything." River defends.

"When did you see her?"

"While on the Island," River answers. "It started as a dream. I was actually talking to her. It was almost a competition on who belonged here, me or her. Then I saw her again, after Dana proposed."

"Are you holding back your feelings because of your past?" Dave asks.

River shakes her head.

"I love Dana, I don't deny that any more, but I don't know if I am supposed to be with him. Sometimes I can't wait to see him or to be with him, and then there are times when I don't want to."

"What are you feeling when you don't want to be with him?"

"Nothing," River said. "I just want to work, write, see Jenny, you. Dana questions my life a lot, he wondered if we never had broken up, would I be who I am today?"

"What did you tell him?"

River doesn't want to answer that question again.

"I don't believe my life would be what it is if we were still together. I know that I don't want to lose myself like I did when I was younger-,"

"But don't hide either,"

"I'm not," River says. "But what I am afraid of is, if I break up with him. Will I hide or will I be okay, and if I stay with him, is that what I am supposed to do, or it this cold feet?"

Dave waits a moment before he speaks.

"I think she came back to tell you that remembering the past is okay, don't let the memories haunt you."

River doesn't respond.

"What are you afraid of?

"Losing what I established,"

"Your success,"

"My sanity," River exclaims.

"River, you're not sane, you are hallucinating yourself," Dave laughs.

"Ha-ha," River mocks.

"I love you," Dave laughs again.

Dave stands up. He takes River's hands and pulls her to stand up and wraps his arms around her.

"Okay, what do you want?" he asks.

"Moments like this," she said enjoying the embrace, "Not to change anything."

"Okay," Dave replies softly.

THE NEXT DAY, DANA is at River's. She grins as she enters her home. She had been working late at the university, going over papers and homework. As she enters her home, Dana sees the tired look on her face. He takes the business case from her.

"This is why you need to slow down," Dana comments.

"I'm sorry?" River questions.

"You working late?"

"I had to finish checking the papers from the literature class and make sure they did their homework assignment. My class is studying Steinbeck."

"When we get married, you're not going to be working those long shifts." Dana said.

"I beg your pardon?" River asks.

"I'm not going to be an appointment." Dana states. "Since you and I got back together I managed to lighten my work load. Maybe you should give up one, teaching or writing."

"I'm not giving up anything, Dana." She states sternly. "My life, writing, school, my friends, family, they are my essence. It's who I am."

"Where do I fit in?" Dana asks.

River takes in a deep breath.

"You don't," River replies. "The type of woman you want is not the woman I am."

A moment passes. River and Dana stand looking at each other. Dana sees a look I her eyes that he doesn't like. River takes in a deep breath.

"Dana, I'm not going to marry you."

Dana stands stunned, not believing what she just said. The love of his life is standing before him telling him that she does not want to marry him. Her face is serious like that cool and stoic River; but her eyes are tender not the blocks of ice. He doesn't know what to say. What happened? River waits a moment before she explains her decision.

"When we broke up I snapped, but that was just one of the elements. I experienced a lot of hurt. My mom died, my grandfather, everything just-," River hesitates. "But I know my life is to do what I am doing, writing and teaching."

"River-," Dana protests.

"I loved you then," she says as tears form in her eyes. "I don't love you; that way now."

Her words are sharp. She takes in a deep breath preparing for her body to feel cold and numb, but her temperature stays the same.

"We don't want the same things." River says. "You want a wife, someone to come home to, someone to be Mrs. Dana Wilson. I don't want to be Mrs. Dana Wilson. I want to be Dr. River Daniels."

"You don't have to change your name." he finally says.

River looked at him feeling stunned that what she just said seemed to go right over his head.

"Fate, you believe in fate, but it was fate that you came back into my life, for us to have the closure that we needed. You missed me, I missed you, but considering the circumstances, we can't be together. I'm not going to change, because I can honestly say that I like my life. I like my friends, I like my family. I enjoy what I do."

"So that's it, you just break up with me and that is supposed to be it," he asks.

River shrugs her shoulders.

"I'm sorry," she says to him.

Dana cannot understand how he thought about her, almost went insane over her, finally had her back in his life and now she is just dismissing him.

River takes her ring off and puts it in Dana's hand. He doesn't want to take the ring back. He sets it down on the table, hoping that in a few days, she'll change her mind. He walks out of her house heartbroken and defeated. He lost the love of his life, that River is gone-forever.

River stands still. She is afraid to look to the left and to the right. She is afraid to look behind her; her friend may be there. She takes a deep breath and quickly turns around, as predicted the pretty girl is standing behind her. River is not afraid. She nods her head welcoming her friend.

"We'll be okay," the pretty one assures her.

"Structure," River warns.

The pretty one nods her head in agreement. She steps forward and walks into River. River closes her eyes welcoming the possibility of both the new and the old. Not forgetting the past but moving forward into the future together. River inhales and then exhales. She smiles

DAVE DOESN'T UNDERSTAND THE strange feeling that has been haunting him. He feels as if he has to see River. With the events of the past year and the engagement and the uncertainty of being engaged, maybe something has happened. He knows something has happened. However throughout the day, Dave shakes his head;

> *You're being paranoid,* he says to himself. *River is fine.*

However, by the end of the work day, he cannot go home. He has to check on River. Even if she is okay, he has to know that she is okay; to see that she is okay. Then he'll go home and see her at work the next day. If not, then he will sleep over, hold her and tell her how strong she is. River will survive.

DAVE KNOCKS HARD, RIVER answers the door looking at Dave as if he lost his mind for banging on the door that way.

He doesn't wait for an invitation to enter. After all they have been through this year; he doesn't have to ever ask for an invite.

He looks her over for a long moment. River doesn't look sad or discouraged, just confused at Dave's behavior. Her eyes ask what is wrong.

"I had this feeling that something was wrong," he confesses.

River smiles.

"I love you," she says. "I love you so much,"

She wraps her arms around him.

"Thank you for being my friend." She says.

Dave is touched by River's affection. He pulls away from her.

"I ended things with Dana," River informs him.

Before Dave can say anything, he looks River over. He didn't notice when he first came in, but he sees something different, something that he hasn't seen in over a decade. She is dressed casual. She wears a pair of jeans and a short sleeve T-shirt; not a pair of slacks and a button up. Her hair is worn down, not in a ponytail or bun. Her eyes are soft and there is light in them.

"Dave, I'm okay," she says smiling. "I really am okay. He was my past. I am to be healed from the past, not to entertain the past, and not run from the past."

Dave nods his head.

"Do you wonder about our little friend?"

River points to her heart.

"She was not so bad," River says being coy.

"What were you doing when I came?" Dave questions.

River sighs.

"I was writing," she says. "A love story,"

Dave grins.

"I'm not Flaming Blue," she says to him.

Dave remembers the art exhibit, the artist that tragically took her life because of a broken heart. He nods his head smiling.

"You're not," he says.

E. Davis

Acknowledgements
My best friend: Jaison Pascuzzi for designing this awesome cover

Dedication
To those that live in the clouds